THE SACKING OF FALLUJAH

A Volume in the Series

CULTURE AND POLITICS IN THE COLD WAR AND BEYOND

EDITED BY
Edwin A. Martini
and
Scott Laderman

THE SACKING OF

FALLUJAH

A PEOPLE'S HISTORY

ROSS CAPUTI RICHARD HIL DONNA MULHEARN

University of Massachusetts Press
Amherst and Boston

ISBN 978-1-62534-438-0 (paper); 437-0 (hardcover)

Designed by Sally Nichols
Set in Minion
Printed and bound by Maple Press, Inc.

Cover design by Thomas Eykemans
Cover photo by Idaho Sagebrush, *Fallujah*, 2004, www.flickr.com/photos/idahosage-
brush/9197397204/. Licensed under https://creativecommons.org/licenses/by/2.0/.

Library of Congress Cataloging-in-Publication Data

Names: Caputi, Ross, author. | Hill, Richard, 1949–author. | Mulhearn,
Donna, author.
Title: The sacking of Fallujah : a people's history / Ross Caputi, Richard
Hill, and Donna Mulhearn.
Description: Amherst : University of Massachusetts Press, 2019. | Series:
Culture and politics in the Cold War and beyond | Includes bibliographical
references and index. |
Identifiers: LCCN 2018051545 (print) | LCCN 2018055901 (ebook) | ISBN
9781613766880 (ebook) | ISBN 9781613766897 (ebook) | ISBN 9781625344373 |
ISBN 9781625344373(hardcover) | ISBN 9781625344380(pbk.)
Subjects: LCSH: Fall?ujah (Iraq)—History—21st century. | Fallujah, Battle
of, Fall?ujah, Iraq, 2004. | Iraq War,
2003–2011—Campaigns—Iraq—Fall?ujah. | IS (Organization)
Classification: LCC DS79.764.F35 (ebook) | LCC DS79.764.F35 C37 2019 (print)
| DDC 956.7044/342—dc23
LC record available at https://lccn.loc.gov/2018051545

British Library Cataloguing-in-Publication Data
A catalog record for this book is available from the British Library.

All photos in the gallery by Donna Mulhearn.

CONTENTS

PREFACE

In this book, a U.S. veteran and scholar, an Australian journalist, and an academic unite to uncover the real story of the sacking of the Iraqi city of Fallujah—a story of enormous historical significance. *The Sacking of Fallujah: A People's History* is the first complete account of the three sieges of Fallujah, from the U.S. operations in 2004 to the Iraqi government siege and the rise of the Islamic State in 2014.

Distinguishing itself from other books on Fallujah, which are predominantly written by military historians or war correspondents, this book draws on a wide range of sources and includes Iraqi voices to draw attention to the untold, often tragic stories on the other side of the conflict. The book also differs from others in that it examines recent events in Fallujah and analyzes the violence of the last five years as a direct legacy of the 2004 U.S.-led attacks.

Above all, *The Sacking of Fallujah* is about how modern wars are waged and, in particular, the use of propaganda campaigns in both legitimating military incursions and mollifying domestic audiences. While the U.S. military has long used such tactics to cultivate an air of legitimacy, the use of propaganda in Fallujah went much further, carefully choreographing justifications for the use of military violence against people and institutions traditionally protected under the Geneva Conventions.

Those of us opposed to aggressive war have a moral and ethical responsibility to ensure that what happened in Fallujah is not forgotten and, equally important, that those responsible for the illegal invasion and occupation of Iraq should one day be held accountable. This takes on greater significance when we consider the many additional problems that have resulted from U.S.-led actions, not least the emergence of ISIS, institutionalized sectarian violence, extreme government repression, and ongoing economic and political instability in Iraq.

We each have a deep personal and intellectual interest in what happened in Fallujah. Donna Mulhearn, a human rights activist and journalist, was one of few foreigners to gain access to the city and witness the first siege in April 2004; she returned several times to document the rise in birth defects. Ross Caputi, a penitent veteran of the second siege, responded to the tragedy of Fallujah by establishing a small campaigning organization called the Justice for Fallujah Project. Richard Hil, an academic and activist, had long been interested in the U.S. occupation of Iraq and in 2010 coauthored *Erasing Iraq: The Human Costs of Carnage.* The three of us joined forces to bring together a clear analysis of the Fallujah attacks, the bloodiest military campaign of the Anglo-American occupation of Iraq, the legacy of which, fifteen years on, is still playing out and will continue to do so for decades to come.

The Sacking of Fallujah is the result of a collaborative effort spanning several years, made all the more challenging by the recent violence, instability, and rapidly changing geopolitical events in the Middle East. This is an ongoing story of calculated violence, propaganda, resistance, and the will on the part of the people of Fallujah to live free of oppression and foreign interference. This book is dedicated to them and the independent journalists and activists who have taken risks to tell their stories.

THE SACKING OF FALLUJAH

INTRODUCTION

The Iraqi city of Fallujah is situated along the Euphrates River at the crossroads of ancient trade routes with Saudi Arabia, Jordan, and Syria. Religiously conservative, tribal, and traditional, Fallujah was something of an urban oasis resting in the secluded, western province of Anbar—the largest of Iraq's nineteen governorates. Long regarded as a backwater of Iraq, Anbar was until recently a vast stretch of desert of little political importance, with agriculture limited to a thin strip of fertile land hugging the banks of the Euphrates. Commonly referred to as *madīnat al-masājid,* "the city of mosques," Fallujah once bristled with over a hundred minarets that defined its cityscape. The famous Omar Bin Khattab Mosque with its beautiful blue minarets sat resplendent in the center of the city, overlooking the dense urban sprawl beneath. Single-family houses built in the traditional Arab style with stucco walls and flat rooftops nestled around the mosque, each jammed against the other, forming a maze of city blocks, walled courtyards, and narrow alleyways. As a thriving center of commercial and cultural activity, Fallujah had a vibrant population, until recently, between 300,000 and 435,000.[1]

Whether because of its proximity to neighboring countries with unguarded borders across vast stretches of desert, its rugged urban terrain, or the character of its people, Fallujah has more than once been the bane of foreign invaders. The city played a leading role in anticolonial struggles against the British in the 1920s, earning itself a reputation throughout Iraq for its patriotism, bravery, and rebellious spirit.[2] Perhaps not surprisingly, when the U.S.-led occupation of Iraq began in 2003 the city reemerged as a key site of armed resistance, as it did a decade later when the Iraqi government vied with the Islamic State for control over Anbar province.

Today, the city is emerging from fifteen years of devastating conflict. At the time of writing (2018), much of Fallujah lies in ruins, its people slowly returning from refugee camps inside and outside of Iraq. The character of the city, its former beauty and vibrancy, are—for now at least—a thing of the past.

The roots of this most recent conflict and ensuing devastation are to be found in the early years of the Anglo-American invasion and occupation. In April 2004, U.S. forces surrounded Fallujah and launched a major assault, code-named Operation Vigilant Resolve, in an effort to bring the recalcitrant city back under the control of the occupation. The operation caused widespread destruction to the city and resulted in hundreds of civilian casualties. Due in part to Arab TV network Al Jazeera's coverage of the operation, which revealed American atrocities to the world, enraging the international community, and partly due to the unexpected skill and tenacity of Fallujah's rebel fighters, the world's most powerful military was forced to retreat. Overnight, Fallujah came to symbolize the struggle of oppressed peoples the world over, a testament to those who refused to be cowed by military might.

The dramatic victory in Fallujah and the high price paid in terms of civilian casualties attracted international attention as well as considerable support to its cause. Muslims from outside Iraq traveled to Fallujah out of solidarity with their besieged brothers and sisters. Others came with their own agendas, including Al Qaeda. Sensing the growing movement of resistance, the Coalition[3] quickly regrouped and began preparing to launch a second assault to recapture Fallujah and bring it back under U.S. military control. In the buildup to this operation, U.S. forces waged a campaign of information warfare—militarized propaganda—in an effort to discredit Fallujah's insurgents, linking them with Al Qaeda and terrorism more generally. In November 2004, the Coalition launched Operation Phantom Fury, the second siege of Fallujah, deploying the full panoply of its military might to destroy the city's resistance and its symbolic power. Vast tracts of Fallujah were flattened, thousands of civilians killed and injured, and tens of thousands more displaced. Despite the unfolding realities on the ground, Western audiences, encouraged by a compliant and uncritical mainstream media, cheered what they believed to be a victory against Al Qaeda—the archenemy of the United States.

These operations came at a time when the strategic focus of the U.S. military shifted from jungles and mountain passes to dense urban centers—the principal sites of contemporary warfare. Fallujah is a potent example of this trend. Indeed, the ancient practice of city sacking has resurfaced, aided by new doctrines of information warfare that legitimize organized state violence and atrocities on a grand scale.

On March 31, 2004, four U.S. "contractors" working for the private security company Blackwater USA were ambushed and killed in Fallujah, their bodies mutilated and hung from a bridge over the Euphrates. Jack Wheeler, a former political advisor to President Ronald Reagan, responded by declaring "Fallujah delenda est!" (Fallujah must be destroyed), echoing Cato the Elder's call for Rome to sack Carthage: "Carthage delenda est!" more than 2000 years earlier. Though Wheeler was writing for a small, far-right-wing online magazine, his rhetoric was more than an isolated case of reactive hyperbole. He was joined by a bipartisan chorus of baying voices calling for Fallujah's total destruction. Sacking Fallujah was widely entertained among media commentators and some politicians as a credible policy option. For some, the city, its residents, and the "insurgents" and "terrorists" who apparently inhabited it were regarded as hostile and dangerous to U.S. and Iraq interests and therefore had to be dealt with as a whole. This of course blurred the lines between those regarded as "civilians" and "terrorists." The symbolism of Fallujah, its cultural importance and historic resistance to colonial rule, was, for the U.S. political and military leadership, as resonant and threatening as the bombs and bullets of insurgents. Something had to be done to bring the city to heel.

And so it was that four days after the Blackwater killings, Coalition forces launched the first siege of Fallujah. It was to prove an assault very different in both method and scale to sieges carried out in antiquity, or more recently in cities like Leningrad. The portents for this modern-day form of siege warfare were evident years before the 2004 operation. In 1996 Major Ralph Peters—now a retired U.S. Army Lieutenant Colonel, author, and regular media commentator—observed that "we may be entering a new age of siege warfare, but one in which the military techniques would be largely unrecognizable to Mehmet the Conqueror or Vauban, or even to our own greatest soldiers and conquerors of cities, Ulysses S. Grant and Winfield Scott."[4] With extraordinary prescience, Peters noted the "diminishing . . . strategic, operational, and even tactical importance" of "nonurban terrain." The new siege warfare, he argued, would focus on achieving "control" over "indigenous populations" through the deployment of a range of weapons, tactics, and capabilities, with psychological operations playing a central role in the military's arsenal.[5]

In 2006 General David Petraeus penned the U.S. Army's much vaunted counterinsurgency field manual, promising a more "humane" form of warfare to meet the U.S. military's strategic objectives in the Global War on Terror.[6] Petraeus's "population-centric counterinsurgency" articulated an evolving trend of warfare that Peters hinted at a decade earlier. Today's wars, he argued, were to be won not simply by capturing and controlling terrain—although these remained critical— but also by achieving political control over *populations*.[7] Despite the platitudinous nature of Petraeus's counterinsurgency manual, and earlier promises from Pentagon bureaucrats that high-tech, precision weaponry would make urban operations more "clinical," contemporary siege warfare has proved no more humane and no less destructive than earlier military incursions. The result has been nothing short of urbicide[8]—the decimation of an entire city, played out again and again in cities like Sarajevo, Gaza, Aleppo, Mosul, Raqqa, and, we argue, Fallujah.

At the same time, the means by which the U.S. military sought to assert itself in Fallujah, to destroy and undermine its enemies, have led to the eradication not of terrorism, but of popular resistance. These operations have split families, neighbors, and communities along the lines of collaborators and patriots: young men have been forced to take on the familial roles of their martyred fathers; women fear bearing children due to a crisis of birth defects allegedly caused by war pollution; and nearly all Iraqis suffer from the traumatic psychological effects of prolonged warfare. The divide-and-conquer tactics of the occupation have plunged the country into sectarian turmoil. Neighbors now fear one another, and religious institutions have become ideological battlegrounds. Schisms, fractures, discord, and distrust are now an endemic feature of everyday life in Fallujah, and Iraq more generally. In short, the Anglo-American occupation of the country has resulted in sociocide—"the obliteration of an entire way of life."[9]

U.S. information operations were instrumental not only in obscuring the vicious nature of the occupation from the American public but in the conduct of the violence itself. What makes the use of propaganda in the second siege of Fallujah in November 2004 unique is that the way in which the story was articulated—the carefully choreographed narrative, the characterization of the actors involved, the focus on strategic themes, the tactical use of language—was as much a part of the battle plan as the use of bombs and infantry. That is, the U.S. propaganda campaign achieved far more than simply legitimizing the operation to domestic audiences. Propaganda was also integral to the violence itself, shaping, facilitating, and motivating it—a point that has yet to be fully appreciated, even by some of the most incisive of observers. Not only was the official story of Fallujah largely false and devoid of reference to Iraqi suffering, but the second siege of Fallujah marked a turning point in the weaponization of information.

To be sure, while in 2004 information operations was at the cutting edge of military thinking, breaking new ground in cooperative military-media relations, the use of propaganda in theaters of war was hardly novel. Armies have long exaggerated their victories and the crimes of their enemies. But as the methods of communication have changed over the years—from couriers, to print journalism, to broadcast crews on the battlefield—armies have become increasingly sophisticated in their messaging techniques. The U.S.-led invasion of Iraq in 2003 occurred after a period of rapid change in U.S. military doctrines, prompted in part by the integration of new information technologies. Information warfare as a form of "soft power" would become "a primary effort of future conflicts" according to the U.S. military,[10] and the pursuit of "information dominance" would lead to ways of thinking that extended warfare well beyond the boundaries of the traditional battlefield to the "hearts and minds" of civilians living in war zones and on the home front. Dr. Dan Kuehl of the National Defense University in Washington, D.C., wrote in 2004 that information warfare takes place in a "battlespace" that reaches into "the 'gray matter' of the brain in which opinions are formed and decisions made," thus elevating information dissemination as "the most, and perhaps only, effective weapon."[11]

The transformation of the battlefield into a battlespace has had far-reaching implications, extending the scope of military operations to actors and domains traditionally thought of as civilian. The hackneyed metaphor of a "battle of ideas" has furnished the U.S. military with the rationale to treat journalists, doctors, clergy, and anyone else in a position to release information about U.S. military actions as combatants if they somehow threaten operational objectives. This is exactly what happened in Fallujah. Yet most of us watched the operation in Fallujah play out on our screens unaware of the doctrines guiding U.S. actions, least of all of our role as civilians in this new battlespace. U.S. information warfare now regards the colonizing of hearts and minds, whether in war zones or on the home front, as a military objective. Arguably, this is just a more aggressive, better organized, and more resourceful attempt by the U.S. military to manufacture consent for its military actions. But these innovations are also deeply antidemocratic and dangerous, denying ordinary citizens the vital, balanced information they need to assess the actions of their governments.

The success of U.S. information warfare in Fallujah is evidenced in the Western world's continued appraisal that U.S. forces *liberated* Fallujah from the control of Al Qaeda terrorists. This self-justifying account was carefully crafted by the U.S. military, disseminated by Western journalists, and mythologized by U.S. military historians who churned out numerous skewed histories of the operations, such as *No True Glory: A Frontline Account of the Battle for Fallujah* (2005) by former U.S. Marine Bing West; *Fallujah with Honor: First Battalion Eighth Marine's Role in Operation Phantom Fury* (2006) by Gary Livingston; *Fighting for*

Fallujah: A New Dawn for Iraq (2006) by Colonel John R. Ballard; *Operation Phantom Fury: The Assault and Capture of Fallujah, Iraq* (2009) by retired Colonel Dick Camp; and *New Dawn: The Battles for Fallujah* (2010) by Richard S. Lowry. Now entrenched in cultural memory, these accounts have found expression in other mediums such as the cinematic blockbuster *American Sniper* (2014), which depicts Fallujah's residents as living sheepishly under the tyranny of extremist warlords until the arrival of American liberators—a story that resonates with the usual hero-villain binary.

When ISIS emerged in Fallujah in January of 2014, the Western mainstream media and political leaders rarely asked why. The image of Fallujah as a city teeming with Islamic extremists was familiar and convenient, dovetailing neatly with Islamophobic sentiments. Western journalists took it as given that ISIS was the cause of this new conflict and not the outcome of one more than a decade old. It mattered little that ISIS had emerged after the Iraqi government had begun laying siege to Fallujah, and it mattered even less that for the entire previous year Fallujah had been at the center of a nationwide, nonviolent protest movement against the Iraqi government's corruption and internal repression. The suffering and resistance of ordinary Fallujans was ignored in favor of a sensationalist narrative that elevated religious extremism over geopolitical maneuvering. This made sense in the dualist vernacular of the mainstream media and to U.S. cinemagoers, but it jarred somewhat with people's experiences on the ground in Fallujah.

The new Iraqi government, dominated by sectarian, Shia political parties, and sponsored by both the United States and Iran, had in various ways contributed to the persecution of Sunnis since 2005. By January 2014, Anbar and other Sunni provinces were in full revolt against the government in Baghdad. At the time, ISIS was simply one militant force among many in this bloody conflict, and its influence was minimal. The ascent of ISIS to a serious military force on par with the armies of neighboring states was far from inevitable. We contend that ISIS's success cannot be attributed simply to the quality of its propaganda videos, its ability to flood internet chat rooms with recruiters, or the allure of its violent ideology. The fundamental questions that need to be addressed here are,

Why were nonviolent protesters in Fallujah willing to partner with an organization whose political goals were inimical to their own? How was ISIS able to grow and eclipse other rebel factions in the Sunni uprising? And why did a medium-sized city like Fallujah become such a strategic possession for them?

The Sacking of Fallujah: A People's History seeks to answer these and many other questions by tracing the roots of the Iraqi government-led siege in 2014–16 back to the U.S.-led invasion of 2003 and the sieges of 2004. One of the challenges of writing a history of this conflict is that so much of the primary source material available was produced by the U.S. military's propaganda apparatus. To counter this, we have relied on mixed methods, combining people's history with "new military history."[12] We center the experiences of Fallujans, include their voices as much as possible, and situate their accounts within the context of evolving U.S. military doctrines, U.S. foreign policy, and the pernicious narratives promoted by the global mainstream media. For too long, Fallujah and its people have been depicted as passive onlookers to the political machinations of Baghdad or as the hapless victims of extremists asserting their will. For these reasons we have chosen to highlight the perspectives of Fallujans and their resistance to occupation and oppression by civil, political, and military means.

The Sacking of Fallujah: A People's History is, however, more than a revisionist history. It is also a call to action. We assert that the way in which this conflict is remembered is of great political, legal, and moral significance, particularly if we are serious about addressing the injustices heaped upon ordinary Iraqis. Current U.S. foreign policy in Iraq continues to ignore how the invasion of 2003 and subsequent occupation contributed to Iraq's ongoing problems, refusing to acknowledge how the crimes of the United States' closest allies in Iraq—the Iraqi government and sectarian militias—are making resolution and reconciliation impossible. The United States' current strategy is in many ways a more limited version of previous mistakes and miscalculations. Its apparent inability or unwillingness to understand how each operation in Fallujah set the conditions for the next, contributing to what became a regional conflagration, has at times been breathtaking. The history of what happened in Fallujah illustrates the time-honored folly of seeking to apply external colonial-military solutions to the complex political problems of other nations—a historical lesson that, sadly, the powerful seem unable or reluctant to learn.

Chapter 1 discusses the sieges of Fallujah in the broader historical context of U.S. foreign policy in the Middle East. It also focuses on Orientalist discourses and their role in shaping the military conflict and U.S. information operations. Beginning with a discussion of U.S. imperialism in the post-World War II era, we focus on how the United States' early and enduring relationships with Middle Eastern states have shaped its contemporary foreign policy in the region.

Chapter 2 focuses on Western media discourses concerning the Fallujah conflict from March 2003 to April 2004, contrasting these with the lived experiences of Fallujans whose voices, we argue, were largely ignored or discredited by the Western media and, as a consequence, rarely reached U.S. domestic audiences. Thus, the story of the conflict was restricted largely to the accounts provided by Coalition spokespersons and embedded journalists.

Chapter 3 details the first siege of Fallujah, beginning on April 5, 2004, followed by the ceasefire and U.S. withdrawal, and ending with the creation of the Fallujah Brigade. Of central importance is the role of the media in representing and shaping this operation. U.S. forces later regarded their inability to control the media as their biggest failure in the operation. This was compounded, as we show, when Al Jazeera began broadcasting footage unfavorable to U.S. military interests. The political backlash forced the United States to negotiate a withdrawal from the city but also set in train the next operation in which the U.S. military would seek to control all media coverage.

In chapter 4 we discuss U.S. information operations in preparation for the second siege of Fallujah. After its experience with Al Jazeera during the first siege, the military came to believe that controlling the information sphere was essential to achieving victory. This led to several specific actions, including a psychological operation that exaggerated the role of Jordanian terrorist Abu Musab al-Zarqawi in Fallujah, allegedly the leader of Al Qaeda in Iraq, as a pretext for a second assault. We also report how the Coalition blocked a peace delegation from Fallujah's leadership, which hoped to negotiate a settlement, and efforts by Kofi Annan, UN Secretary General, to broker peace.

Chapter 5 examines the nature and consequences of the second military assault on Fallujah and the U.S.-imposed media blackout on outlets deemed hostile to American interests. We detail the work of several Fallujans who sought to document the human rights violations committed by U.S. forces. We also draw attention to several controversies surrounding the operation, including the United States' use of white phosphorous weapons, the reported use of "excessive force," and the prosecution of individual soldiers for crimes caught on film.

The impact of toxic weapons is explored in chapter 6. We investigate allegations linking the increased rate of birth defects in Fallujah to the U.S. military's use of depleted uranium, military burn pits, and conventional munitions, as well as the possibility of unknown weapon systems that used "slightly enriched" uranium. We also detail the work of Dr. Samira Alaani, chief of pediatrics at Fallujah's Maternity and Children's Hospital. She is the lead author of several reports on Fallujah's birth defects and has done more than anyone to alert the West to Fallujah's predicament. Such insider information has been vital to understanding the nature and scale of the health challenges confronting Fallujah, particularly when we consider how Iraqi authorities repeatedly sought to block epidemiological studies.

Chapter 7, covering the third siege of Fallujah, begins by discussing the Iraqi Spring protest movement in 2013 that connected nonviolent protest groups in Fallujah, Ramadi, Mosul, Baghdad, and other cities throughout Iraq. We document the underlying motives of these protests and how, following the Iraqi government's attack on protest camps in December 2013, this led to the Sunni uprising of 2014. This uprising ended with Iraqi security forces placing Fallujah under siege. It is against this backdrop, we argue, that ISIS first established a presence in Iraq and slowly came to dominate the uprising by waging war on other Sunni militias.

We further contend that the sensationalist media coverage of the Islamic State has obscured the extent to which it was a by-product of specific social and political conditions, rather than simply a movement peddling a messianic vision. Drawing on the available evidence, we show that while the campaign to drive out the Islamic State was applauded in the Western media, the Iraqi-led coalition destroyed entire cities and killed thousands of civilians—all of which served to further inflame an already explosive situation.

Between our chapters we have included short, first-person accounts from Fallujans and other eyewitnesses to the conflict, including brief reflections from students in Fallujah collected and translated by Dr. Asmaa Khalaf Madlool of the University of Anbar; ethnographic interviews conducted by Kali Rubaii with Fallujans living in refugee camps in 2014–15; testimony from Ross Caputi, a U.S. Marine who participated in the second siege of Fallujah (and a coauthor of this book); and short-form journalism from Donna Mulhearn (also a coauthor of this book), who returned to Fallujah in 2012 and 2013 to report on the crisis of birth defects. These accounts paint a vivid, multilayered picture of what happened in Fallujah, how its residents experienced repeated military incursions, and what these events meant to them.

Despite the fact that reconstruction projects in Fallujah are slowly underway, most Fallujans continue to live in an environment of fear and trepidation. Sectarian politics and unaccountable, government-aligned militias remain a constant threat to peace and stability. The conditions that caused Fallujans to rise up in 2014 still exist. For them, the current "peace" feels fragile and transitory. Until the underlying causes of this conflict in Iraq are adequately addressed, future insurgency and bloodletting seem inevitable.

The Sacking of Fallujah: A People's History casts a critical light on a tragic conflict founded on questionable, self-serving motives, which, despite all the lofty rhetoric about "freedom" and "liberty," has delivered anything but. The conflict has lingered for fifteen years, primarily because of a lack of accountability and a failure to pay heed to the needs and aspirations of the Iraqi people. One of the intentions of this book is to establish exactly that—accountability, and to contribute to a lasting memory of what was done to Fallujah.

The Sacking of Fallujah is intended, in part, to provide further impetus for an ongoing, grassroots project to document the experiences of a people subject to aggressive war and to support other forms of solidarity work, including the pursuit of reparations for Iraqi victims. This is the necessary groundwork for peace—peace with justice.

CHAPTER 1

THE ROAD TO FALLUJAH

The city's history is defined by foreign occupation, and the animosity and distrust of the Fallujah people towards the new U.S.-U.K. occupation (2003–2011) was not without reasons and historical roots.

—Dr. Muhamad Al-Darraji, *Fallujah' Secrets and Nuremberg' Barrier*

The story of the sieges of Fallujah has several historical starting points. It could, for instance, begin with the killing of the Blackwater USA "security contractors" in late March 2004, the massacre at Fallujah's al-Qa'id school in April 2003, the Anglo-American invasion of Iraq in 2003, or even the Gulf War of 1991. Like the confluence of the Euphrates and Tigris Rivers, Fallujah is where many histories converge and clash. Yet the conflict that began sixteen years ago was hardly inevitable. War came to the doorsteps of Fallujans for reasons largely beyond their control, not least of all the imperial ambitions of the George W. Bush administration and the attacks on 9/11 that sparked the so-called Global War on Terror. But while the Bush Doctrine can be understood as an extremist foreign policy, the wars in Iraq and Afghanistan are in many ways a continuation of the last seventy years of U.S. intervention in the Middle East. And the preparedness of U.S. political and military elites to engage in such actions harkens back to the earliest times of a fledgling empire.

American imperialism is notably distinct in character from its European counterparts. It developed in the context of settler colonialism, when European pioneers believed they were destined to rule over indigenous lands. From its earliest days, providential iterations of "exceptionalism" and "manifest destiny" informed U.S. foreign policy ambitions and legitimated all manner of incursions into the affairs of foreign nations. The United States' self-declared mission was founded on a deeply held belief that because of its military and economic strength, and adherence to Judeo-Christian values, it had a God-given right to assert its leadership over other nations. The United States has, therefore, sought to impose particular social, political, and cultural values, as well as "free market" doctrines, as universally applicable and desirable markers of civilization. The "American way of life" has been equated with the spread of freedom and liberty, when in reality the United States has used its military strength to coerce other nations into a global economic order that privileges American interests. Military incursions into other sovereign nations have been repeatedly justified on the grounds of national security, deterrence, and a desire to establish a world order congruent with U.S. national interests, understood euphemistically as a Pax Americana.

Perhaps the clearest, and most recent, example of such thinking is the Project for the New American Century (PNAC), a far-right think tank with several members in the presidential administration of George W. Bush. In its "Statement of Principles," PNAC declared its desire to maintain the United States' position as "the world's preeminent power" and to promote "American global leadership." Significantly, the statement asserts that "the history of the 20th century should have taught us that it is important to shape circumstances before crises emerge, and *to meet threats before they become dire*. The history of this century should have taught us to embrace the cause of American leadership."[1] These affirmations of imperial ethos would later inform a policy document aimed at putting its vision of U.S. global domination into action.

In September 2000, the PNAC published "Rebuilding America's Defenses: Strategy, Forces and Resources for a New Century."[2] This document reiterated much of the organization's "Statement of Principles," claiming that the "political and economic principles" that the United States fights for around the globe "are almost universally embraced."[3] With this in mind, it was argued that America's future security obligations should be devoted to homeland security, war fighting capabilities, global policing, and the continued transformation of the U.S. military consistent with the "revolution in military affairs." The document makes repeated reference to Iraq (as well as other nations, such as Iran, Libya, and North Korea) as a threat to U.S. interests and promotes political and economic transformation throughout the entire Middle East in accordance with U.S. national interests and security concerns.

Many commentators have argued that this document is evidence of the extent to which the 2003 invasion of Iraq was premeditated, more specifically, that leading neoconservatives in the Bush administration—Paul Wolfowitz, Dick Cheney, Elliot Abrams, and others—seized the opportunity provided by the tragic events of 9/11 to put their policy vision, expressed in this document, into action and invade Iraq. Whether or not this is the case, the dangers of this preemptive doctrine are glaringly apparent. Although considered extreme in some quarters, the policy ambitions of PNAC were hardly new. In fact, the organization's nomenclature echoes the title of Henry Luce's famous 1941 essay, "The American Century," which called for the United States not only to enter World War II but to assume the role of imperial superpower.[4] Such chauvinistic ideas have been articulated in different ways throughout much of American history, chiefly to legitimate all manner of interventions into the affairs of foreign nations.

Since the Declaration of Independence in 1776, America has invaded over seventy countries, financed pro-American paramilitaries, toppled democratically elected leaders, engaged in targeted assassinations, and imprisoned and tortured its opponents without trial.[5] Prior to World War II America's imperial ambitions were mostly limited to the Western hemisphere. After 1945, however, it emerged as the world's leading economic and military power, eclipsing the British Empire as it sought to protect Western (and especially its own) interests in the Middle East.

The single most important strategic and economic factor in the region was oil. Professor of Political Science Irene Gendzier writes, "In the immediate postwar years, the United States defined its policy in the Near and Middle East in terms of assuring unimpeded access and control by U.S. oil companies of its great material prize, petroleum. Congressional hearings on the role of petroleum and the national defense envisioned petroleum as a weapon of war. It followed that ensuring the presence and stability of compatible regimes was an essential dimension of policy, as was containing and crushing those whose nationalist and reformist orientation rendered them suspect."[6] Military and business interests overlapped as the United States sought to establish favorable economic conditions abroad, often propping up autocratic and corrupt governments to achieve this end. It was precisely these motives that made the Arabian American Oil Company (ARAMCO) a strategic priority and that positioned the United States as one of the earliest and most ardent supporters of Israel—a vital military ally in the region.[7] Oil was also a primary motivator of the Anglo-American coup that overthrew Iran's democratically elected prime minster, Mohammad Mosaddeq, in 1953 and reinstated the corrupt and oppressive Shah.[8]

The United States' strategic alliance with Israel, Iran, and Saudi Arabia would have the most lasting impact on U.S. policy in the region. During the Cold War the United States embraced the tactic of fostering regime change, directly or indirectly, to create a favorable geopolitical environment for its military and business interests. Indeed, the United States engaged in dozens of such actions between 1947 and 1989. Drawing on documents contained in the National Archives, National Security Archive, and presidential libraries, Assistant Professor of Political Science Lindsey O'Rourke notes that the United States attempted regime change in at least seventy-two countries during this period, with the majority of such operations ending in catastrophic failure as well as contributing to deteriorating social, economic, and political conditions in the victim nations.[9]

A decade after the CIA-backed coup d'état in Iran, Iraq too would suffer regime change instigated by the Americans. The Iraqi Revolution of 1958 overthrew the country's monarchy and put in its place the Iraqi Republic. Fearing the strength of the Iraqi Communist Party and the demand of the prime minister, Brigadier General Abd al-Karim Qasim, that a greater share of the revenue from the then Anglo-American-owned Iraq Petroleum Company go to the Iraqi state, the United States "adopted [the Ba'ath Party] as one of their key agents of influence in Iraq, starting in the early 1960's."[10] Saddam Hussein emerged on the scene for the first time in 1962–63 as a CIA affiliate plotting to assassinate Iraq's prime minister, only to fail and flee the country.[11] General Qasim was eventually killed, and the Ba'ath Party assumed power and went on to murder hundreds, possibly thousands, of Iraqi communists with the help of the CIA.

This relationship between the United States and Iraq persisted and then strengthened after the Iranian Revolution of 1979 that ousted the brutal, U.S.-backed Shah and replaced him with an "Islamic Republic" that took a firm stance against Western influence. In a State of the Union address on January 23, 1980, President Jimmy Carter responded to the Iran hostage crisis, announcing that the United States would use military force in the Persian Gulf if its economic interests came under threat. This would come to be known as the "Carter Doctrine," which Andrew Bacevich, former army colonel and professor of international relations and history, argues constituted the first instantiation of a U.S. policy toward the Middle East.[12] Until this point, U.S. actions in the region had often been opportunistic, even spontaneous, and more often than not characterized by covert actions and indirect methods of influence. But the Carter Doctrine would lead to a series of major military actions, each one setting the stage for the next, beginning with the Iran-Iraq War, in which the United States armed both sides and gradually became a full party to the conflict.[13]

After the collapse of the Soviet Union, the United States turned on its longtime ally, Saddam Hussein, following Iraq's invasion of Kuwait. This led to the Gulf War of 1991, resulting in the expulsion of Iraqis from Kuwait and a sustained campaign of aerial bombardment, followed by a lengthy period of sanctions that reduced the Iraqi people to desperate poverty. Then, with the fall of the Iron Curtain in 1989, the United States' obsession with diminishing the power of the Soviet Union shifted to a focus on transforming the Islamic world to fit its economic and security agendas. This shift in strategy is partly attributable to the popularization of Samuel Huntington's "clash of civilizations" thesis and what came to be known as the "new barbarism thesis." Both theses predicted a world of conflict driven by the tribalism and the atavism of third world cultures.[14]

Both focus squarely on Islam as a future source of conflict and a threat to U.S. security. Despite the fact that the United States had, since the end of World War II, built close strategic relations with Saudi Arabia—mainly to ensure the flow of oil to the West, but also to counter communist expansionism and Iranian influence—relations with Islamic nations deteriorated significantly over this period. This had not always been the case, however. Immediately after World War II, public opinion in the Middle East toward the United States was generally favorable. America was viewed as being different from the European colonial powers, and the anticolonial rhetoric of the 1941 Atlantic Charter, signed by President Roosevelt, resonated with the Islamic world. However, decades of covert action and support for repressive regimes in the Middle East fed increasing anti-American attitudes and Islamic militancy throughout the region.

A radical expression of such sentiments emerged in the form of Al Qaeda, a network of Islamic militant groups whose mujahideen, "holy warriors," once received U.S. support to fight the Soviets in Afghanistan. The U.S. invasion of Iraq in 1991, followed by the brutal regime of sanctions that starved half a million Iraqi children to death,[15] along with America's continued support for the Israeli occupation of Palestine, and the presence of U.S. military bases in Saudi Arabia were decisive factors in turning Al Qaeda into a powerful and ultimately lethal oppositional force. Following NATO's involvement in the Balkan wars and the launch of the Global War on Terror, the United States continued with its interventionist approach, destabilizing nations, instigating internecine conflicts, and creating new enemies to be fought in new wars. According to independent journalist Glenn Greenwald, "Syria has become at least the 14th country in the Islamic world that U.S. forces have invaded or occupied or bombed, and in which American soldiers have killed or been killed. And that's just since 1980."[16] These countries include Libya, Lebanon, Kuwait, Iraq, Somalia, Bosnia, Saudi Arabia, Afghanistan, Sudan, Kosovo, Yemen, and Pakistan. Such military actions, along with attacks by U.S. allies and sponsored military coups, have resulted in extreme repression in many of these countries.

The resulting death toll, given the number of civilians who have died from avoidable war-related harm, is staggering. And if one were to include the untold numbers of people suffering long-term disabilities and illnesses and the destruction to infrastructure, environment, cultural heritage, and so forth, what emerges is a picture of incalculable harm, widespread mayhem, pain, and suffering.

CIVILIZING THE BARBARIANS

The events discussed above would not have been possible were it not for pervasive mythologies, attitudes, tropes, and patterns of reasoning that rationalized *our* use of violence against *them*. For example, it is widely believed in the West that the Middle East is a chaotic and dangerous place, that Muslims are driven to violence by ancient hatreds and scriptural injunction, and that *we* ought to intervene and bring stability and democracy to this troubled part of the world. Such stereotypes not only characterize the Middle East and Arabs in essentialist terms but also draw a rigid psychosocial divide between "us" and "them" and frame Western intervention as being responsive to the volatile nature of Arabs, Muslims, and the region itself, rather than it being the cause of much of the region's instability. Such beliefs are indicative of how the Arab world has been viewed by the West in homogenized and racist terms over many centuries, and how such representations have served to legitimate much of the violence and subjugation inflicted upon Arab countries, including the more recent attacks on Iraq.

Renowned cultural scholar Edward Said argued forcefully in *Orientalism* that the broad categories of the "Middle East," "Arabs," and the "Arab world" have over the centuries been subjected to various negative representations, often reducing complex, differentiated cultures, institutions, and practices to simple, invariably racist, assertions about the "Arab Other." Crude dichotomies have positioned the Christian West against Islam, civilization against barbarism, progress against stagnation, modernity against antiquity, and, more recently, good against evil, and freedom against terrorism. Core to these dualisms is the entrenched belief that Arab nations and the people who inhabit them are fundamentally different—less refined, cultured, and civilized than "us"—and therefore more prone to actions that accord with the supposedly aberrant characteristics of a homogenized population.

Historically, these ways of thinking have made it possible for colonizing powers to justify military incursions into various parts of the Middle East, including Mesopotamia, in order to appropriate lands and resources for economic and strategic purposes. In short, perceived divisions between the Orient and the West have served to legitimate and deflect attention from the cruel, degrading, and exploitative actions of colonizing powers. More recently Orientalist thought has been rearticulated in "the new barbarism thesis," which seeks to explain conflicts as the product of cultural propensities and tribalistic impulses that emerge in the context of weak state power and resource scarcity.[17] Many have criticized this view, arguing that historical and political analysis is brushed aside in favor of culturalist explanations that posit the perceived essence or nature of groups as the origin of their violent behavior. Islam has become the main target of new barbarism theorists, who see the conflicts plaguing the Middle East as an expression of the region itself, Arab culture, and, in particular, the tenets of Islam. Within this framework Arabs and Muslims are seen as naturally inclined to violence, and the political instability of the region reflects their tribalistic and aggressive impulses.

After the attacks of 9/11 the new barbarism thesis was adopted by the mainstream media as a convenient explanation for the phenomenon of Islamic terrorism and the region's tumultuous history. Professor of Conflict Studies Tim Jacoby argues that pundits and politicians found that the new barbarism discourse resonated with their interests and preconceptions because it did not portray political violence in the Middle East as a reaction to Western intervention or as "a more diffuse expression of the politics of a post-colonial world order." Instead, he claims, the violence plaguing the regions was "regarded primarily as a product of Muslims' singular and invariably bellicose cultural reference point: the purportedly reactionary tenets of Islam."[18] Thus, focusing the blame for the Global War on Terror on Islam served to deflect attention away from the destructive legacy of U.S. imperialism in the region and frame the U.S. interventions in Iraq and Afghanistan as liberalizing and democratizing missions in a region crippled by backwardness and chauvinism. As Dag Tuastad, researcher in Middle East studies, put it, "In the same way that Orientalism once served the policies of colonial powers, the new barbarism thus serves the political interests of people who are aware of the need to produce images of a conflict as one between civilisation and barbarism."[19]

The U.S.-led assaults on Fallujah in 2004 were in many respects a continuation of these historical practices, reinforcing the Western tendency to regard armed resistance to imperial adventurism as acts of unwarranted opposition and barbarism. Author and journalist Matt Carr argues that the attacks on Fallujah were in part sanctioned by a narrative based on the assumption of a Global War on Terror between the countervailing forces of good versus evil and civilization versus barbarism. The deployment of such binaries, he says, served to "provide the U.S. military with the appearance of moral legitimacy, as it turned the city [Fallujah] to rubble in order to 'save' it."[20] According to geographer, Stephen Graham, this way of thinking has dovetailed with a new trend of urban warfare that is legitimized through "indiscriminate, Orientalist, categorizations."[21] Graham suggests the new urban warfare blends Orientalism, dehumanization, and Islamophobia, rendering the Islamic Other as "terrorist" to justify military and other actions against Islamic cities and their inhabitants. In effect, entire populations of city dwellers are lumped together as legitimate targets of military action.[22] Such assertions are what philosopher Eduardo Mendieta refers to as the "babel of rhetorics"[23] that ultimately serve to rationalize the use of massive, indiscriminate military force in cities such as Fallujah, cleansing them—as one would cleanse a garden of insects—of undesirable elements. In representing the barbarian as one with whom no rational discourse or common ethical framework is possible, gross acts of violence appear morally justifiable, even essential. This view tended to underpin U.S. propaganda in the buildup to the sieges Fallujah in 2004, leading to demands that the city be obliterated.

OPERATION IRAQI LIBERATION, CODE NAME OIL

The official story of the U.S.-led operations in Fallujah in 2004, and indeed of the 2003 assault on Iraq, was a cover for a host of ulterior motives. The Bush administration's original pretext for the invasion was that Saddam Hussein was stockpiling weapons of mass destruction (WMDs) in defiance of UN Security Council resolutions and that Al Qaeda had cells within Iraq that could gain access to these weapons. Hence, a "preemptive" strike on Iraq was necessary, the administration claimed. There were other pretexts too: that regime change would liberate the Iraqi people from a wicked dictator and that building liberal and democratic institutions in Iraq could spark similar transformations throughout the entire region. Yet as the accumulated evidence demonstrates, the United States had for many years courted friendly relations with Iraq under Hussein's rule, sending political emissaries, economic advisers, trade delegations, and others to cozy up to the Baathist regime. It also supplied the regime with WMDs that were used in numerous attacks on its own people, including the helicopters that dropped chemical weapons on the Kurdish city of Halabja in the late 1980s.[24]

The deceit and illegality associated with the Anglo-American invasion of Iraq in 2003—initially named Operation Iraqi Liberation (OIL) but later changed to Operation Iraqi Freedom—have been well documented. Declassified U.S. and British documents clearly show that during the buildup to the invasion the intelligence communities of both the United States and the United Kingdom were highly skeptical of the information that was being presented to the public as justification for the removal of Saddam Hussein.[25] The notorious 2002 "Downing Street Memo" asserted plainly that "Bush wanted to remove Saddam through military action, justified by the conjunction of terrorism and WMD. But the intelligence and facts were being fixed around the policy."[26] Thus, a selective vetting of intelligence was presented as a clear-cut case for war, and ongoing UN inspections were ignored, thereby deliberately misleading the American public and proceeding with the supreme crime against humanity: a war of aggression.

All this was done in spite of mass international opposition to the invasion of Iraq that culminated in the largest ever global antiwar protest of February 15, 2003. The mainstream media, however, rarely questioned the legitimacy of the U.S.-led mission in Iraq. But they did want to see a successful regime change with minimal casualties and a smooth transition to a democratic Iraq, commensurate (of course) with U.S. interests. Occasionally, the mainstream media displayed a willingness to criticize the Bush administration and the U.S. military for failing to achieve these goals. Yet allegations that the invasion and occupation of Iraq were illegal under international law rarely reached most Americans, despite declarations from figures such as Richard Falk, professor emeritus of international law and practice at Princeton University, who characterized the invasion as "a flagrant example of aggressive war making," adding that "the subsequent military occupation is thus illegal and aggravated by abuses of the Geneva Conventions of 1949 governing the duties of an occupying state."[27] It follows from this that every minute of the U.S. occupation was illegitimate, as was every action linked to the sieges of Fallujah: from aerial bombings, individual house raids and checkpoints, to everyday street patrols.

However, Bacevich argues that doubts over the legality of the invasion understate the United States' radical ambitions in the Iraq theater. The Bush administration's penchant for "preventative war," he states, was intended to set a precedent that would exempt the United States from the constraints of international law.[28] The United States claimed for itself the right to global, unilateral military action, justified by the need to confront threats before they arose. Thus, one of the war's objectives was to render its illegality irrelevant.

Despite the officially stated goals of liberation, nation-building, and the creation of a liberal democracy, the U.S.-led Coalition's incursion into Iraq failed by almost every measure. Shortly after the invasion, U.S.-led forces established the Coalition Provisional Authority (CPA), a "transitional" government led by politicians from the occupying countries. Under the stewardship of Paul Bremer, a U.S. diplomat appointed by George W. Bush as presidential envoy to Iraq, the CPA initiated sweeping changes to Iraq's infrastructure with, first, "state destruction" and then reconstruction as its key policy objectives.[29] The architects of the invasion sought to fashion Iraq into a "model state" in the Middle East that would "set off a series of democratic/neoliberal waves throughout the region."[30] But first this required that most of Iraq's institutions, industries, and laws be torn down or recast so that the state-building process could begin.[31]

As head of the CPA, Bremer made his first priority "economic transformation," casting aside the wishes of Iraqis and challenging the notion of democracy itself. Canadian independent journalist, Naomi Klein, noted the contradictory nature of Bremer's authoritarian reforms with the CPA's stated goal of building a democracy. "Before the invasion," she observed, "Iraq's economy had been anchored by its national oil company and by two hundred state-owned companies, which produced staples of the Iraqi diet and raw materials of its industry, everything from cement to paper and cooking oil. The month after he arrived in his new job, Bremer announced that the two hundred firms were going to be privatized immediately."[32]

In addition to imposing new economic laws, which Bremer attempted to unilaterally insert into Iraq's new constitution,[33] the CPA introduced a new currency and granted immunity to Coalition forces in Iraqi courts. Bremer went even further, launching a campaign of "de-Baathification," officially known as "CPA Order Number 2: Dissolution of Entities." This order disbanded much of Iraq's security forces, including the military, and barred former members of the Ba'ath Party from holding state jobs.[34] But since the Iraqi government had formerly been the largest employer in the country, and given that Ba'ath Party membership was necessary to become eligible for state jobs, this move effectively laid off the majority of the Iraqi workforce.[35] Bremer's reforms also extended to the political system, notably by prohibiting local elections[36] and instead installing handpicked Iraqi politicians, many of whom had lived in exile for most of their lives and were referred to by many Iraqis derisively as "imported Iraqi politicians."[37]

Under Bremer's watch, the occupying forces determined the sort of future Iraq could have and what role its citizens were allowed to play in shaping their nation's future. Iraqis could participate in the political process only as long as their demands did not run counter to the goals of the Coalition. By limiting Iraqi participation in the remaking of their country and by imposing limits on acceptable political thought, the Coalition effectively created the conditions for the emergence of an enemy that refused to accept those constraints.

INFORMATION WARFARE

It is difficult to appreciate how new and innovative the use of propaganda in Fallujah was, given the media environment that we live in today and considering the long evolution of military propaganda. The Uncle Sam posters of World War I no longer exist; contemporary U.S. propaganda is brought to the public via choreographed information to the news media. This is considerably different from the U.S. military's attitude toward the media during the Vietnam War, which regarded the presence of journalists on the battlefield as a nuisance, at best, but more often as a liability. With the arrival of the Information Age, the availability of new communication technologies during the 1991 Gulf War gave the U.S. military more leverage in their relationship with the media and brought significant change to their thinking about soft power and media relations. They came to see the news media as a "strategic enabler,"[38] that is, as a minimally critical platform they could use for "perception management" by influencing the images that domestic audiences see and the stories they hear of U.S. military actions around the world.[39] These breakthroughs, along with the spectacular use of high-tech weaponry in Iraq, prompted a period of rapid doctrinal and technological change within the military, which was heralded as a revolution in military affairs.[40]

By the time of Operation Iraqi Freedom I and II, the U.S. military was incorporating propaganda into its day-to-day operations in an effort to influence how domestic and foreign audiences perceived their conduct. Military historian Stephen Badsey observed, "US troops [in Iraq] were being trained to view their relationship with the media not as a constitutional or ethical issue, but as an aspect of warfighting, and as a tool enabling them to accomplish their self-defined missions more effectively."[41] During the 2004 sieges of Fallujah, propaganda played an integral and decisive role in military operational success.

Predictably, the U.S. government does not refer to its activities as propaganda, but rather as "strategic communications." Jeffery B. Jones, former director of strategic communications and information on the U.S. National Security Council, has defined strategic communications as "the synchronized coordination of statecraft, public affairs, public diplomacy, military information operations, and other activities, *reinforced by political, economic, military, and other actions,* to advance U.S. foreign policy objectives."[42] In other words, strategic communications constitutes an organized effort across governmental agencies and the military to influence foreign and domestic audiences alike, using various forms of soft power (i.e., propaganda and diplomacy), supplemented by hard power (i.e., military action). Under this doctrinal umbrella, various military and state operations are coordinated and conducted, each with distinct messaging goals. Of these, the military's disciplines of information operations (IO) and public affairs (PA) were key in shaping how the media represented the Coalition's operations in Iraq to the world.

IO refers to the coordination of a number of military capabilities—including electronic warfare, computer network operations, military deception, and psychological operations (PSYOP).[43] But the activity most concerned with the dissemination images and narratives was PSYOP,[44] which involved a broad set of activities such as sponsoring news media companies in Iraq to produce U.S.-friendly news, feeding false information to enemy forces about American military activities, playing inflammatory messages in Arabic through loudspeakers to provoke an enemy reaction, and dropping leafleted messages in civilian neighborhoods. PA on the other hand was concerned primarily with messaging domestic audiences. This involved appointing specially trained military spokespersons, organizing press information centers where news conferences could be staged, and embedding journalists in military units. Broadly speaking, PSYOP focused on messaging foreign audiences, while PA messaged domestic audiences; but it was through IO and, at the highest level, strategic communications that these different efforts were planned and coordinated.

Not that strategic communications sought to, or was even capable of, *controlling* media content. Rather, its role was to *influence*—in subtle but powerful ways—how individual journalists and media networks represented conflicts to the public. For example, the Coalition opened several press information centers during the early days of the Iraq conflict, where press conferences were held. These served mainly as official platforms from which military spokespersons could frame issues and narrate battlefield events. IO also had the benefit of making some events appear more prominent in news coverage than others by selectively leaking intelligence or giving individual journalists special access to stories that the Coalition wanted to promote.

Perhaps the most significant method adopted by the Coalition to influence the media's representation of the conflict was to embed journalists within military units. In so doing, the military was able to restrict access to certain aspects of the conflict and cultivate a perspective from which audiences at home would receive information—a perspective that they believed to be the "ground truth."[45] In reality, this meant the foregrounding of the American military experience at the expense of ordinary Iraqis, whose voices were ignored almost entirely. Predictably, many critics charged that the embedding process caused journalists to "go native" and adopt the worldview of the troops upon whom they relied for their protection, thereby limiting their ability to remain impartial.

While the U.S. military is open about its efforts to influence the media (although it would say it seeks only to inform the media), it insists that it does not interfere with the editorial practices of media networks. In fact, the nature and quality of media coverage during the conflict varied significantly, with some networks able to exercise a degree of independence when it came to the interpretation of information provided by the military. Many from within the strategic communications community even complained of partisan journalism, asserting that different networks aligned their coverage of the war with the ideological orientation of one or another of the major political parties. For example, Lieutenant Commander Steven Tatham, who was media spokesperson and head of maritime media operations for the British Royal Navy in 2003, was highly critical of Fox News' coverage of the war, arguing that the network's reporting was often "uniformly subjective, ultra-patriotic and hugely biased in favour of the President's actions."[46] Leaked Fox News internal memos suggest that it was an editorial decision to disassociate from those who "decry the use of 'excessive force'" in Fallujah rather than external military influence.[47]

Although the military's influence on media content is often referred to as "spin," officials assure the public that propaganda directed at domestic audiences is always true and intended to inform audiences, while propaganda aimed at enemies, which can contain misinformation, saved lives.[48] Emma Louise Briant, author of *Propaganda and Counterterrorism*, explains that this notion of "propaganda boundaries"—the division between domestic, foreign, and enemy audiences and the practice of messaging them according to different ethical standards—is aimed at reconciling the professed commitment to democratic values and the use of propaganda.[49] But she cautions that "when America and Britain's propaganda apparatus makes claims about 'truth' it is crucial that we remember that this 'truth' is negotiated within ideological boundaries influenced by the institutions and wider society."[50]

However, Badsey notes that these boundaries began to seriously erode with the introduction of the concept of "offensive information operations" in 1998, which was aimed at "shaping and misleading enemy perceptions." The introduction of offensive information operations into the strategic lexicon provoked a debate within the military about the ethical boundary between PSYOP and PA.[51] Many were concerned that propaganda intended for America's enemies might now make its way to the American public. Since the United States' propaganda apparatus is a "cross-government" activity, different military units involved with IO communicate with various government agencies to develop a consistent messaging strategy.[52] Traditionally, a doctrinal "firewall" has existed between PSYOPs and PA to maintain these propaganda boundaries.[53] However, with a new globally connected internet and news media, offensive PSYOP could now easily reach domestic audiences.

Under the leadership of Defense Secretary Donald Rumsfeld, propaganda boundaries continued to erode. Rumsfeld was a noted enthusiast for the technocratic vision of war promised by the so-called revolution in military affairs and an advocate for a more aggressive use of propaganda.

When appointed secretary of defense in 2001, he used his "indomitable bureaucratic presence"[54] to enact controversial reforms to the organizational structure of the military and increase the role of propaganda in U.S. diplomacy and military operations. Thus, by the time of the 2003 invasion, propaganda and "perception management," exercised through manipulation of the media, became favored tactics in the U.S. military's day-to-day operations.

Rumsfeld was also primarily responsible for the way in which Operation Iraqi Freedom was fought. Ignoring the advice of his generals, he adopted a theater strategy, which became known as the Rumsfeld Doctrine, "based on speed, maneuver, shock effect, extensive covert preparation of the battlefield, precision strikes at strategically significant targets, and information dominance."[55] He also distributed a seventy-four-page directive within the U.S. government in 2003 entitled "Information Operations Roadmap," now declassified and widely criticized, that was intended to facilitate coordination between IO and PA.[56]

The United States' defeat during the first siege of Fallujah in April 2004, Operation Vigilant Resolve, advanced these operational concerns from a matter of doctrinal debate to strategic necessity. The unpalatable prospect of being forcibly ejected from a country the U.S. leadership claimed to be liberating suddenly became apparent, and many within the U.S. military and government felt an urgent need to implement changes to IO practices. The U.S. military duly obliged, launching a major campaign of "aggressive information operations" leading up to Operation Phantom Fury in November 2004.[57] Badsey notes that by the time of the second siege, "any distinctions between information operations and public affairs had largely vanished from US senior officers' thinking and planning."[58]

This determination arose, in part, because of the widely held belief within the U.S. military that the first siege stalled because of a failure to control the "informational realm."[59] It was argued that the information war was lost to the insurgents by allowing the Arab TV network Al Jazeera and other media outlets to report civilian casualties and failing to provide the Western media with an "alternative" perspective that would portray U.S. actions in a more flattering light. Lieutenant General

Thomas F. Metz, commander of the Multi-National Corps—Iraq in 2004, would later argue that the first siege of Fallujah presents "a cautionary tale for anyone who would downplay the significance of information in modern warfare."[60]

This view was shared by Robert D. Kaplan, best-selling author and former chief geopolitical analyst for Stratfor (a private intelligence firm that contracts with the U.S. government). Kaplan is also credited with one of the early articulations of the new barbarism thesis.[61] In a 1994 essay entitled "The Coming Anarchy," Kaplan envisioned a chaotic, post-modern future in which the breakdown of state power lets loose an array of regional disputes, internecine conflicts, and tribalistic violence.[62] Long an advocate of U.S. imperialism, Kaplan argues that the U.S. military is perhaps the only force capable of staying such anarchy. He sees the world outside the American imperium—what he terms "Injun Country"—as dangerous and despotic, full of confusion and savagery.[63] At the frontier of Injun Country and civilization are U.S. forces, fighting to bring order and stability to the more barbarous areas of the world.

Kaplan was embedded with the 1st Battalion 5th Marines in Fallujah on the frontlines of what he viewed as a global imperial project. After all, he notes, "The War on Terrorism was really about taming the frontier."[64] Like many of the regions he has written about, Kaplan viewed Iraq as a geographically incoherent land of clashing identities, urban decay, and inhospitable terrain. "Adam and Eve," he writes, "did not live in a garden paradise but in a turgid mud swamp."[65]

On the first day of the siege, Kaplan recalls, "I looked around in broad daylight to see the roofscape of Al-Fallujah covered with thousands upon thousands of old mufflers and tailpipes, guarded by U.S. Marines, standing atop this part of the city with fixed bayonets. Mosques and factories loomed in the distance. It was truly ugly: the classic terrain of radicalism, occupied by the lumpen faithful."[66] The explanation for the violence is summed up in his pejorative description of the city: Fallujah—violent by nature, its residents driven by religious extremism. But perhaps what is most concerning about Kaplan's account is his enthusiasm for his role in the information war:

Because the battles in a counterinsurgency are small scale and often clandestine, the story line is rarely obvious. It becomes a matter of perceptions, and victory is awarded to those who weave the most compelling narrative. Truly, in the world of postmodern, 21st century conflict, civilian and military public-affairs officers must become war fighters by another name. They must control and anticipate a whole new storm system represented by a global media, which too often exposes embarrassing facts out of historical or philosophical context.

Without a communications strategy that gives the public the same sense of mission that a company captain imparts to his noncommissioned officers, victory in warfare nowadays is impossible. Looking beyond Iraq, the American military needs battlefield doctrine for influencing the public in the same way that the Army and the Marines already have doctrine for individual infantry tasks and squad-level operations . . .[67]

Kaplan's notion of a "sense of mission" betrays any journalistic pretension. He fully embraces his role, not just as a conduit of official propaganda, but as a belligerent in a conflict that blurs the line between violence and information. His observation that operational success depends in large part on his work, however, is correct.

Kaplan brings us full circle as an unapologetic defender of U.S. imperialism, a progenitor of the new barbarism thesis, and a self-conscious propagandist. Long before he set foot in Fallujah as a willing participant in U.S. information warfare, his writings paved the way for a new generation of journalists that would explain Middle Eastern events as a function of the harshness of Arab culture and Islamic teachings. When violence erupted in Fallujah, American audiences were already primed to accept racist and essentialist explanations for the conflict that attributed blame to Arabs and Muslims—inherently violent and opposed to Western freedoms and modernity. This was a narrative all too readily latched onto by foreign aggressors whose fortunes were soon to take a turn for the worse.

PEOPLE'S STORIES

Part I

I cry as I type out these true stories, which I have collected from my college-level English students in Fallujah. I have decided to give you these eyewitness accounts to challenge America's false claims about human rights and justice in Iraq. I used to have faith in human rights, but now it is politicized and manipulated by the powerful and used according to their benefit. Human rights have been buried in Iraq forever, and you can see the grave in the innocent eyes of my poor people.

Forgive me for this question: Where are you when our blood is shed? Where are our so-called human rights? Where are the true Christians when we in Fallujah are hit with illegal bombs by America?

All of the following stories are true. They occurred in the same neighborhood. You can check the credibility of these stories by asking anyone from Fallujah. There are millions of American crimes that are engraved in our minds. These are just a small part of the pain that is locked inside the bottom of my heart. Our responsibility is to be faithful and convey the truth to the coming generation. I ask every country that participated in the aggression against Iraq to present a political apology to the Iraqi people, not the government of Iraq. Perhaps Iraqis will accept your apology.

> Dr. Asmaa Khalaf Madlool
> University of Anbar
> Fallujah, Iraq

CRUSADER'S WAR

Our religion orders us to respect and believe in all heavenly religions and books, from the Torah to the New Testament. Throughout the whole of history it is impossible to find evidence of a Muslim making fun of any Christian prophet. Yet we find that Christians mock our prophet and the Qur'an. Bush referred to the American war in Iraq as a crusade in one of his visits to a base. Perhaps this encourages American soldiers to attack our mosques and kill the religious men inside them. When the Americans withdrew from Fallujah, the owner of the building that they occupied came to check his property. He was surprised to such extent that he called for all religious men to witness what he found. The soldiers used the pages of Qur'an as toilet paper and left them soiled on the ground. Not only this, but the remainder of Qur'an was left in the toilet and the soldiers drew a big cross on the wall inside the mosque. The people of Fallujah regard this crime as the worst, even worse than the many killings that they committed around our city. Another man checked his garage that was used by the Americans for training, and he found that the Qur'an was used as a target for gun training. The man found a hole in the middle of the holy book. Is this the war that God ordered Bush to wage?

UNLUCKY BRIDE

One day a very beautiful woman was hired in our school to teach English. Everyone was attracted to her appearance. She was a good woman, very religious, always wearing the Islamic veil. And she loved her cousin, to whom she was engaged to be married soon. She worked hard as our new English teacher, and she was fond of her specialization. But her fiancé ordered her to leave her work, so she built her life around her new family. She found great happiness in her marriage. Her new family, like mine, refused to leave Fallujah during the second battle with the Americans. Perhaps they made this decision due to the large size of their family. Toward the end of the battle, the soldiers called through their microphones for everyone to leave their homes and go to the central road. After promising our safety, we went to the road. My brother saw the family of the teacher, including her father and mother and the families of their sons and a young unmarried son. The teacher had given birth to a beautiful baby, and she carried it with her. They went to the road too, following orders. But they did not hear the new order to walk. Thus, as usual, without any warrant the Americans shot the whole family. The teacher held her baby strongly to protect him, but the shooting was heavy. She and the child fell to the side of the road. The old father was hit too. He tried to bandage his wound on his side, but he then received a new shower of bullets and fell with the rest. The older son, my friend, died too. The old father and the mother died. The youngest son's head was cut in half leaving a horrible scar on his handsome face. All that was left of this family was the wife of the oldest son and the husband of the teacher. As usual the Americans wanted to hide any sign of this crime by throwing the bodies in the river or in the desert. But they did not realize that we would remember all these stories and tell the coming generation to show the criminality of America. While writing this story I heard that the husband of the teacher died from depression and regret for leaving his little daughter in the field of war. He looks in vain for her body. All he wants is a grave for his dear daughter to be visited every Friday. She left the world silently without a funeral. She left no sign and no grave save the love in our heart.

CHAPTER 2

CONFLICTING NARRATIVES

How could you have control in Iraq when you have this cancer called Fallujah? So it had to be eradicated before you could even conceive of having a successful election in January [2005].

—Major General Richard F. Natonski, Commanding General,
1st Marine Division, Multi National Force, West

On March 31, 2004, four U.S. mercenaries with the Blackwater USA private military contracting company were ambushed and killed, their bodies burned, mutilated, dragged through the city, and hung from a bridge over the Euphrates River. The bodies were still hanging when news of the ambush began to spread around the world. Brigadier General Mark Kimmitt, then deputy director of operations and chief military spokesman in Iraq, initially tried to play down the significance of the ambush, calling it an "isolated" incident.[1] But the graphic nature of the images coming out of Fallujah prompted a torrent of "fantasies of punitive annihilation" in the media, which likened Fallujans to "thugs," "savages," and "barbarians" and called for the city's destruction, invoking Dresden and Hiroshima as precedents.[2]

This was not the first time Americans had been killed in Fallujah. Much of the outrage over this incident stemmed not just from the manner in which these men were killed, but from the media's portrayal of the victims as innocent civilians. A *Washington Post* headline read, "US Civilians Mutilated in Iraq Attack," while the *Chicago Tribune* declared "Iraqi Mob

Mutilates 4 American Civilians." The *Miami Herald* put it more concisely: "Americans Desecrated."[3] From mainstream media headlines to right-wing internet forums, a consensus of rage and retaliation was forming. On Fox News, the conservative anchorman Bill O'Reilly exhorted the U.S. military to a "final solution," declaring, "You're not going to win their hearts and minds. They're going to kill you to the very end. They've proven that. So let's knock this place down."[4] One of the more frenzied reactions came from Jack Wheeler, a former advisor to Ronald Reagan, who proposed the Roman sacking of Carthage as a model to deal with Fallujah. Wheeler called on U.S. senators and congressmen to conclude every speech with the exhortation "Fallujah delenda est!" ("Fallujah must be destroyed"), a reference to Cato the Elder's invocation, "Carthage delenda est!"

> Fallujah must be destroyed. I don't mean metaphorically, I mean for the entire population of the city, every man, woman and child, given 24 hours to leave and be dispersed in resettlement camps, moved in with relatives in another village, wherever, and the town turned into a ghost-town. Then the entire city carpet-bombed by B-52s into rubble, the rubble ground into powdered rubble by Abrams tanks, and the powdered rubble sown with salt as the Romans did with Carthage. Fallujah must be physically obliterated from the face of the earth.[5]

In Wheeler's view, the Blackwater "contractors" were not mercenaries but defenders of Western civilization. Since the 9/11 attacks, the idea that America should act like Rome and impose a "benevolent hegemony" on a disordered world has been a recurring theme among neoconservative intellectuals. Wheeler's proposal for a "Carthaginian" response to the killings at Fallujah was no exception.

This media frenzy provoked a visceral response down the chain of command, starting in Washington. The killings were regarded as a test of the American will, comparable to the "Black Hawk Down" battle in Mogadishu in 1993 when images of dead U.S. airmen being dragged through the streets had similarly horrified the American public. Journalist Jeremy Scahill labeled the Fallujah killings the "Mogadishu moment" of the Iraq war but noted that the murdered men were neither U.S. soldiers nor civilians.[6] In the eyes of many Fallujans, the heavily armed security contractors, driving into their city at a time of intense violence, were in all likelihood CIA operatives or some kind of "special forces."[7]

Despite spokesperson Kimmitt's initial downplaying of the ambush, the White House and the Coalition Provisional Authority (CPA) knew the incident constituted an embarrassing blow to the public image of the occupation, a blow that warranted an equally strong political and military response. "The images immediately became icons of the brutal reality of the insurgency," wrote Paul Bremer, arguing that they "underscored the fact that the coalition military did not control Fallujah."[8] On April 1, Bremer gave a speech to the first graduating class of Iraq's new police academy in which he described the previous day's events as "a dramatic example of the ongoing struggle between human dignity and barbarism." He added, "These acts are also a crime under law and a crime against the future of Iraq. The coalition, Americans and others came here to help the people of Iraq. They came to help Iraq recover from decades of dictatorship, to help the people of Iraq gain the elections, democracy and freedom desired by the overwhelming majority of the Iraqi people."[9] Even though several U.S. generals argued against a rash, retaliatory operation, the American political leadership caved to public pressure and called for an operation to sweep and clear Fallujah of insurgents[10]— the first siege of Fallujah, also known as Operation Vigilant Resolve or the First Battle of Fallujah. On April 5, General Kimmitt announced the initiation of operations in Fallujah, "to kill or capture anti-coalition elements and enemies of the Iraqi people."[11]

Suddenly, Fallujah was positioned front and center in the minds of the U.S. public—emblematic, apparently, of all that was wrong with Iraq. The city and its residents were now cast as problems that had to be suppressed or eradicated altogether. For many outside observers the attack on the Blackwater personnel seemed unprovoked and could only be explained by the barbarous nature of Fallujans themselves, their anti-American sentiments and religious extremism. The U.S. response must have appeared a rational way of dealing with such hatred. However, for the residents of Fallujah, this conflict had a long history.

More than a decade before the 2003 invasion during Operation Desert Storm, Fallujah suffered one of the highest civilian death tolls of that war.

Two separate failed bombing attempts on the main bridge across the Euphrates River hit crowded markets, killing an estimated 130 civilians.[12] In an age of "smart weaponry," the city had experienced a shocking loss of civilian life.

Then, after the fall of Baghdad on April 14, 2003, Fallujah quickly established its own local government and security forces. As a result, the city never experienced the looting and chaos that afflicted many other parts of Iraq.[13] Although there was no need for forces to maintain security, the 82nd Airborne Division moved into the city on April 23, meeting no local resistance, at first. But the attitudes and behaviors of the soldiers soon began to cause offense. There were complaints about Humvees speeding up and down streets, the humiliation of local people at checkpoints, inappropriate treatment of women, and reports of soldiers urinating in the streets.[14] Perhaps most importantly, the Americans did not appreciate the cultural importance of privacy to Fallujans; consequently, they failed to comprehend just how provocative it was for them to place soldiers on rooftops with binoculars. Within just a few days, a clear consensus was building in Fallujah that the U.S. troops should at least withdraw to the city limits.[15]

The tension culminated on April 28 when angry crowds began to protest, first in front of the former Ba'ath Party headquarters building, which the soldiers had commandeered as a base. The protest began in the evening, but when the soldiers fired warning shots, the crowd dispersed. At around 10:00 p.m. the crowd reconvened in front of the al-Qa'id primary school, a two-story compound that the soldiers had converted into a barracks, the roof of which was being used as a surveillance position. Classes were scheduled to reopen on April 29, and residents wanted the soldiers out of the school and out of residential areas all together. As the curfew imposed on the city passed, the angry residents chanted anti-American slogans and demanded that the soldiers leave and the school be reopened. Almost immediately, soldiers fired on the crowd, killing at least thirteen people, including six children, and wounding more than seventy.[16]

The details of this event are disputed. The American soldiers claimed they were responding to gunfire from the crowd, while the protesters deny that they were armed. Human Rights Watch noted that there was no evidence of bullet marks on the al-Qa'id school to support the U.S. Army's allegation that they were fired upon.[17] However, perceptions mattered more than reality. If the residents of Fallujah ever believed that they were being liberated, the encounter at the al-Qa'id school convinced them otherwise, with many reliving their experiences of British colonialism.

Two days after the shootings another protest occurred in front of the Ba'ath Party headquarters building, and U.S. soldiers again fired on the crowd, killing three more and injuring at least sixteen others.[18] Just as before, U.S. commanders claimed their forces acted in self-defense, and again their story was contradicted by eyewitnesses and journalists. The veracity of these claims was of secondary importance, however, given that there was widespread and growing opposition in Fallujah to a military occupation of their city. This was fueled by the 82nd Airborne's refusal to heed the will of the local population. By not respecting their wishes, the American soldiers were bound to come into conflict with Fallujans. But their resort to deadly force, whether in self-defense or not, aggravated an already volatile situation and gave birth to the armed resistance movement in Fallujah.[19]

An agreement was later reached between the 82nd Airborne and the local police, who consented to work with the Americans. However, the police were unwilling to allow them to use their station as a base out of fear that it would make them a target "of what was seen within the city, to an increasing degree, as a legitimate resistance."[20] So the Americans finally agreed to station themselves outside of the city and limit their patrols. Even Sheikh Abdullah al-Janabi, the head of the newly formed Mujahideen Council, urged residents to give the Americans six months to do their work and leave.[21] This agreement led to a dramatic decrease in clashes between armed groups and U.S. forces.[22]

Another initiative was promoted by Colonel Brian Drinkwine of the 82nd Airborne to form a city council composed of local leaders. One such individual was Muhamad Tareq Al-Darraji, who at the time was a thirty-one-year-old graduate student working toward a doctorate in biotechnology at the University of Baghdad. Al-Darraji was born and raised in Fallujah, the youngest of five children in his family. When we spoke with him in 2017, he told us that he was raised in an apolitical family and that he had planned to live a simple life. His adolescent ambition was to earn a science degree and put his knowledge to agricultural purposes. But the occupation changed everything for him. Al-Darraji became active in the political resistance in Fallujah, and he would become one of the city's leading human rights activists. In 2003 he became executive director of the Study Centre for Human Rights and Democracy, which was affiliated with the al-Hadhra Mosque in Fallujah. That same year he was appointed to the newly formed city council. "The idea behind establishing this Council," Al-Darraji told us,

> was to give the people of Fallujah more freedom in managing their lives by themselves, with some technical help from the American forces, in services and maintenance of security. The purpose behind establishing this Council, as the American leader suggested and [Fallujans] and [their] civil leaders agreed on, was to let Fallujans run their affairs by themselves. The Council started with such good steps like forming a local police force and a city-protection force that was comprised of Fallujans, and the results were good in maintaining security and restoring life to the city.[23]

However, the existence of a self-governing city whose security improved by minimizing the Coalition's involvement in its daily affairs seemed to fly in the face of Paul Bremer's claims that they were morally obligated to remain in Iraq in order to maintain security and assist the country in its transition to democracy. Bremer was unwilling to cooperate with the local leadership. He viewed compromise with anyone who was critical of the occupation not as the accommodation of local opinions but as capitulation to the Baathists, and he insisted that the only way to remove all forms of resistance was to "clean out Fallujah."[24]

In November 2003, Bremer deployed newly trained units of Iraqi police and the Iraqi National Guard to bring Fallujah under the control of the CPA. However, the Fallujah City Council refused to accept the authority of these new forces in their city. This resulted in renewed clashes between armed groups and the new Iraqi police and U.S. forces.[25] It was at this point that the violence spiraled out of control, with an increasing number of Fallujans viewing armed resistance against the occupation as both a religious and national duty. However, during these first several months of the occupation, the Coalition denied they were facing an insurgency. Rather, armed groups in Fallujah and elsewhere were depicted as being nothing more than criminals or "former regime elements."[26] The Coalition insisted on framing themselves as liberators and the armed groups in Fallujah as criminal gangs who were "enemies of the Iraqi people" and who did not represent the *true* residents of Fallujah.

Accordingly, bringing security to Fallujah was seen as just a matter of swaying the *real* Fallujans away from the influence of those illegitimate elements within their city. As noted by Bing West—a former assistant secretary of defense in the Reagan administration, former RAND analyst, Vietnam veteran, and an embedded journalist during the second siege—the Coalition tried "winning over Fallujan hearts and minds by infusing jobs, repairing infrastructure, and building relationships with the mayor, the sheikhs, and the clerics."[27] It was further assumed that by simply improving the quality of interactions between Iraqis and the Coalition it would be possible to persuade Iraqis to view the occupation more favorably. Vincent L. Foulk, an Army Civil Affairs officer working with the CPA, later wrote that, "the Marines trained for several months on how to win over Iraqis to the Coalition cause by politely inspecting vehicles, smiling, and waving."[28]

Yet, much to the consternation of military leaders, most Iraqis, especially in Fallujah, were reluctant to cooperate. Foulk observed that "a common statement heard at the unit level was, 'These people are used to force and don't understand much else' . . . The soldiers themselves felt they were bringing something of value and could not understand the lack of enthusiasm by the Iraqis. Democracy was a given good, and the Americans resented the lack of acceptance and gratitude."[29] The belief that the Coalition's attempted nation-building project was motivated by goodwill was articulated by Lieutenant Colonel Eric Wesley, executive officer of the 3rd Infantry Division in 2003, who advised city elders in Fallujah: "You have a stake in a better future, and we as American soldiers are here only to help you. We have no designs upon this city."[30]

While such sentiments were consistent with the Coalition's claim that its mission was guided by the will of "the overwhelming majority of the Iraqi people," the institutional, political, and economic changes imposed by the occupiers were largely informed by a U.S.-centric neoliberal ideology and certainly without the consent of ordinary Iraqis.

Many Americans, civilian and military, simply did not see their actions in Iraq as a violation of Iraqi sovereignty and, therefore, failed to understand or acknowledge how nationalist sentiments fueled the insurgency. This was especially true in the case of Fallujah, whose residents were proud of the reputation their city earned for its role in the anticolonial struggle against the British in the 1920s and who perceived continuity between that struggle and their opposition to the American-led occupation.[31] Muhamad Al-Darraji writes that "[Fallujah's] history is defined by foreign occupation, and the animosity and distrust of the Fallujah people towards the new U.S.-U.K. occupation (2003–11) was not without reasons and historical roots."[32] For most Iraqis, a foreign military occupation was tantamount to an assault on their sovereignty and independence. Yet the Coalition, either mistakenly or strategically, characterized the uprising as being driven by a combination of former regime elements, "hardened terrorists," "criminals and malcontents,"[33] or simply "bad guys."

Bing West summarized the conflict thus: "In Fallujah and Ramadi, sheikhs and former Baathists enriched under Saddam encouraged the imams to call for jihad, insisting it was the duty of every Muslim to take up arms against the infidel invaders. The American occupation had shoved from power both the Sunni clerics and the Baathist officials. Now Sunni nationalism and religious extremism had converged, resulting in calls from the mosques to kill the infidels."[34] This sort of reductivist narrative proliferated through the mainstream media and found further expression in the accounts of military specialists and in veterans' memoirs. However, the few independent journalists who reported the voices of Fallujans painted a very different picture. Journalist Nir Rosen, for example, describes a popular resistance throughout Fallujah with nearly every institution in the city supporting the mujahideen, including mosques and the local police force.[35] Another independent journalist,

Dahr Jamail, reported that "most inhabitants of the city supported the resistance."[36] Zaki Chehab, a U.K.-based journalist and author of *Inside the Resistance*, noted that because Coalition forces did not understand or respect the tribal culture in Fallujah, this inevitably turned entire tribes against them. During one incident when the head of the Abu Al Bourissa tribe was arrested along with his four sons, the result was that "the entire tribe became a fighting unit."[37]

In Fallujah there were a dozen or more militias operating throughout the city, the vast majority of whom described themselves—and were regarded by the majority of the city's residents—as part of a national liberation movement.[38] Al Qaeda was a marginal military force at the time and was situated at the ideological fringes of Iraqi society. From the Coalition's perspective, the widespread, popular support for resistance against the occupation never contradicted its devout belief in the inherent moral legitimacy of its mission. The "hearts and minds" of Fallujans were regarded as a strategic objective to be won, not an end in themselves. If Fallujans were more supportive of the local armed groups in their city, the Coalition only interpreted this as being temporary and indicative of the enemy's thus far superior use of propaganda to sway the people to their cause. But until Fallujans were persuaded to accept foreign occupation and the new political and economic system created for them, their opinions mattered little, if at all.

The power to speak for the civilians of Fallujah—to decide what was in their interests and to claim protectorship over them—and to represent them to Western audiences was central to the Coalition's military strategy. Additionally, a great deal of information operations was directed at Fallujans in the form of Coalition-sponsored news media, pro-Coalition graffiti spray painted on city walls, leaflet drops, and loudspeaker announcements. Robert D. Kaplan describes how the Coalition conducted information operations in Fallujah to convince "the city's inhabitants that the Marines now represented the 'superior tribe' there" and that it was in their interest to cooperate with them.[39] He recalls how an officer told him about their "flash-bang strategy" in which they would "stun the bad guys with aggressive fire, then Psy-ops the shit out of them, always coming back to the theme of the inevitability of the superior tribe."[40]

In this "new kind of war,"[41] victory was just as contingent on persuading the civilian population to participate in the newly created Iraq as it was on destroying the armed resistance. As Vincent L. Foulk put it, "the population was in fact the prize for both sides" of the conflict.[42] However, the more the Coalition tried to play a civic role in Iraqi society—through what the military calls civil military operations (policing, public works, etc.)—the more civilians were drawn into the violence.

Perhaps not surprisingly, Coalition forces on the ground were constantly in a state of confusion when it came to who exactly constituted "the enemy." Some argued that there was "no way to distinguish neutral Iraqis from potential insurgents" while insisting that the distinction was real.[43] Military leaders frequently employed the metaphor of "cancer" to emphasize their ability to draw such a distinction. For instance, Lieutenant Colonel Drinkwine likened the armed groups in Fallujah to a cancerous tumor in an otherwise healthy body. He explained, "When you have a friend who has cancer, you go and carve out the heart of it."[44] General Metz described the city of Fallujah itself as a "cancerous safe haven" that needed to be "taken out."[45] Major General Richard Natonski also referred to the city as a cancer that needed to be "eradicated" before it spread.[46]

The Coalition's confusion around its own categories of "civilian" and "insurgent" was indicative of a more general problem with counterinsurgency warfare. Historian Hannah Gurman observes that "the very idea of a neat physical divide between the insurgency and the people understates the role of family and kinship ties across these categories, while the idea of a clear ideological chasm between insurgents and the population often minimizes the degree of support for 'insurgent' ideas among the people."[47] In other words, this division was more rhetorical than real. Nonetheless, the use of such crude binaries was essential to the Coalition's pursuit of political legitimacy.

In the twelve months between April 2003 and April 2004, five different U.S. Army units had been rotated in and out of Fallujah as the city remained a constant challenge to the occupying forces.[48] Finally, in March 2004, military governance was turned over to the U.S. Marine Corps with a fresh resolve to stamp out resistance. In a message to arriving troops, Marine commander Major General James Mattis likened their mission to battles in World War II and Vietnam. "We are going back to the brawl," he said. "This is our test—our Guadalcanal, or Chosin Reservoir, our Hue City . . . You are going to write history."[49] True to his word, a more aggressive occupation of Fallujah began immediately, involving daily raids, arrests, and firefights that resulted in civilian casualties.[50] Major General Paul Eaton, tasked with training Iraqi forces at the time, remarked on the rapidly escalating conflict, "This thing evolved in front of us. And each day it got incrementally worse, until it exploded."[51]

PEOPLE'S STORIES

PART II

HANDICAPPED VICTIM

Throughout our childhood we became used to seeing crazy Hazim who guarded the secondary school for girls for free. He was fond of this school, and everyone in the school liked him. Even the headmaster liked him and asked him to protect the school. In spite of his mental illness, he has made himself a member of the community, and everyone in Fallujah knew him. He was one of the brave people who refused to leave the city when the Americans attacked. His father was killed in the Iraq-Iran war. Unfortunately, his fate was similar to his father's. When the Americans entered our neighborhood like monsters, they shot Hazim in spite of his handicapped appearance and hid his body.

POOR GIRL

In our city a poor family can live in a school and work as servants or janitors. When I was a student, there was a poor family that lived in the Al-Fallujah Secondary School. I met [the daughter] once when she was looking for the time table of her final exam. She surprised me because she seemed older than her age. I admired her determination to overcome her bad circumstances. One day the Americans burst into the school shouting. Her father and mother did not have the courage to open their door, so the poor girl decided to open it to let the soldiers search because they had nothing to hide. The poor girl seemed to believe in the false slogan of American justice. She behaved as a leader for her family when she decided to open the door. But when the Americans heard the sound of the key, they shot the door to kill the person behind it. They made her body vanish and they arrested her family.

TWO OLD LADIES

Everyone in Fallujah knows the two brave old ladies who behaved strongly and nobly against injustice. In spite of their poverty, they had pride in their morals and traditions. When most of the Fallujan people decided to leave the city before the battle with the Americans, these two women refused because they regarded it as a sign of old age, frailty, and cowardice. They said, "Who could kill old women?" Their appearance brought sympathy because they wore the mourning dress for their dead sons. They were not sisters, but relatives. They both lost their sons, who were killed in different events in their homes. Then the Americans came to our neighborhood to knock on their door. The two ladies were very brave. They hurried to open the door, but the soldiers threw a grenade over the heads of the women. Their bodies appeared on TV with their blood and flesh scattered horribly. The "virtue" of the soldiers was leaving the bodies of the dead women.

CHAPTER 3

THE FIRST SIEGE OF FALLUJAH

> . . . Fallujah soon became a symbol not just of resistance to the occupation but to U.S. hegemony. By and large, Fallujah began to be seen as an island of proud resistance backed by strong tribal and religious affiliations. History was poised to repeat itself in Fallujah, eighty-four years after the rebellion against the British.
>
> —Dahr Jamail, *Beyond the Green Zone: Dispatches from an Unembedded Journalist in Occupied Iraq*

Four days after the killing and mutilation of the Blackwater mercenaries, Fallujah was surrounded and sealed off by Coalition checkpoints. On the evening of April 4, 2004, Operation Vigilant Resolve began with 2nd Battalion 1st Marines attacking from the northwest and 1st Battalion 5th Marines pushing into Fallujah's industrial zone from the southeast, and the 1st Reconnaissance Battalion serving as a screening force from the south.[1] Later these units would be reinforced by 3rd Battalion 4th Marines and 2nd Battalion 2nd Marines.[2]

Fallujah's armed resistance was composed mostly of local militias. Certain mosques controlled their own groups of mujahideen, such as the Al Hadra Muhamadia mosque. The Association of Islamic Scholars—headed by Sheikh Harith Al Dhari, the grandson of Sheikh Suleiman Al Dhari who led the uprising against the British in the 1920s—and the Mujahideen Council, headed by Imam Abdullah al-Janabi, commanded militia forces as well.[3] Additionally, there were a few groups of international mujahideen operating within the city, including Al Qaeda. However, Al Qaeda came to Fallujah with its own religious and political agenda and would not "recognize the authority" of the local leadership.[4] The relationship between Al Qaeda and local armed groups was at times antagonistic, and by 2007 Al Qaeda would be expelled from Fallujah completely by Iraqi tribal forces.[5] But in 2004 they were united with the local mujahideen against a common enemy: the U.S.-led occupation.

Once the cordon around the city was in place, Coalition forces forbade all military-age males from fleeing the city. While this raised concerns that all men between fifteen and fifty-five were treated as legitimate targets, it also created unanticipated hardship for women and children. Local customs forbade women from traveling unaccompanied by their husbands, brothers, or fathers. Many women could not or refused to leave their male family members behind.[6] Consequently, the vast majority of Fallujah's residents had to wait out the siege in their homes.

On April 5, the Iraqi police dropped off leaflets at the city's mosques, announcing a curfew and prohibiting residents from carrying weapons.[7] The Coalition explained that the curfew and the weapons ban were intended to help the Marines distinguish between insurgents and civilians. According to Colonel John Ballard, commander of the Marine Corps' 4th Civil Affairs Group in Iraq at the time, the U.S. military also "broadcast techniques for residents to stay sheltered in their homes and ways to safely approach coalition forces."[8] This tactic, however, also created a situation in which civilians who left their homes were treated as legitimate targets. Indeed, numerous reports from independent journalists and aid workers claim that civilians were being gunned down in the streets while trying to reach doctors, find food and water, or reach a relative's house.

Jo Wilding, a British citizen who volunteered to travel to Iraq with a small circus to perform for Iraqi children, witnessed just such a tragedy. As the siege was unfolding, Wilding separated from her troop and volunteered to help bring medical aid into Fallujah and evacuate patients. Once in the city she worked with a small volunteer staff who transported the sick, injured, and dead around the city by ambulance. On one run they came across the body of a man in the middle of the street, shot in the back with no weapon in sight, his children hiding in a nearby house. They were too afraid to come out to recover the body, fearing they would be shot too.[9] This was not an isolated incident. Doctors, patients, and other volunteers reported numerous similar incidents. Wilding and her colleagues came under fire too. On more than one occasion the ambulance they were riding in was shot at by U.S. Marines, even when the vehicle's lights and sirens were on and megaphones were used to announce the vehicle's transit. Wilding's reports were sent to the Pentagon for comment. Without investigating the incidents in question, the Pentagon replied that U.S. troops only shot at ambulances when they were carrying weapons or fighters.[10]

As the operation progressed, Coalition forces deployed ground troops, tanks, and air support, and were known to use "suppressive fire"— volleys of unaimed fire in the general vicinity of the enemy.[11] Insurgent groups operated in units of twenty or forty, using assault rifles, rocket-propelled grenades, and mortars—an indirect fire weapon, too imprecise to discriminate targets in urban areas.[12] Inevitably, the heavy firepower, imprecise weapons and tactics, and intense firefights in largely residential neighborhoods resulted in high numbers of civilian casualties.

On the very first day of the operation, Coalition air strikes destroyed four houses in two neighborhoods, killing twenty-six people, including women and children, and wounding thirty more.[13] By the third day of fighting, an estimated 280 civilians had been killed.[14] At the time, Al Jazeera was the only media organization to have a broadcast crew within the city, and the televised images of dead and wounded civilians spurred international outrage and condemnation of the American-led operation. The Coalition dismissed these images as "insurgent propaganda"[15] and accused Al Jazeera of being invited into Fallujah by the insurgents to broadcast false reports and "unsubstantiated" figures of the civilian dead and wounded.[16] The Coalition Provisional Authority (CPA) claimed that Al Jazeera broadcast thirty-four stories that "misreported or distorted battlefield events."[17]

Ahmed Mansour, the lead anchor for Al Jazeera in Fallujah, a veteran war correspondent who had covered previous conflicts in the Balkans and Afghanistan and host of the weekly Arabic-language current events program *Without Frontiers,* was a particular irritant to the U.S. military authorities. In his memoir, *Inside Fallujah,* Mansour describes being led into Fallujah by a resident on a backroad often used for smuggling.[18] He makes no mention of being invited by or coordinating with any armed groups and, in fact, has few good things to say about the mujahideen in Fallujah. Instead, Mansour recounts the interviews he conducted with ordinary citizens about their experiences living under siege. Because U.S. forces had taken control of the bridge to the main hospital on the other side of the Euphrates River, doctors and residents had to convert neighborhood clinics and small garages into field hospitals to treat the wounded. Mansour's presence at these field hospitals allowed him to bear witness to the incredible toll the operation took on civilians.

Some of the more gruesome events he reported were of two men bombed in their vehicle while driving to a field hospital during curfew hours, an eighteen-year-old girl and her father shot dead as they were standing by a window, twenty-four civilians killed in a single house by an air strike, and the use of cluster bombs in residential neighborhoods.[19] Mansour also conveyed the difficulties that residents experienced in burying their dead. Because there were so many casualties and given that access to the city's main cemetery was cut off by U.S. forces, the city's only soccer stadium was dug up and converted into what became known as the Martyrs Cemetery. This was done mainly to avoid sanitation problems, although the poignancy of turning a place of pleasure and joy into a site of heartache and grieving was not lost on Fallujah's denizens. In all the rush and confusion, many bodies were buried before they could be identified in unmarked graves.[20] Independent journalist Toshikuni Doi captured some dramatic footage of this cemetery shortly after the first siege. He filmed scenes of graves with incomplete remains marked, for example, as "the arm of Waseem Sadoon," mass graves filled with various body parts from several different bodies, the graves of young children, and crowds of grieving men who were furious with the United States and its allies.[21] One grieving resident told Mansour:

> Americans keep crying "foul" to the rest of the world when they're faced with violent resistance in Fallujah. Who is the aggressor here? Are we attacking them in their cities? Are we placing their families and

children under siege? No. They're the ones who've traveled thousands of miles and crossed continents and oceans to come here to wage war against us. We're obviously in a self-defense situation. They have no right to cry "foul" regardless of what the resistance does to them. If they don't like the way our resistance works, then they need to leave the country. They can't tell us what's moral or immoral in terms of resistance when they are illegally occupying our land.[22]

The images aired by Al Jazeera generated enough international pressure to force the Coalition to end its siege. Not surprisingly, U.S. forces came to see Al Jazeera as an enemy in its information war, as well as an obstacle in their mission. Coalition forces eventually demanded that Mansour and his crew leave Fallujah as a condition for a ceasefire. However, Mansour's reports were corroborated by a handful of independent journalists and activists who also found their way into Fallujah. One such journalist was Dahr Jamail, who had abandoned his job as an Alaskan hiking guide to report on the occupation out of a sense of civic duty. Jamail's background as a communications major in college led him to believe that the mainstream media was deceiving the public through uncritical reporting of the U.S. military's actions in Iraq. While working out of his hotel in Baghdad, he received a tip that an aid convoy was being organized to break the siege around Fallujah. Earlier attempts at this had provoked fire from U.S. troops.[23] But on the fifth day of the siege, Jamail managed to ride in one of sixty trucks in an aid convoy from Baghdad.[24] Only three of these trucks were allowed to pass into Fallujah. Jamail happened to be in one of them.

Upon arriving in Fallujah, Jamail and his colleagues took their supplies directly to one of the field hospitals where they found the doctors working without electricity because Coalition forces had cut all power to the city. Jamail reported that doctors immediately tore into the packages of badly needed supplies and turned their attention to the steady stream of injured civilians arriving at the field hospital. Jamail witnessed a father carrying his dying son and an eighteen-year-old girl who had been "shot through the neck." The injured also included a small child with a gunshot wound to his head who later died of suffocation because the doctors could not vacuum the vomit from his throat without electricity.[25]

Jamail also reported that the field hospital's last functioning ambulance returned pockmarked with bullet holes. The other ambulances had also been fired upon or were bombed by the U.S. Marines and were no longer functioning. The head of the field hospital complained to Jamail that,

> [U.S. soldiers] shot the ambulance and they shot the driver *after* they checked his car, inspected his car, and knew that he was carrying nothing. Then they shot him. And then they shot the ambulance. And now I have no ambulance to evacuate more than twenty wounded people. I don't know who is doing this and why he is doing this. This is terrible. This has never happened before. And I don't know who to call because it seems that nobody is listening . . . For all my life, I believed in American democracy . . . For forty-seven years, I had accepted the illusion of Europe and the United States being good for the world, the carriers of democracy and freedom. Now I see that it took me forty-seven years to wake up to the horrible truth. They are not here to bring anything like democracy or freedom . . . Now I see it has all been lies. The Americans don't give a damn about democracy or human rights. They are worse than even Saddam.[26]

Donna Mulhearn, an Australian journalist and peace activist (and a coauthor of this book), made it into Fallujah on a later aid convoy and witnessed similar conditions. Mulhearn too bore witness to the desperate conditions that the doctors in Fallujah were working under: "the clinic had no disinfectant and no anesthetic and lacked much of the other vital equipment required for the type of surgery the horrific wounds demanded. And as a form of collective punishment all electricity to Fallujah had been cut for days. The clinic had a generator, but when the petrol ran out the doctors had to continue surgery using the glow from cigarette lighters, candles and torches."[27]

In the midst of worsening conditions in the city, Mulhearn reported that whenever residents had to leave their homes for medicine or supplies, they were in constant danger from American snipers and air strikes. She and her colleagues were also shot at by American soldiers even after clearly identifying themselves as aid workers when trying to accompany an ambulance to a field hospital on the other side of the city. She met dozens of frustrated and traumatized residents who could not understand why the Coalition would want to do this to them. One local sheikh told her, "The nature of the people of Fallujah is that they like peace. But after this the Americans have lost their only friends in Fallujah. Now all the people in Fallujah hate the occupation and the US soldiers. All the men are fighting, not just those who are army-trained. Even those who co-operated with the Americans are fighting. We are willing to fight to the last minute even if it will take a hundred years. We are all fighting in a different way."[28]

Another Westerner who made his way into Fallujah was Rahul Mahajan—an American academic, blogger, and activist. His description of the situation in Fallujah differed markedly from the Coalition's official account:

> Among the more laughable assertions of the Bush administration is that the mujaheddin are a small group of isolated "extremists" repudiated by the majority of Fallujah's population. Nothing could be further from the truth. Of course, the mujaheddin don't include women or very young children (we saw an 11-year-old boy with a Kalashnikov), old men, and are not necessarily even a majority of fighting-age men. But they are of the community and fully supported by it. Many of the wounded were brought in by the muj and they stood around openly conversing with doctors and others. One of the muj was wearing an Iraqi police flak jacket; on questioning others who knew [him], we learned that he was in fact a member of the Iraqi police . . . The muj are of the people in the same way that the stone-throwing shabab in the Palestinian intifada were. A young man who is not one today may the next day wind his aqal around his face and pick up a Kalashnikov.[29]

Mahajan also found the Coalition's assertions that Fallujah was a "bastion" of support for Saddam Hussein and the Ba'ath Party to be false. The head of a field hospital told him that "the people of Fallujah refused to resist the Americans just because Saddam told them to" adding that, "If Saddam said work, we would want to take off three days. But the Americans had to cast us as Saddam supporters. When he was captured, they said the resistance would die down, but even as it has increased, they still call us that."[30]

Mansour, Jamail, Mulhearn, Doi, Wilding, Mahajan, and others enabled the voices of ordinary Fallujans to reach international audiences, creating outrage at the humanitarian catastrophe caused by the American operation. U.S. forces, on the other hand, had few journalists embedded with units in Fallujah. The strongest advocate for the U.S. Marines in Fallujah was Robert D. Kaplan, who was embedded with the 1st Battalion 5th Marines. Kaplan offered an alternative explanation for the high number of civilian casualties, claiming, "Almost all the fire and explosions I heard were incoming. The [mujahideen] could fire indiscriminately and blame collateral damage on the Americans, whereas the Americans picked and chose their shots carefully. There was zero tolerance for civilian casualties, though it was impossible to meet the standard always."[31]

In purporting to offer a neutral eyewitness account of unfolding events, Kaplan's reporting went some way toward helping pacify American audiences about the nature of the U.S. intervention in Fallujah and Iraq more broadly. The problem, however, for both the U.S. military and political leadership was the insistent presence of alternative narratives emanating from independent journalists and Fallujans themselves. Faced with these competing narratives, the question of who to blame for civilian casualties became the central factor in legitimizing one side of the conflict and delegitimizing the other.

HUMAN SHIELDS

U.S. forces claimed that the insurgents used "human shields,"[32] asserting that they "deliberately fought from sensitive areas such as mosques, schools and residential areas," using "the Coalition's concern for collateral damage" as an "asymmetric advantage" to limit their "combat capability."[33] Thus, the insurgents, it was argued, were to blame for placing civilians in harm's way. However, the assertion that the insurgents "deliberately fought from sensitive areas" implied that they had a choice. In reality, U.S. forces had encircled Fallujah virtually overnight, trapping all military-age males within city limits.

Historically, one of the only ways guerrilla rebels have been able to defeat the better equipped armies of their foes has been by making use of rugged terrain, often mountains or jungles. Consequently, combat generally occurred in remote areas away from civilian populations. This was not the case in Iraq, however, and combat often took place within the confines of densely populated cities. The Iraqi desert offered little cover that the mujahideen could use to wage war against their occupiers without endangering civilians. While the United States charged the Mujahideen with bringing the violence to urban centers, Fallujans felt the responsibility belonged to the occupiers, not the occupied.

That said, the Iraqi resistance adopted the tactic of planting improvised explosive devices (IEDs) along highways and detonating them when Coalition convoys passed to try to keep the fighting out of civilian neighborhoods as much as possible, because U.S. soldiers, they charged, often responded to ambushes in residential areas with indiscriminate, suppressive fire,[34] which regularly killed civilians.[35] In fact, Ballard notes that the very first IED attack against Coalition forces happened outside of Fallujah.[36]

However, the actual evidence of U.S. aggression mattered little. The outrage elicited by the bloodshed in Fallujah demanded that someone be held responsible, and the Coalition desperately needed to quell public criticism lest their military failure in Fallujah endanger their political goals as well. The Coalition sought to delegitimize Al Jazeera by continually countering its version of events and portraying the insurgents as a cruel and brutal force preying on the civilians of Fallujah by using them as cover. The accusation that the insurgents had used human shields served to legitimate the violence of occupying forces at the same time as it demonized resistance fighters. In the world of binary reportage, such accounts served the occupation well.

Much of the controversy was focused on the fighting that took place in and around mosques, with some accusing the United States of war crimes for targeting mosques with air strikes and others accusing the insurgents of fighting from mosques and using the protection that the Geneva Conventions was supposed to afford these structures to their strategic advantage. Kaplan echoed the latter interpretation, claiming, "The public was never made to feel just how much of a military threat the mosques in Fallujah represented, just how far Marines went to avoid damage to them and to civilians . . . The news photos of holes in mosque domes did not indicate the callousness of the American military; rather the reverse."[37]

Fallujans never denied that the mosques played a role in the fighting.[38] However, there are many conflicting reports about specific instances of combat. For example, on April 7, U.S. forces bombed the Abdul-Aziz al-Samarrai Mosque in Fallujah. Military authorities claimed that they fired a Hellfire missile and two 500-pound bombs at the mosque compound, first in an attempt to kill a sniper who was firing at them from its minaret, and then targeting the retaining wall around the mosque to stun the insurgents before the Marines entered the compound.[39] Major Ben Connable claims that the insurgents must have fled when they saw a drone circling over the mosque, because they found no bodies at the scene. However, the initial news reports of this event asserted that forty Iraqis, who were in the mosque praying, were killed.[40] Others argue that this report misidentified the bodies of insurgents as civilians and that their comrades came and "carried off the casualties" before U.S. forces could get there to assess the scene.[41] Ahmed Mansour, who covered this event for Al Jazeera, contends that there were no combatants in the mosque, not even the sniper, and that "the Americans had either taken the opportunity to bomb a sacred Iraqi relic for satisfaction of revenge or had not truly had sufficient evidence to assume this mosque to be a dangerous hiding place for the enemy."[42]

These conflicting accounts exemplify the way in which competing perceptions of battlefield events were guided by differential assumptions about the legitimacy of violence in combat situations. The official line that insurgents were *attacking* from mosques, schools, and residential areas, rather than *defending* themselves from the United States' attack rested on the belief that the armed groups in Fallujah were, ipso facto, the aggressors. Similarly, the representation of Operation Vigilant Resolve as a "battle" as opposed to a "siege" hinged on the belief that the militants chose Fallujah as the battlefield upon which they would fight the Americans. These claims made sense in the context of the occupiers' rationale for the Iraq mission. Yet for many others, especially those living in Fallujah and Iraq more generally, the reality of life under occupation was undeniable: fresh cemeteries full of civilian dead, homes obliterated, and displaced families.

LOSING CONTROL

Rather than isolating and weeding out the militants in Fallujah, Operation Vigilant Resolve actually united various resistance movements across Iraq that together seriously challenged the authority of the CPA. Uprisings in solidarity with Fallujah broke out in several cities, including Samara, Ramadi, and Najaf. Fallujah had become a symbol of resistance that was bringing Iraq's disparate religious and ethnic groups together in opposition to their occupiers.

As the Coalition was positioning troops around Fallujah on April 2, the CPA decided to close down the newspaper of the immensely popular Shia cleric Muqtada al-Sadr, who preached resistance in the slums of Baghdad. CPA head Paul Bremer called al-Sadr an "outlaw" and ordered the arrest of his top aide. This prompted Sadr to mobilize his militia, the Mahdi Army, and to encourage uprisings in Kut, Kufa, Najaf, Nasiriyah, Sadr City, and several smaller towns.[43] The Coalition suddenly found itself fighting on several fronts.

When reports about the tragedies unfolding in Fallujah emerged, the Mahdi Army sent troops to the city and its surrounding areas in order to help their besieged countrymen. Armed groups in Fallujah reciprocated by sending fighters to Najaf.[44] In addition to armed resistance, there were also nonviolent uprisings. On the fourth day of the siege, thousands of Iraqis from all sects and ethnicities marched from Baghdad to Fallujah in protest of the siege.[45] Further, several members of the Iraqi Governing Council resigned in protest. Even the 2nd Battalion of the new Iraqi army, which was ordered to go to Fallujah to assist the American forces, deserted on the grounds that they felt their orders were "an American plot for Shiites to attack Sunnis."[46]

With uprisings all across Iraq, allegations of war crimes from the international community, increasing criticism at home, and dissent within the Iraqi Governing Council and the Iraqi army, the Coalition's political project in Iraq was beginning to unravel. On April 9, the United States declared a "unilateral suspension of offensive operations" in Fallujah.[47] Although some interpreted this as a ceasefire, all it meant for the Coalition was a decision not to push any further into the city.

Coalition forces held their positions for the next nineteen days. This did not prevent civilians from being killed and wounded, as Coalition forces continued to attack the city, albeit from static positions.

Then, on April 28, dramatic photographs of Iraqi prisoners being tortured in Abu Ghraib were broadcast on *60 Minutes II*.[48] These images outraged Iraqis and created a political firestorm for the U.S. government and the CPA. The Coalition could no longer sustain its operation in Fallujah, but it needed to find a way to end it without losing face. If U.S. forces simply retreated, this would be regarded as a defeat that would damage the image of the United States and, worse, could embolden resistance in other Iraqi cities seeking to emulate Fallujah's example. Faced with a possible public relations disaster, the U.S. military sought an agreement with the leadership in Fallujah that would disguise their withdrawal from the city as a diplomatic maneuver.

The eventual agreement was that Fallujah's "security" would be handed over to the Fallujah Brigade, a newly formed unit composed of former Iraqi soldiers, Iraqi police, and mujahideen.[49] Coalition forces would withdraw outside the city, and the Fallujah Brigade would take control of the city. Many within the Coalition criticized the initiative, claiming the city was being handed over to the very people they had just been fighting, which was indeed correct. The point was to save face by framing their retreat as "an Iraqi solution to an Iraqi problem" and disingenuously asserting that the Fallujah Brigade would police anti-Coalition elements.[50]

On April 30, Coalition forces withdrew completely from Fallujah and formally handed over control of the city to the Fallujah Brigade.[51] According to official U.S. estimates following the siege, 220 civilians lost their lives,[52] although human rights and solidarity groups have *counted* between 572 and 749 civilians killed, including at least 300 women and children.[53] Despite these enormous losses, the American withdrawal was followed by citywide celebrations and parades. Fallujans felt that they had liberated their city. Fallujah was the only city in Iraq that was allowed to manage its own affairs with some degree of autonomy from the occupation. Not surprisingly, the city became internationally renowned as a symbol of resistance to the U.S. empire. Nir Rosen later recalled, "In 2005, while working in Mogadishu, Somalia, I would see a shop named after Falluja and men wearing 'Falluja' T-shirts. In Pakistan I would later purchase an Urdu-language Magazine dedicated to the hero and martyrs of Falluja. A new myth had been created."[54] However, Fallujah's reputation as a center of resistance posed a danger to the Coalition, and in particular to its American military and political leaders. For them, the withdrawal from the city was an acute embarrassment, made worse by the prospect that Fallujah was likely to encourage other rebellions against the occupation and American power more generally.

Despite official assertions that Coalition authorities were seeking a diplomatic solution to the situation in Fallujah, the internal discussions among senior policy makers and military leaders indicated that they were "merely postponing action" by working with the Fallujah Brigade.[55] Just as the first siege of Fallujah ended, another more determined operation was being planned to retake the city. But first, U.S. forces would need to devise a new information campaign in preparation for the coming assault, one that would propagate the most dangerous myth of the entire conflict: the myth of Abu Musab al-Zarqawi.

SAMI

Part I

Kali Rubaii

Sami was seven years old when the first siege of Fallujah began. At the time, he was in the city and eventually joined many others fleeing to his mother's village, located in the rural area surrounding Fallujah.

This is a monologue composed of several partial interviews that I conducted with Sami, always surrounded by one or two of his friends. It would have been impossible, for both cultural and psychological reasons, for Sami to tell this story in a linear way, but he was generous and gave me the time to ask questions and piece the story together into a composite of his unedited sentences. He did not tell the story in this order, nor did he volunteer as many personal details as appear here. I have edited out the questions and prompts that elicited these details to make his story as understandable as possible to those of us accustomed to chronology. I have also edited out most side comments from his peers, but the reader should know that person-centric narratives are rare among Iraqi people. When I asked to hear people's stories individually, I got a shrug and a comments like, "The general picture is more accurate," or "Why my story? It is not a special story. It is like the others." What follows is a composition of my interviews with Sami. All of the words are his own.

———

They wanted revenge, the Americans. The Americans wanted revenge for the Blackwater men. They told us to leave the city and to abandon the people who were fighting to protect the city. It was really strange because they would not allow the men to leave. My father tried to leave with us, but they stopped him. Can you imagine, Kali, the Anbari men sending their women alone outside of the city! We went home and stayed together. I don't remember that day myself. What I remember is the American snipers would play a game, they called it the Family Game I think. I remember that the building was crumpled, but no one was hurt. We saw some fluid on the ground leaking and it smelled strange, not like gas, but then it seemed to change color and turn purple or blue when it waved up from the ground. We were afraid of the gas it made, so we started to run out into the street.

A sniper shot my sister and I saw the hole in her belly grow red, you know, growing round and round and round, bigger. (I am her big brother. She was a good girl.) My father ran out to get her. She was screaming. But when he ran out to get her, the sniper shot him in the leg and he fell. He tried to crawl toward her, and they shot his hand. There was blood all over and I never heard my father scream before. He was so gentle, quiet. My sister was getting quiet, but my father kept reaching for her. They shot him in the neck and he stopped screaming. Blood gurgled out and he turned to face us. My sister was still alive and she was whimpering. I know that the pain in her abdomen was great. We understood they did not want us to save her, and that they would kill us. We were trapped and slept the night there.

In the morning, my sister was dead and my father was dead. We stayed inside the part of our house where we could still light the stove and my mother made some warm food and we had tea and were quiet all night. We heard the noises of war all night. Big low sounds, and short shot sounds, but it was still in our area. There were many bodies in the streets. They, the Americans, rested too. In the morning we heard a shot and my neighbor screaming. Someone else was trying to collect the body, the arms and the parts, of her husband. I think they shot her too.

Dogs were running in the street and sometimes they would try to eat the bodies. A dog tried to drag my sister by the arm, and we threw rocks and pieces of concrete at it. My father's eyes were open, and his mouth. My mother wanted to go and close his eyes. My older brothers would not let her go and she was crying. We were trapped there. I think another day went by but I am not sure.

I remember that the sun was low and my two brothers were whispering together at the end of the opened wall in the building. They decided to drag in the bodies and try to wash them so we could pray. My two brothers decided to go at one time. They thought that if there is just one sniper, at least one of them could get the bodies back. The Americans did this all over, the Family Game. They would try to kill one family person, and then wait and kill one at a time until none were left. My oldest brother stepped out and they shot him in the head right away. He never made any sound. He just fell in slow motion and died before he even touched the bodies. My second brother, Hameed, was my best friend. He got to my sister and turned to bring her body to us. He stopped to close my father's eyes and they shot his ankle—the Americans did that while a son was closing his father's eyes. Not even trying to wash his body, just to close his eyes. He fell but he got back into the house. My mother washed my sister's body. My youngest sister, she was very little, was crying and my mother was trying to get her to be quiet.

My brother's ankle was really hurting. My mother heated up those things, what are they, tongs? For cooking? She made them sterile. She tried to pull out the bullet. It was a special bullet I think. It had shattered in many parts, but she got most of it and treated the wound. We laughed that we should keep alcohol in our house! We could tell our neighbors, "It's for war! It's for medicine."

There was a lot of activity the next day and we crouched low in the back of the place. We saw more gas, and bombs, and heard a lot of noise. I remember hearing the sound in my sleep. I still hear it sometimes, but this is not the worst thing that would come. That is why we say, "Today is better than tomorrow." We think we are sad, and then we become more sad.

My brother could not move and we could not escape. The freedom fighters were active in the city center somewhere. Our street seemed quiet, but we dared not go out or try to leave because of my brother. All that was left now were us. My mother, my baby sister, me, and my big brother,

Hameed, the best one for me. I don't remember how time passed because it is war, but it was real agony. Worse than death. It was a very long time. Hameed started getting little drops on his forehead and my mother said, "That is because his temperature is very high." She said it was an infection from his ankle, or maybe some poison on the bullet, because we don't know how that bullet is. She pulled up his pants and I saw streaks on his skin coming from inside. We did not know what it was.

My mother said his brain would cook if we did not lower his temperature. She taught me to make a fan out of some papers, and we made a fan for his face. That was my job. I fanned his face, and sometimes he looked at me and said nice things, but most of the time he was not there. He started to hallucinate and see things and shout very loud. We tried to make him be quiet, because he was scaring our sister and we did not know when the soldiers would come back. My sister was really very quiet the whole time, watching. We were all waiting, and we could not go anywhere or do anything. Hameed was in a lot of pain, and he would fall out of consciousness. When he did that, his head rolled back on his neck like this, with his mouth open. I never saw before he had a bad tooth in the back. His breath was very strange, like sickness. Later, when my mother opened his bandage to see the ankle, his ankle looked green and open, and I could see some of the bone. It had some black parts that my mother said were very bad.

In the daytime it smelled very bad. I remember we drank water that smelled very bad, but it was worse in the daytime with the sun. The bodies of the dead were all around us, but at some separation from us. My father's body and my brother were swelling up in the abdomen and dogs were fighting over the pieces. I remember that the smell of death is very hard to wash. But the sickness smell, the flesh that is rotting and living at one time . . . it is in the middle of living and dead . . . it smells much worse. I don't know if it was fear or fatigue or hunger or dehydration, but I always remember that the sickness smell made me wretch. I had to run out to vomit and my mother stopped me and grabbed me and I did it on the floor right there. I had forgotten about the snipers and would have run out into the street to die! But now we had vomit and urine, and we had all made an accident in our clothes at the beginning . . . My mother said she could not stand the smell of Fallujah any more, that the smell of death would never be washed away from the streets. She wanted to run to her family village, in the direction of Saqlawiya.

We heard a mosque speaker announce the hospital was bombed, so we had no hope to bring my brother there. My brother was moaning a lot. Hameed, he was not a fighter, not angry, but his fever made him angry sometimes, and sometimes not. I wanted to help him die. Even as a small boy I knew he should die, and that all these days it was taking for him to die was a kind of torture, not inside a jail, but still a torture. I did not have the words for this feeling then, but now I have these words, to say this was the American torture system.

Hameed, he died. It was very sad, a very painful way to die in the heat and shivering. I wanted to kill him. Maybe you should not say that in the book, because they will say, "See, even the Anbari are wanting to kill their own brothers!" But it was not like that. I wanted to kill him because I loved him. But finally, he did not wake up.

My mother said it was time to go. We went out in the street. I felt there was always a sight on my back, that any second I would fall like my oldest brother with a bullet in my head. I imagined the scenario a lot. But we were okay. We did not run because there were many things all over the ground, pieces of the city, and we stepped over some human bodies too. My mother said to stay away from the power lines because they were electric maybe. We got to a place in the city where we could go out through a bridge.

———

> Sami, his mother, and his toddler sister left Fallujah and made it back to his uncle's [mother's brother's] house outside of Saqlawiya. They lived there for years, and Sami continued school a year behind his grade level, with his cousins in Saqlawiya, until war followed them.

CHAPTER 4

THE INTERSIEGE INFORMATION CAMPAIGN

Operation Vigilant Resolve offers a cautionary tale for anyone who would downplay the significance of information in modern warfare.

—Lieutenant General Thomas F. Metz, commander
of the Multi-National Corps—Iraq in 2004

After Coalition forces withdrew from Fallujah in April 2004, deputy director of operations and chief military spokesman in Iraq, General Kimmitt, asserted publicly that "the Marines remain more than capable of continuing the operation to complete the military return of Fallujah to coalition control." He further insisted that U.S. military forces were choosing to withdraw from Fallujah in order to "pursue the peaceful track" and that only when political and diplomatic means had been exhausted would they consider "using the Marines to go back into Fallujah."[1] However, by forcing the world's most powerful military to retreat and negotiate, Fallujah had become more than just a hot spot of resistance against the occupation. It was now a resonant symbol of resistance that unified various other national liberation movements across Iraq. Its pushback against the U.S. military had the capacity to inspire uprisings throughout the country, a prospect that the occupiers could not entertain.

Despite General Kimmitt's claims, the U.S. military's actions in the months following the first siege suggest that the withdrawal from Fallujah was less a compromise and more a change in tactics. A second operation was needed not simply to defeat the insurgency in Fallujah, but to crush it in a spectacular fashion, sending a clear message to armed groups throughout the country that resistance was futile. This was the goal from the moment "control" of the city was ceded to the Fallujah Brigade. The United States' withdrawal was, in effect, a temporary maneuver to regroup, rethink the battle plan, and "shape" the battlefield and, equally important, the political environment for the ensuing operation.

In doing so, the Coalition took certain lessons to heart from what they considered to be a humiliating defeat. Colonel Ballard notes that "by the end of April [2004] the MEF's [Marine Expeditionary Force] lack of robust Public Affairs (PA) and Information Operations (IO) activities had become obvious in relation to the effective efforts of the insurgents. So the MEF placed new emphasis on those techniques, and they began to figure much more prominently in the scheme of maneuver than they had in the initial operations order."[2] In other words, U.S. military leaders viewed their failure to silence Al Jazeera or to provide a credible alternative account of the operation to international audiences as problems that had to be urgently addressed. Moreover, military leaders and analysts agreed that they had allowed the attack on the Blackwater mercenaries to provoke them into launching a hastily planned operation. Lieutenant General Sattler, commanding general of the 1st Marine Expeditionary Force in Iraq in 2004, remarked that "[we] did not have an opportunity to shape the battle—only to deal with the enemy's activities. So we took the lessons learned, such as how the enemy used information operations [IO] to stop the battle, to set the stage for Fallujah II."[3]

With this in mind, the U.S. military then launched a major campaign to "shape" the battlespace in anticipation of a second siege. The military term "shaping operations" refers to a number of activities including strategic communications, direct attack, and other "lethal and nonlethal activities" to both influence the enemy's decisions and the media environment.[4] Above all, the U.S. military sought to avoid the impression that the coming attack was a vindictive operation fought simply to avenge the United States' tarnished image and to force Fallujah to accept a government created by the occupying powers. Instead, the operation was justified as a last resort following the exhaustion of all diplomatic and peaceful efforts to restore "security" so that Iraq could have a free election in January 2005.

The information campaign unfolded gradually, first with a change in how it characterized the enemy from "former regime elements" to Al Qaeda militants led by the Jordanian militant Abu Musab al-Zarqawi. While this rhetorical shift was barely noticeable to the American public, it created a dangerous and misleading public discourse. Military spokespersons and media commentators were now using labels like "jihadists," "thugs," "terrorists," "insurgents," and "Al Qaeda" interchangeably, conflating and demonizing all Islamic militant groups, regardless of their political goals or choice of tactics. Political scientist Emma Louise Briant argues that obscuring the differences between militant groups in order to create a "homogeneous other" was characteristic of the Bush administration's post-9/11 rhetoric.[5] Kevin McCarty, the former National Security Council director for global outreach, rationalized this rhetorical strategy, recalling that "the bad guys in our mind were Al Qaeda, which is a very loose term for a whole bunch of bad guys doing different things. I mean, there wasn't really an Al Qaeda, there just were a lot of different bad guys. Some of them used the name, some didn't."[6] While McCarty might regard all military forces opposing the United States as "bad guys," the American public was not given the information needed to decide for themselves whether a morally relevant distinction should have been drawn between the nationalist forces in Fallujah and other groups self-identifying as Al Qaeda.

No longer Baathist loyalists, the rebels in Fallujah were now reduced to jihadists with links to Al Qaeda. By September the shaping operations had intensified and included air strikes, the disbanding of the Fallujah Brigade, and the beginning of a psychological operation aimed at prompting civilians to flee the city.[7] Describing this "new kind of war," Lieutenant General Sattler observed,

> When we bombed targets during the shaping phase, whatever target we hit, even though we did positive identification, we did the collateral damage assessment to make sure there wouldn't be collateral damage

to noncombatants, and we deconflicted friendly forces . . . We watched the hit and we knew who we killed, and we knew what collateral damage was done.

The next day there was going to be a press release coming out from the insurgents that would show [that] we killed women, children, and elderly men. And there would always be pictures of hospitals with children, women, and old men in it as they talked about who we had bombed, and that [our bombs] never killed any insurgents, they never killed any of [Abu Musab al-] Zarqawi's [Al Qaeda] network. It was always a standard thing.

And then we would try to rebut that.[8]

Ahmed Mansour also wrote about this "standard" procedure:

The hunt for al-Zarqawi began an endless cycle in Fallujah: American forces would bomb a civilian house and declare they'd just bombed an al-Zarqawi hideout; reporters would snap pictures and shoot footage of dead civilians; and the phantom al-Zarqawi would not be found. The bombings intensified in July and reached their peak in mid-October, immediately after Allawi threatened Fallujans to hand over the enemy . . .

This intensified bombing caused some Fallujan families to flee the city again, only six short months after they had returned in the aftermath of the first battle. These families considered the escape to be temporary. Since family ties are very strong in that region, they had no problem finding relatives outside Fallujah to stay with. But many Fallujans had trouble getting to those relatives safely because migrating convoys of civilians were often bombed. On October 12, one entire family (including young children) was bombed on the way out of Fallujah, and images of the bombed car were broadcast by news networks across the world.

One of the more gruesome crimes US forces committed while "looking for al-Zarqawi" took place on October 8. American forces claimed to have directed an accurate surgical strike on an important al-Zarqawi hideout. Iraqi doctors who treated the wounded later revealed the target to have been a civilian house where a wedding had just taken place. The bride was injured, along with nine other women and six children. The groom was killed along with ten other people. Out of the eleven killed there were eight from the same family: a father and his seven children . . .

In another case, a family who had left the city to escape the wrath of the bombs, decided to return home to pick up some things. On that night of October 19, their house was bombed by two massive rockets and killed them all. Reuters correspondent Yasser Faisal confirmed that he'd seen all six members of the doomed family—two parents and four children—being pulled from the rubble. Neighbors told the same story. But spokespersons for American forces once again claimed that the strike targeted, with surgical accuracy, a house that sheltered al-Zarqawi's men.[9]

How can we explain these very different accounts of the same battlefield events? Was the insistence of American military leaders that "every bomb . . . we dropped has been a precision munition"[10] and that civilian casualties were "almost zero"[11] a sincere belief in the infallibility of their methods, or a deliberate act of deception? Is it possible that there was a flaw in their process of selecting targets and collateral damage assessment?

To complicate matters further, armed groups in Fallujah also saw themselves as being locked in an information war with the occupying forces. It was understood that the reports they released about civilian casualties, or the crimes of the occupying powers, would have a direct bearing on battlefield events. Colonel Ballard points to one incident when insurgents released a stock image of a "bullet-ridden" ambulance when in fact the Coalition had targeted that ambulance—which they claimed was being used to ferry weapons—with a laser-guided bomb.[12] This inaccuracy in the insurgents' press release was seized upon by the United States to discredit all claims coming out of Fallujah about civilian casualties. These conflicting accounts make it extremely difficult to know who is spinning the truth or to ascertain the outcome of every air strike conducted by the Coalition. However, dismissing all or even most of the reports of civilian casualties in Fallujah as "enemy IO" flies in the face a lot of evidence, including the dead bodies of women and children filling the Martyrs Cemetery.

It was General Sattler's task to give the final approval for air strikes against all targeted individuals, houses, and infrastructure.[13] In response to accusations that U.S. forces had bombed Fallujah indiscriminately,

Sattler invited Martha Raddatz, journalist for ABC News, to his workshop where he and his staff analyzed intelligence and selected targets for air strikes. Sattler wanted to, "show 'em the whole targeting procedure, show them how we build targeting orders, show them how we update the folders, and when we hit the culmination point, when the positive identification and the criteria that we've established for that particular target's met, how we clear it, how we discuss it quickly, and how we strike it."[14] However, instead of offering transparency, Raddatz's visit was turned into a PR exercise in which she investigated nothing and uncritically relayed Sattler's words to American audiences. She later wrote in a short article for ABC News that "the military says great care is taken to avoid killing innocent civilians" and that "the military says the numbers [of innocent civilians killed] have been greatly exaggerated," making little commentary of her own on the matter.[15]

General Sattler may well have believed that the houses selected were legitimate targets that held only evil men and that their air strikes were precise. The assessment of who constituted a threat and the outcomes of the strikes, however, is worth questioning. In fact, the extreme pragmatism of information warfare in this period raises many questions. By treating unflattering facts, reports, and statements as enemy activities that require a combative response, much of this information was disregarded simply for its impertinence to U.S. operational objectives. The possibility that it might have been true does not seem to have even been considered. Perhaps for some in the IO community it was inconceivable that U.S. air strikes had in fact resulted in the reported number of civilian casualties. Perhaps for others such claims had to be rebutted as a matter of standard operating procedure. In any case, the real tragedy of what was happening to Fallujans was lost in this war of spin that so easily dismissed their death and injury as "enemy IO."

Indeed, Lieutenant General Thomas F. Metz, commander of the Multi-National Corps—Iraq, recalls that reports of civilian causalities were regarded as "IO challenges" that were addressed militarily rather than through humanitarian efforts. For example, Metz claims that the Coalition "took control of the hospital the evening before the main attack on Fallujah, removing it from the enemy's IO platform."[16] The

U.S. military had long assumed the doctors at Fallujah's hospital to be a "terrorist-supportive staff"[17] and the hospital itself to be "little more than a nest of insurgent propagandists," because "that April they [the insurgents] had used the facility to issue claims of non-existent civilian casualties."[18] But did the U.S. military ever investigate the accuracy of the Fallujah hospital's reports? Or were these reports defined as IO challenges, ipso facto, because they highlighted civilian deaths and, by extension, were attributed to the U.S. military?

Further preparations for IO challenges included the Coalition's decree that only embedded journalists would be allowed inside Fallujah for Operation Phantom Fury. The Media Commission in Iraq, which was established by Order 65 of Bremer's 100 Orders, sent out a brazen warning to all journalists in Iraq that they should "stick to the government line on the U.S.-led offensive in Fallujah or face legal action."[19] Journalists who tried to enter Fallujah without being embedded with Coalition forces were detained.[20] This time around, ninety-one journalists were embedded with Coalition units inside Fallujah to "[offer] a rebuttal" to the "Arab media," whereas in the first siege there were only a few such journalists.[21] The objective of these increased placements was to show American audiences what the Coalition believed to be the "ground truth"—that is, the operation as seen through the eyes of the U.S. military.[22]

Encouraging civilians to flee Fallujah "amid general threats of an imminent US attack"[23] was another way in which Coalition forces responded to "IO challenges." Leaflet drops were used to warn civilians of the coming assault, a PSYOP that Lieutenant General Metz described as "very successful" because "almost 90% of the population departed Fallujah."[24] General Sattler believed that Fallujans left "voluntarily" because the PSYOP alerted them to the fact that "we're going to come, and you probably don't want to be here."[25] Also, the electricity and water supply to the city were cut "to induce the few remaining civilians to leave."[26] This provided a practical solution to the problem of crossing the "IO threshold," which General Metz describes as "the boundary below which the media is not interested and above which they are."[27] In other words, the IO threshold was not about the actual level of violence used, but rather about limiting the extent to which it was reported in the media to avoid an "adverse political and public reaction" so that the "US shaping operations and later attacks could be conducted with impunity."[28]

General Metz later argued that the IO campaign leading up to the second siege could serve as a model for the integration between IO and PA. That said, he considered a "firewall" between IO and PA essential to ensure that "PSYOP, Deception Operations, EW [electronic warfare], and CNO [computer network operations] do not migrate into PA and discredit the PA effort." Metz believes that IO officers could serve as a "bridge" by getting "images and stories that the media could use" to the PA officers.[29] During the campaign, however, "exaggerated" reports were intentionally fed to American journalists, and by extension, to U.S. audiences. This misinformation was directed at both Iraqis and the U.S. domestic media and served to create one of the most pervasive and destructive myths about the U.S.-led occupation of Iraq, a myth that became a conventional wisdom among American soldiers, journalists, and policy makers. Crucially it was mythmaking that legitimated future military actions, resulting in the loss of thousands of lives.

THE MYTH OF ABU MUSAB AL-ZARQAWI

Abu Musab al-Zarqawi was born Abu Hilalah Ahmad Fadil al-Nazal al-Khalayleh in Zarqa, Jordan.[30] When Colin Powell addressed the UN Security Council in 2003 in an attempt to garner international support for the invasion of Iraq, al-Zarqawi's alleged presence in the country was cited as a justification for the U.S.-led invasion. At that point, it was believed that al-Zarqawi had already been a mujahideen fighter for over ten years, with combat experience in Afghanistan and ties to Osama bin Laden. Powell claimed that al-Zarqawi was commanding a cell of jihadist fighters linked to Al Qaeda in the northeast of the country and that he had been offered safe haven there by the regime of Saddam Hussein.[31] After the invasion, there was little mention of al-Zarqawi in the media for almost a year, until February 9, 2004, when a "selective leak" was made by the U.S. military to an American journalist.[32]

By mid-May of 2004, allegations began to surface in the media about al-Zarqawi using Fallujah as a base for military operations. Rahul Maha-jan noted the suspicious timing of al-Zarqawi's reemergence in media reports, "at a time of maximal Shia-Sunni unity."[33] It was rumored that al-Zarqawi bore an intense hatred for Shia Muslims and hoped to pro-voke a Sunni-Shia civil war in Iraq. Then, in the midst of the first U.S. siege, a video emerged entitled "Abu Musa'b al-Zarqawi slaughters an American" showing the decapitation of Nicholas Berg, an American contractor in Iraq, by masked mujahideen, one of whom was assumed to be al-Zarqawi. Some Coalition intelligence analysts believed that the video was *probably* filmed in the Jolan neighborhood of Fallujah, though the evidence was inconclusive.[34] Regardless, rumors soon emerged connecting al-Zarqawi with Sheikh Abdullah al-Janabi and other local mujahideen in Fallujah, like Omar Hadid. No proof that al-Zarqawi had even set foot in Fallujah was ever provided, yet the mainstream media repeatedly aired these rumors as if they were fact.[35]

Speculations about al-Zarqawi's presence in Fallujah soon morphed into conventional wisdom, and before long the Coalition boldly asserted that al-Zarqawi was indeed in Fallujah, using the city as a base from which his organization—dubbed "Al Qaeda in Iraq" by the occupiers but in actual fact going by the name *Jama'at al-Tawhid wal-Jihad* ("orga-nization of monotheism and jihad")—was launching attacks all across the country. Independent journalist Jeremy Scahill notes that "Zarqawi became a propaganda bonanza for the Bush administration because it could now characterize the resistance in Iraq as being led by al Qaeda."[36] This became a common belief among U.S. soldiers, from the lowest ranks to the highest levels in the chain of command. And to this day al-Zarqawi remains a potent myth in the collective memory of the U.S.-led occupation of Iraq. He has been featured in films and literature about the War on Terror, most notably in the 2014 film *American Sniper*, as the head terrorist in Iraq leading the insurgency from Fallujah.

Yet in 2006 it was revealed that U.S. forces had been conducting a PSYOP campaign that intentionally exaggerated the role of al-Zarqawi in the insurgency, including making a "selective leak" about al-Zarqawi to *New York Times* journalist Dexter Filkins.[37] Army Colonel James Treadwell denied that this PSYOP was aimed at deceiving the American public. The leaked military documents show that the goal was to elicit a "xenophobia [*sic*] response" in Iraqis by characterizing the Sunni resistance as both foreign and extremist. And Brigadier General Kimmitt claimed that "the Zarqawi PSYOP program [was] the most successful information campaign to date." However, the measure of success for this operation is unclear. Those targeted most directly (Fallujans) were skeptical that al-Zarqawi even existed, let alone was in their city; while those allegedly not targeted (the American public) had come to believe that al-Zarqawi constituted an existential threat. But the most obvious result of the operation was increased paranoia between Sunni and Shia Iraqis, bringing the country closer to civil war.

What is clear, however, is that with the porous boundary between IO and PA, the al-Zarqawi PSYOP, and the air strikes on Fallujah, were essential and interrelated components of the shaping operations that fed off of each other in a lethal way. According to Sattler, the "theme" of al-Zarqawi justified the air strikes to Americans and Iraqis alike through the IO/PA nexus:

> There has to be public affairs, and I know public affairs and IO are separate; they have two different missions in life. The way you attack a theme is different when you're IO or public affairs, but the themes can be relatively the same. And they need to know each other's themes so they can play off 'em inside their own arena. So we had public affairs, civil affairs, and IO all sitting down at the same table, working through themes, to make sure we were getting the effect that we wanted.
>
> What we basically did, before we dropped a bomb, after about the two-week mark, [a] press release went out from us, telling what we did, why we did it, [that] the individual was a thug, a two-bit criminal who has killed "X" number of Iraqi civilians . . . So every time we struck, we told 'em who [we] went after, who we thought we killed—i.e., a member of the Zarqawi network—and then we were able to also remind everybody that this is not Robin Hood . . . We twisted that over time; we turned it around to play the way it should be played. And believe it or not, after about a week of us getting the first shot out, their IO campaign fell apart . . . We started to drive a wedge between the terrorists and the local residents, and then we drove a wedge between [Omar] Hadeed, one thug lord; Zarqawi, another thug lord; and [Abdullah al-] Janabi, another thug lord.[38]

Sattler's analysis is wrong, however. There is significant evidence to suggest that the Mujahideen Council led by Sheikh Abdullah al-Janabi was antagonistic to the Al Qaeda–aligned militias that had made their way into Fallujah, and this antagonism arose not out of the American IO campaign but out of incompatible interests and goals with the local militia groups. It is difficult to tell from the interview quoted above whether the myth of al-Zarqawi was believed to be true even by the IO officers working with Sattler or whether al-Zarqawi was nothing more than a theme used to justify military action in Fallujah.

To begin with, Sheikh al-Janabi publicly disavowed any connection with al-Zarqawi, stating, "We don't need Zarqawi to defend our city . . . The Iraqi resistance is something, and the terrorism is something else. We don't kidnap journalists, and we don't sabotage the oil pipelines and the electric power stations. We don't kill innocent Iraqis. We resist the occupation."[39] This public statement appears to be genuine, according to the work of independent journalists, like Nir Rosen, who documented evidence of the growing animosity between the foreign, Al Qaeda–aligned militias in Fallujah and the local, nationalist militias. Tracking a Coalition bombing campaign that began on July 19 and claimed to target al-Zarqawi and his Fallujah-based network, Rosen reported that this campaign killed "scores of civilians."[40] He also reported that by late July, "the leadership in Falluja met with foreign fighters in the city and expelled about twenty-five of them, including Syrians, Jordanians, and Saudis." In fact "several resistance groups . . . issued a joint declaration calling for the blood of Abu Musab al-Zarqawi to be spilled. Their declaration also declared their friendship with Iraqi Shias and called for cooperation with the new Iraqi government led by Prime Minister Ayad Alawi."[41] Such reports indicated that the insurgency in Fallujah was not dominated by foreign fighters like al-Zarqawi; rather, local armed groups were not only hostile to al-Zarqawi but also had the capability to eject foreign fighters from the city.

An even more complicated picture is painted by journalist, Michael Ware, who was embedded with Coalition and insurgent forces alike and probably knew more about al-Zarqawi's network than most U.S. intelligence operatives. In fact, Ware had unusual access to this otherwise highly secretive network. In the summer of 2004, al-Zarqawi's network reached out to him with a propaganda video that they wanted reported in the media. A working relationship developed, and Ware was able to meet and interview several members of this network, though he never met al-Zarqawi, who, he said, "operates in a stratosphere that is beyond my experience and is beyond the experience of, I'd vouch, almost every insurgent commander and leader in the country. The number of people who would have sat and met face-to-face with Zarqawi would be very, very small."[42] Ware was also careful to note that he was investigating an insurgent network that bore al-Zarqawi's name, even though little was known about Zarqawi himself. In fact, while al-Zarqawi's name is associated with the propaganda video, Ware states that "what is believed to be Zarqawi's voice is heard only once."[43] While al-Zarqawi does indeed appear to have been an insurgent leader in Iraq, there is very little real evidence connecting him to Fallujah. Indeed, his alleged leadership role in Fallujah's insurgency and his relationship with Sheikh Abdullah al-Janabi's Mujahideen Council are more myth than reality.

MANUFACTURING LEGITIMACY

Another goal of the shaping operations was to put an Iraqi face on the second siege of Fallujah. Even before the city had been turned over to the Fallujah Brigade in April, the Coalition Provisional Authority (CPA) knew that defeating the insurgency in Fallujah would be politically impossible without the support of the Iraqi government and its military. In June, the CPA granted "sovereignty" to the Iraqi Interim Government (IIG), which was to govern Iraq until the country's first election under their new constitution in January 2005. All members of this IIG were appointed by the CPA, including Prime Minister Ayad Allawi, a native of Baghdad who lived in exile for almost thirty years and was on the CIA's payroll for most of the 1990s.[44]

Although the Coalition claimed they had handed sovereignty over to Iraq, the interim government had little real power of its own and was completely dependent on Coalition forces for security. The interim government was hugely unpopular among Iraqis and would have been quickly overthrown were it not for the presence of U.S.-led forces.

However, the IIG and the Coalition needed one another to survive. Various tasks had to be initiated by Iraqis so as to create the appearance of an independent Iraqi democracy and, above all, to mask the unsavory reality of foreign occupation.

For example, it had long been on Bush and Rumsfeld's agenda to silence Al Jazeera, even though this was far from being politically expedient. Such an act of outright censorship would have merely supported the widely held view that the Coalition's mission was driven by imperialist ambitions. So Allawi ordered the closure of Al Jazeera's Baghdad bureau on August 7, 2004, repeating the lines of Bush and Rumsfeld that the station's reporting "incites violence and hatred."[45]

Allawi did the Coalition another favor by dissolving the Fallujah Brigade.[46] He and the Coalition accused the Brigade of having failed to police the city, of being in full collaboration with the insurgents, and of harboring terrorists like al-Zarqawi. The Fallujah Brigade was duly disbanded on September 11, 2004.[47] Nonetheless, the Fallujan leadership sent a delegation, led by Sheikh Khaled Hamoud Al-Jumaili, to begin peace negotiations with Iraqi defense minister Hazim al-Shalan in mid-October. The negotiations were briefly suspended by the Mujahideen Council because of the Coalition's "continuous bombing in Fallujah."[48] However, when the negotiations resumed, many viewed their progress as hopeful. The *Washington Post* reported, "Local insurgent leaders voted overwhelmingly to accept broad conditions set by the Iraqi government, including demands that they eject foreign fighters from the city, turn over all heavy weapons, dismantle illegal checkpoints and allow the Iraqi National Guard to enter the city. In turn, the insurgents set their own conditions, which included a halt to U.S. attacks on the city and acknowledgment by the military that women and children have been among the casualties in U.S. strikes."[49] Some former CPA officials saw the peace negotiations as "a potential breakthrough that could avert not only an assault on Fallujah but also a violent aftermath, when insurgents might take the fight elsewhere."[50] But Allawi demanded that Fallujah's leadership turn al-Zarqawi over to the Coalition, effectively ending the peace negotiations.[51] It was a demand that Fallujans could never meet, an impossible condition for peace.

In response, Kassim Abdullsattar al-Jumaily, the president of the Study Centre of Human Rights and Democracy based in Fallujah, wrote an open letter to Kofi Annan, then UN secretary general on October 13, 2004, pleading that he intervene to stop U.S. air strikes, which had killed and injured "hundreds of innocent people," and to stop the coming assault "to prevent a new massacre." The letter went on to affirm the right of Fallujans to resist the occupation, according to international law, and deny that al-Zarqawi was in Fallujah:

> On the night of the 13th October alone American bombardment demolished 50 houses on top of their residents. Is this a genocidal crime or a lesson about the American democracy? It is obvious that the Americans are committing acts of terror against the people of Fallujah for one reason only: their refusal to accept the Occupation . . .
>
> We know that we are living in world of double standards. In Fallujah, they have created a new vague target,: AL ZARQAWI. This is a new pretext to justify their crimes, killing and daily bombardment of civilians. Almost a year has elapsed since they created this new pretext, and whenever they destroy houses, mosques, restaurants, and kill children and women they said "we have launched a successful operation against Al-Zarqawi." They will never say that they have killed him, because there is no such a person. And that means the killing of civilian [sic] and the daily genocide will continue . . .[52]

In response Kofi Annan wrote an open letter to George W. Bush, Tony Blair, and Ayad Allawi, asking them to renew peace negotiations with the help of the UN.[53] All three rejected the offer and asked the UN for "noninterference."[54]

Allawi's actions were essential in making the operation look like an "Iraqi call," as General Sattler explains:

> Prime Minister [Ayad] Allawi had to be the one that set the conditions, with not only the Iraqi people, both the Shi'a and the Sunni. He had to exhaust all opportunity for a peaceful conclusion, and then he had to let the international community know he had done so; mainly the GCC [Gulf Cooperation Council] countries, which surround Iraq. He had to let Muslims worldwide know that he was only going to fight other Muslims because it had to be done. We had to paint the picture

of what was going on inside Fallujah, and was being exported out of Fallujah.[55]

This sort of messaging was extremely important for the Coalition, with Iraq's first elections coming up in January. Allawi was capable of selling this message in a way that the Coalition simply could not. The Coalition wanted the world to believe that Iraq embraced the political changes that were being put in place. Fallujah's violent rejection of the Coalition's political project sent a message that was unacceptable for U.S. military and political leaders. General Richard Natonski put the danger that Fallujah posed this way: "How could you have control in Iraq when you have this cancer called Fallujah? So it had to be eradicated before you could even conceive of having a successful election in January [2005] . . . by taking out Fallujah, I think we then had the momentum in the rest of the country, that the Iraqi people understood that we meant business . . ."[56] The elections would enable the Coalition to create the appearance to the world of a successful nation-building project in Iraq, rather than the creation of a client state. Political allies like Allawi gave the occupation the facade of Iraqi approval and the practical collaboration they so badly needed.

The original name given to the second siege by the Coalition was Operation Phantom Fury. However, two days before the operation began, Ayad Allawi requested that the operation be renamed Operation Al Fajr, "new dawn," to better appeal to the Arab world.[57] On November 7 Allawi declared martial law throughout Iraq and gave the go-ahead for Coalition forces to conduct the operation.[58] On November 8, as the ground offensive of Operation Phantom Fury began, Donald Rumsfeld announced that "every effort has been made to persuade the criminals running roughshod over Fallujah to reach a political solution, but they've chosen the path of violence instead."

PEOPLE'S STORIES

PART III

FAITHFUL FATHER

He was an old man who worked all his life to provide for his humble family. His youngest son was in his final stage of secondary school. His son liked to study, and he wanted to get high grades and go to a good college. Before the battle with the Americans, the father tried to convince his son to postpone his studies and to leave Fallujah with his family, but the boy asked to stay at school for just a few more weeks to finish his final exams. He promised to come and join the family as soon as possible. So the family left town and the son stayed. After a week, the father heard about the American crimes in Fallujah. He returned to force his son to leave. Unfortunately, when the father had almost reached his home, he was shot and fell near his door. The son heard the shots and went out to see what happened. He saw his father's body cut into two, his two legs in one place and his body in the other. With the help of relatives he carried his father's body to the hospital. They found Dr. Rafiaa, but there was not a free bed in the whole hospital because of the incredible number of injuries. Dr. Rafiaa completed the operation in the corridor and saved the father's life. But to this day the son lives with the guilt for his father's lost legs.

A CIGARETTE

During the battle we were imprisoned inside our homes for months. When the battle began, we did not know we would remain in our homes for such a long time. Eventually, our food was finished and our supplies ran out. Many smokers become very angry because they did not have cigarettes. Our neighbor could not endure it any more. His son saw him suffering, and like a good boy he offered to help. The father asked the son to cross the main road and bring a pack of cigarettes from the broken shop. The poor boy agreed and was ready for this venture. He did not know that the American sniper was waiting for him. The father thought that the Americans would not kill a child. The boy was hit by the American and left on the road like a dead bird. The father heard the noise of people who saw the crime. He ran to collect the body of his dutiful son. After the end of the second attack I visited the boy`s grave, but I withdrew when I noticed someone approaching. It was the boy's father. I barely recognized this ghost of a man, crying and blaming himself for sending his dear son to death for a cigarette.

FORBIDDEN BOMBS

Al-Julan is an important neighborhood of Fallujah. The people of Julan decided to protect themselves from the Americans, since they were certain that in any case they would face death. During the battle, the American soldiers played with the dead bodies there. They tied injured people to the front of their tank to serve as human shields. In spite of these monstrosities, the Americans faced a lot of difficulties entering this part of town. Halfway through the battle they withdrew all their troops from this neighborhood. Everyone was surprised by this sudden withdrawal, and then planes dropped strange bombs that produced heavy smoke. In the days after this attack, many people entered Julan to save the injured. All the first responders were surprised to see that the dead bodies appeared melted. The strange thing was that the clothes of all the victims were not affected. We do not have information about the type of bomb, but when the battle ended many foreign groups came to visit Fallujah. They inspected Fallujah with machines, and they were shocked to find high degrees of radiation in the schools and homes of this neighborhood. They forced the teachers to close the schools and leave the city to clean it from the effect of these forbidden bombs. The effect still lives among us. The Americans left Fallujah, but they left cancer behind them to kill the survivors. Many children are born with defects. With this bloody story I hope to shock the silent, cowardly world with this appalling question: Why has America not been judged for using forbidden bombs in Fallujah? The painful irony is that the reason given for their horrendous aggression was to remove forbidden weapons from Iraq, but then the Americans themselves used forbidden weapons to kill us. Many foreign researchers have visited my town to prove the use of forbidden weapons. Where is the international court's judgment about these crimes?

A DEAD VISITOR

During the battle we tried not to let our brothers go outside our home. Once we opened our door after hearing faint knocks, and we found a young boy with one leg begging for treatment. But it was too difficult to give him a hand because of the snipers. After the shooting stopped we pulled him in only to find him dead. After a period of quiet in our neighborhood my brother insisted on burying him in the nearby grave-yard. He wanted to keep something from the boy to identify him so he could tell his family about his grave. We could not find anything except for his unique belt. After the end of the second attack, his mother came to thank us for granting him a grave. We give her all that remained of her son—his belt.

CHAPTER 5

THE SECOND SIEGE OF FALLUJAH

A lot of the marines that I've had wounded or killed over the past
five months have been by a faceless enemy. But the enemy has
got a face. He's called Satan. He's in Falluja. And we're going to
destroy him.

—Lieutenant Colonel Gareth Brandl, Battalion Commander,
1st Battalion 8th Marines, to his troops prior to battle

In Staff Sergeant David Bellavia's memoir of Operation
Phantom Fury, *House to House: An Epic Memoir of War*, he
describes a grueling first day of battle in which he and his
men encounter booby traps and a trained and capable enemy
willing to fight to the death. During a pause in the fighting, Bellavia and
members of his squad strike up a conversation with an embedded journalist, Michael Ware. They are soon taken aback by his assessment of
the Iraqi insurgency. Bellavia recalls Ware elaborating on "the different
groups" they believed they were fighting.

He talks about Hezbollah, and the type of training the Iranian Revolutionary Guard gives to the insurgents. That leads him into a tactical
discussion. He compares the insurgents who fought in Samarra to
those in Najaf. He speaks of the Iranian influence on Sunni Wahha-
bis . . . In Fallujah, we face an insurgent global all-star team. It includes
Chechen snipers, Filipino machine gunners, Pakistani mortar men,
and Saudi suicide bombers. They're all waiting for us down the street.

Ware is an authority on the enemy. He knows more about them

than our own intelligence officers. I hang on every word and try to remember everything he tells us. It is the best, most comprehensive discussion I've heard about the enemy since arriving in Iraq.

And it comes from a fucking reporter.[1]

Bellavia most likely misunderstood Ware—Hezbollah and the Iranian Revolutionary Guard had no relationship with the insurgency in Fallujah. But what is obvious is that Bellavia, like most of the American soldiers who participated in the operation, had little or no understanding of who their enemy was or what its motivations were. They often had to rely on indirect sources of information, such as conversations with embedded journalists or the news media playing on television sets in their chow halls, to understand the context of what they were being ordered to do, and why.

Bellavia's memoir depicts the second siege of Fallujah as a hard-won victory for a just cause, made possible by the courage and sacrifices of U.S. soldiers. No doubt, it appeared to him as such. Although Bellavia was mostly oblivious to the historical and political context of the operation, he was, however, keenly aware of the historical importance of the moment, likening the assault on Fallujah to the invasion of Normandy. Thus, when the bombing campaign climaxes, Bellavia does not see an unfolding tragedy, but rather history in the making. He recalls that "every weapon available in our arsenal short of nukes is turned on Fallujah. The pre-assault bombardment is unrelenting. Jet after jet drops its bombs and rockets. Warthogs—the big, bruising A-10 Thunderbolt II close-support aircraft—strafe the main avenues into the city with their 30mm antitank cannon. Fallujah is smothered in bombs, shrouded in smoke. Buildings collapse. Mines detonate. Artillery roar."[2] Of course, for Fallujans, the assault was interpreted very differently.

The bombing and shelling had picked up dramatically in October and peaked on November 7, as Staff Sergeant Bellavia looked on from just outside the city. From inside Fallujah, Burhan Fasa'a, an Iraqi journalist working for the Lebanese Broadcasting Company, recalled that "rarely a minute passed without the ground's shaking from the bombing."[3] This unrelenting volume of airpower was being used despite uncertainty as to the number of civilians remaining in the city, least of all their locations.

Yet U.S. Defense Secretary Donald Rumsfeld remained confident, stating that "there aren't going to be large numbers of civilians killed and certainly not by U.S. forces." His confidence was based on his belief that U.S. forces were "well led" and "well trained" and that "they [were] using precision and they have rules of engagement that are appropriate to an urban environment."[4] General Richard Natonski did not share Rumsfeld's confidence, however, recalling that on the eve of the ground assault he was worried about civilian casualties, because "we really didn't know what we were going to find in the city."[5]

In his book *The Battle for Fallujah: Occupation, Resistance and Stalemate in the War in Iraq*, former Army civil affairs officer Vincent L. Foulk writes that intelligence imagery "suggested" that the military's "warnings" to civilians to leave the city "had been nearly completely successful." He added that "the place looked deserted from the air," and their "guess" was that probably only a few thousand civilians "might be in the way, maybe not even that."[6] These "warnings" included leaflet drops and broadcasted announcements to inform civilians of the coming operation. Later measures included cutting the electrical and water supply to the entire city in order to "to induce the few remaining civilians to leave."[7] The city's communication lines were also cut.[8] The Emergency Working Group on Fallujah—comprising UN and Red Cross/Crescent workers and relevant Iraqi Ministries—condemned this action, stating that it "directly affects civilians (approximately 50,000 people inside Falluja) for whom water is a basic need and a fundamental human right."[9] Indeed, cutting the electricity and water supplies appears callous, regardless of how many civilians remained in the city. But the electricity and water were cut on November 8, after the air assault had finished.[10] This suggests that these measures were taken chiefly to create further hardship for the insurgents, disregarding the impact this would have on the civilians hoping to survive the operation in their homes.

Much of the Coalition's process of selecting targets for air strikes remains obscure. Their inability to do anything more than guesstimate the number of civilians still in the city, let alone determine their whereabouts, raises questions about their assertions of "precision strikes." The military's confidence that they could attack a city and keep collateral damage to a minimum, despite not knowing how many civilians remained, persisted even after November 6, when Coalition forces bombed the Nazzal Emergency Hospital, leaving the building in "rubble."[11]

This sort of destruction was not an isolated incident. Several civilians have testified to the indiscriminate nature of the air campaign. Iraqi journalist Burhan Fasa'a reported that he saw "at least 200 families who had their homes collapsed on their heads by American bombs."[12] One woman stated that her house was bombed even though there were no insurgents in her area. She lost her pregnant sister, who was killed in the blast. She told journalists, "I cannot get the image out of my mind of her foetus being blown out of her body."[13]

Others reported that the bombing was so severe that residents still trapped in the city became convinced that "American and Iraq forces were bent on killing anyone who stayed in Fallujah." Many tried to swim to safety across the Euphrates River at the city's western limit.[14] A man using the pseudonym Abu Hammed said that "even then the Americans shot them with rifles from the shore."[15] Another man reported that he considered swimming, "but I changed my mind after seeing U.S. helicopters firing on and killing people who tried to cross the river."[16]

Three days into the ground assault, the Emergency Working Group on Fallujah estimated that up to 50,000 civilians remained trapped in the city. The report also stated that it was "unaware" of any "response plan matching the scale of anticipated need."[17] The Coalition claimed to have "a robust civil affairs program for the postbattle period."[18] However, reports soon emerged of an overflow of refugees, well surpassing the ability of the UN to provide shelter and care for everyone. Some were lucky enough to be able to stay with family members in nearby cities, but many others had to squat in abandoned buildings or find some other way to survive the onslaught. On November 9, the UN High Commissioner for Refugees expressed "extreme concern over the fate of tens of thousands of Iraqis who have fled the city of Fallujah."[19]

U.S. forces also prevented aid convoys from entering Fallujah.[20] Part of the reason for this was to exclude any competition in the fight for the "hearts and minds" of the civilians and to highlight the efforts of Colonel Ballard's civil-military operations center, which would disperse all humanitarian aid (the same Colonel Ballard who later went on the write *Fighting for Fallujah: A New Dawn for Iraq*).[21] But U.S. forces were also suspicious that aid convoys would be used to smuggle supplies to the insurgents. In fact, they accused the Iraqi Red Crescent Society of attempting to evacuate military-age males in ambulances, claiming that "the Marines knew from previous operations that the organization used ambulances to transport enemy fighters and supplies."[22]

The ground assault began in the early hours of November 8, when nine U.S. infantry battalions and six Iraqi battalions (12,000 soldiers in total) lined up on the northern edge of the city and began sweeping south, accompanied by tanks, D-9 bulldozers, AAVs (amphibious assault vehicles), air support, and special operation forces, including SEAL sniper teams.[23] Although the rules of engagement clearly stated that "no forces are declared hostile," and that positive identification of all targets as legitimate military targets was required before anyone could pull a trigger, several accounts suggest widespread confusion on these points, or ambivalence toward the rules of engagement in practice.[24]

For example, Ross Caputi, a coauthor of this book who was then a Marine infantry private, recalls being told by his command prior to the assault that *all* civilians had left Fallujah and that only enemy combatants remained in the city.[25] Petty Officer Zollie Goodman reported that Fallujah had been declared a "free-fire zone."[26] Additionally, Kevin Sites stated that large parts of Fallujah were declared a "weapons-free" zone, meaning "the marines can shoot whatever they see—it's all considered hostile."[27] Even the official account of the operation, published by the Marine Corps History Division, notes that "because of the heavy concentration of insurgent forces, southern Fallujah would remain a kill zone subject to Coalition air and artillery strikes until the soldiers and Marines of the 1st Marine Division assault force attacked into southern Fallujah later in the battle."[28] These reports suggest that the U.S.-led Coalition proceeded in many instances as if there was no need to safeguard civilian life, utilizing a volume of airpower that was anything but proportionate or precise and that frequently eschewed the need for positive identification of targets.

Intense house-to-house combat persisted for several days as infantry units swept the city. The most dangerous moment for U.S. soldiers was when they would kick in the door of a house and rush a fire team inside. If a group of insurgents were waiting for them behind a sandbag bunker with their rifles fixed on the doorway, the soldiers stood little chance of beating them to the draw. Bing West, who was embedded as a historian with U.S. forces, wrote that "with scant civilians in the city, the usual tactic was to throw grenades over the courtyard wall, blow the lock on the metal gate, rush a four-man fire team into the courtyard, and shout and bang on the windows and door to the house to draw fire."[29] Thus, by provoking enemy fire, as West describes, the Marines were able to discern the dangerous houses from the empty ones. The only other way that the Marines knew when to proceed more cautiously was if civilians "waved white flags when they heard the platoon approaching."[30] Not all families were able to do so, however, and many were put in serious danger as U.S. forces fired their rifles or threw fragmentation grenades to test for insurgents as they entered each and every house in the city.

Caputi testified that as U.S. forces took more casualties, they also took fewer and fewer precautions to safeguard civilians when entering houses. He describes an atmosphere in which destructive tactics became more casual as the operation went on, and infantry units began disengaging from firefights to let tanks fire main gun rounds into houses or use AT4 rocket-launchers to fire shoulder-launched multipurpose assault weapons (SMAWs) or SMAW-NE ("novel explosive")[31] rounds into houses to kill everyone inside. In the case of smaller buildings, bulldozers were used to knock the buildings down on top of the insurgents. Caputi recalls,

> At this point we knew that there were still civilians in the city, but we began using a tactic called "reconnaissance by fire" anyway, which is when you fire into an area or building to see if people are there. If you hear silence after your firing, then everything is clear. If you hear otherwise, if you hear screaming or moaning, then there are either combatants or civilians there. This tactic is always indiscriminate, which would make it illegal, and our command was very aware that we were using it . . .
>
> I watched as the carnage changed the people around me and a violent hysteria developed in my unit. At a certain point during the assault I had to carry the radio up to a rooftop, and there were two guys that I knew sitting up there with their rifles aimed out into the street. They turned and looked at me, and one of them said "Hey Caputi, did you kill anyone yet? I only got one kill, but this guy next to me got nine."

Later, a friend of mine came up to me and told me about how his team leader had been cutting up the dead body of a resistance fighter looking for the adrenal gland, and how he tried to drag another dead body in front of an AAV for it to be run over. People were bragging about posing for pictures with the dead bodies of resistance fighters, and about the things that they had stolen out of houses or found in the pockets of the dead.

One day I was up on a rooftop with the radio, and I saw a unit to our right flank bulldozing an entire neighborhood. They were moving fast, and I know they were not checking inside the houses to see if civilians were inside. On one of the last days of the assault, we came across a house with two resistance fighters and a young boy bunkered inside. The boy was about ten years old. I do not know if any attempts were made to negotiate or to try to get that boy out of that house in some way and save his life. All I know is that we fired grenades into that house until it collapsed, killing all three of them inside.[32]

Coalition ground troops moved at a rapid pace, clearing hundreds of buildings a day, until dusk when each unit would capture a building—sometimes abandoned homes—and use them as defensive positions for the night. As in the first siege, the combat that took place in and around mosques, hospitals, residential neighborhoods, and other structures normally protected under the Geneva Conventions became particularly controversial. In fact, the initial targets of the ground assault included the Fallujah General Hospital, the city's train station, the al-Hadrah Mosque, and the mayor's complex. Colonel Ballard explains that these "normally restricted locations" became "tactical objectives," because the insurgents were using them as "command and control nodes," causing these structures to lose their protected status under the Geneva Conventions.[33]

According to the *New York Times* the operation began with "ear splitting bangs" as Iraqi troops, accompanied by U.S. special forces, broke down doors and rushed into the Fallujah General Hospital, which was "considered a refuge for insurgents and a center of propaganda against allied forces."[34] Dick Camp, former Marine colonel and author of *Operation Phantom Fury*, writes that the Iraqi soldiers "hustled patients and doctors out of their rooms, flexcuffed them with plastic zip-ties, and put them under guard in the hallways."[35] There are conflicting accounts of what happened next. Colonel Ballard claims that U.S. soldiers "rounded up nearly 40 military aged males in the hospital who were neither staff nor patients."[36] According to Camp, Coalition forces apprehended "five men suspected of being foreign fighters" and after an hour the hospital's staff and most of the patients were uncuffed and went back to work.[37] But staff at the hospital felt under attack. As one staff member recalls, "I was taking care of a woman who was giving birth and the baby was still connected to its mother through the umbilical cord. The U.S. soldier asked the National Guardsman to arrest me, and the guard tied my hands with ropes."[38]

The Coalition anticipated that the capture of the Fallujah hospital might raise questions about the Geneva Conventions. To deflect potential criticism, U.S. forces paired the capture of the hospital with a delivery of "emergency prepackaged medical supplies and humanitarian assistance kits" that same day.[39] Camp claims that "the insurgents attempted to portray the hospital as a monument to American brutality but were stymied when the embedded news media countered with stories about how the hospital was being supplied and equipped by U.S. forces."[40]

Richard A. Oppel Jr., the *New York Times* correspondent who accompanied Coalition forces on this operation, never investigated the U.S. military's claims about the "regular flow" of "propaganda" and "inflated civilian casualty figures" coming out of the hospital. Instead, he just repeated the Coalition's assertions. The Coalition also maintained that mosques should be regarded as legitimate targets. In Vincent L. Foulk's assessment,

> Each of the mosques was an outpost for the insurgents. But they were also command and control centers as well. In each were snipers that would serve as forward command posts. As the American troops and Marines approached, the snipers would take the attackers under fire. The small force in the mosque then raised a black flag and started to call on others in the city to come to the battle using the loud-speakers each mosque had for the call to prayer. Groups of insurgents, sometimes as many as fifty, more often in the tens or only a few, would race to the battle and counter-attack in a disjointed manner.[41]

For the people of Fallujah, however, none of the buildings in their city constituted a legitimate target. Fallujans believed that their entire city was under attack and they defended all of it according to the means available to them. While many Fallujans chose to pick up a weapon against the Americans, the vast majority of the city's residents chose other forms of resistance. The United States' imposed categories of "civilian" and "insurgent" did not neatly map onto this reality of popular resistance, which pervaded all aspects of daily life in every corner of the city. Mosques were a perfect example of the ubiquity of Fallujah's resistance and its diversity of tactics. As both a social and spiritual space for their congregation, it only made sense that they would address the most pressing concerns of the city and become a site of resistance as well. In the months leading up to the sieges, sermons could be heard regularly in the many mosques throughout the city denouncing the crimes of the Americans and calling on Fallujah's able-bodied men to defend their neighbors. And when the Americans attacked, the mosques allowed their buildings to be used for the defense of their flock. It is hardly surprising then that the Coalition found evidence that "63 of 133 recognized mosques" in the city "had been used as fighting positions or weapons caches and documented 24 separate cases of foreign fighter involvement."[42] But the Coalition portrayed the use of mosques by rebel fighters as the callous, cold-hearted actions of religious extremists who took advantage of these sacred spaces and the Geneva Conventions in order to kill Americans. This became a resonant, though entirely misleading, theme in the U.S. information campaign.

By November 12, Coalition forces had successfully pushed from the northern edge of the city all the way to its southern limits.[43] They then began back-sweeping and searching for pockets of resistance fighters who survived the initial push. Operation Phantom Fury lasted forty-six days in total, at the end of which all civilians were allowed to return to their ruined city, where they were given a "wheelbarrow" full of "food, water, and fuel"[44] and a $200 humanitarian assistance payment to "buy" their "good will."[45]

As Bing West observes, "The rationale for stopping the attack in April was a perception that the damage being done was too great. In the month of April, 150 air strikes had destroyed 75 to 100 buildings. In November the damage was vastly greater. There were 540 air strikes and 14,000 artillery and mortar shells fired, as well as 2,500 tank main gun rounds. Eighteen thousand of Fallujah's 39,000 buildings were damaged or destroyed."[46] While independent journalists sought to report the brutality of the first attack on Fallujah, embedded journalists argued that this operation was necessary and just, despite being far more destructive than the first assault.

A MEDIATED OPERATION

The Western world learned about the second siege of Fallujah through a number of media genres, but initially via news journalism. In a study of the American, British, and German news media's coverage of the second siege, Florian Zollmann, journalist and lecturer at Newcastle University in the United Kingdom, concluded that "official explanations [for the sieges] attained higher prominence and news stories were mostly built on official perspectives."[47] Any negative reportage was largely concerned with "procedural or tactical" matters, typically asking whether the operation could have been conducted in a less destructive manner, but rarely (if ever) challenging its fundamental legitimacy.[48] Zollmann argued that it was "quasi off debate, that the Fallujah 'operations' could have been launched in order to crush a popular resistance which aimed to prevent the West from accessing the mineral resources of its country. Instead . . . the Western press largely transported the official ideology."[49]

Mainstream U.S. accounts of the operation were thus reported within a narrow interpretive framework that privileged the triumphalist version of events that U.S. strategic communications sought to disseminate, omitting any reference to American atrocities and the experiences of Fallujans. Those media criticisms that managed to pass through this filter tended to focus on the use of excessive force, the improper use of certain weapons, and individual violations of the rules of engagement— criticisms of the operation that failed to challenge its claimed legitimacy. Nonetheless, a small number of residents, independent journalists, scholars, and international solidarity organizations managed, amid intense censorship, to put out counternarratives that urged Western audiences to focus less on those instances when Coalition forces exceeded their self-imposed limits and standards of conduct, and to see the operation, and the occupation more generally, as a violation of Iraqi sovereignty.

Again, Muhamad Al-Darraji at the Study Centre for Human Rights and Democracy was prominent among those seeking to make plain exactly what had occurred in the wake of the second siege. The Centre published the first report on the damage done to the city in early January 2005. By Western standards, the report was hastily done, with no photographic evidence and only a casual collection of testimonies and observations. However, the report is characteristic of much of the work that would be undertaken in Fallujah over the coming years—conducted under dangerous and difficult circumstances with few resources and little institutional support. Nonetheless, the report offers many valuable insights into the conduct and consequences of the operation. On the topic of civilian casualties, the report states, "On 25th and 26th of December 2004, the emergency teams of Fallujah hospital had lifted 700 dead bodies from six residential quarters only—Fallujah is consisted of 28 residential quarters— among those bodies 504 were of children and women the remaining belong to old men and mid-aged people, all are Iraqis."[50] Based on these figures, Al-Darraji estimates that the true number of civilian casualties during the second siege could be as high as 4,000 to 6,000.[51]

Al-Darraji would go on to head the Conservation Center of Environment and Reserves in Fallujah and the Monitoring Net of Human Rights in Iraq. Much of the material from Al-Darraji's first report would later be reprinted in a larger report and submitted to the United Nations High Commissioner for Human Rights.[52] Al-Darraji's Monitoring Net of Human Rights in Iraq would over the next year submit three additional reports on human rights violations in Iraq.[53]

Sadly, none of these reports ever made their way through the bureaucratic channels of the UN. Al-Darraji recalls,

> we found out later that there were political parties, whether UN officers or senior staff like Ms. Louise Arbour, who prevented not only the information from circulating but prevented others from taking necessary measures as well . . . After the second battle, for example, I met the UN representative in Iraq Mr. Ashraf Qazi in Amman and

showed him a documentary film by a British journalist about the reality of Fallujah after the second battle. He was stunned and said that this
was not what the Americans had told him. As a result, he requested to
send two teams to Fallujah, one from the WHO and the second from
the Office of Human Rights in the Human Rights Commission. Both
teams were denied entry by American forces under the pretext of the
security situation. This pretext continued until 2008. Unfortunately,
the UN has not taken any measures to investigate the violations of
human rights so far. And we discovered in 2010 that the reports we
used to send did not even reach Geneva or the office of Special Measures which takes legal action in the event of any serious violations.[54]

Bilal Hussein, a native of Fallujah, was working as a photographer for
the Associated Press at the time of the second siege. He volunteered to
stay in his city during the operation. "Destruction was everywhere. I saw
people lying dead in the streets, wounded were bleeding and there was
no one to come and help them," he told AP. "There was no medicine,
water, no electricity nor food for days."[55] Hussein eventually ran out of
supplies and had no choice but to try to escape. He went to the bank of
the Euphrates thinking he would swim to safety but changed his mind
when he saw U.S. soldiers gun down a family half way across the river.
Instead, he walked for hours through the brush of the river bank and
managed to slip out of the city.[56] Eventually, Hussein made his way to
AP's Baghdad office.

He thought he had made it to safety; however, the photographs he
took of the fighting led to his detention in a U.S.-run prison in Iraq. The
rationale given for his arrest was, vaguely, "reasons of security," presumably because of suspected "links with Iraqi insurgents." Hussein was held
without charge for two years.[57] The Committee to Protect Journalists noted
that Hussein's case "illustrated the U.S. military's alarming tactic of holding
Iraqi journalists in open-ended detentions without due process. The Committee to Protect Journalists has documented dozens of these detentions
without charge, but no journalist spent as long in prison as Hussein."[58] His
photographs of Fallujah under siege later earned him a share in a 2005
Pulitzer Prize[59] and an International Press Freedom Award in 2008.

While the works of Muhamad Al-Darraji and Bilal Hussein never
reached a mainstream Western audience, one issue that did receive such

attention regarded the use of white phosphorous munitions in Fallujah. White phosphorus munitions ignite on contact with oxygen and burn at extremely high temperatures until deprived of oxygen. While it is permissible to use white phosphorus to illuminate the battlefield, burn foliage, disable military vehicles by melting the engine blocks, and create smoke to screen troop movements; the Geneva Conventions prohibit its use as an offensive weapon on troops and civilians.[60] Following the second siege of Fallujah, considerable public attention was drawn to the use of white phosphorous as an offensive weapon.

Reports of its impacts began with an article in the *Washington Post* on November 10, stating that rebel fighters in the city claimed they had been attacked with a substance that melted their skin.[61] The article quoted Kamal Hadeethi, a physician at a regional hospital, who said, "The corpses of the mujaheddin which we received were burned, and some corpses were melted."[62] But the U.S. State Department denied that white phosphorous munitions were used as an offensive weapon in Fallujah, insisting that it was only employed "to illuminate enemy positions at night" and that U.S. forces used them "very sparingly."[63]

However, a year later in November 2005 the U.S. military was finally forced to retract its earlier denials and admit that white phosphorous was indeed used as a direct fire weapon in Fallujah. This admission came only once it was clear that the cumulative evidence presented by journalists, statements from soldiers, and eyewitness reports were simply too compelling to dismiss. First, an Italian documentary, *Fallujah: The Hidden Massacre,* by directors Sigfrido Ranucci and Maurizio Torrealta, aired in early November 2005 on the Italian state channel *RAI*, containing testimony from eyewitnesses and a U.S. veteran that the military did in fact use white phosphorus as an offensive weapon in Fallujah, killing and injuring insurgents and civilians alike.[64] The documentary prompted further media scrutiny of the issue, and on November 15, 2005, U.S. Department of Defense spokesman, Lieutenant Colonel Barry Venable, confirmed to BBC Radio that white phosphorus had been used as an incendiary weapon during the siege but denied claims that it killed civilians. He explained that "one technique is to fire a white phosphorus round into the position because the combined effects of the fire and smoke—and in some case the terror brought about by the explosion on the ground—will drive them out of the holes so that you can kill them with high explosives."[65] When asked directly if white phosphorous was used as an offensive weapon during the siege, Venable replied, "Yes, it was used as an incendiary weapon against enemy combatants."

That same month an official Army publication, *Field Artillery Magazine*, disclosed that the Army had used white phosphorus in Fallujah and that it "proved to be an effective and versatile munition. We used it for screening missions at two breeches and, later in the fight, as a potent psychological weapon against the insurgents in trench lines and spider holes where we could not get effects on them with HE (High Explosives). We fired 'shake and bake' missions at the insurgents, using WP [white phosphorus] to flush them out and HE to take them out."[66] In response to these admissions, a spokesman at the U.K. Ministry of Defense told the BBC that the use of white phosphorus is permitted in battle situations when there are no civilians near the target area.[67] However, there was no way of knowing where civilians might have been seeking refuge at the time of the assault, and the Italian documentary presented evidence that white phosphorous maimed and killed civilians in Fallujah. When the filmmakers asked an American veteran if he saw white phosphorous kill civilians, he replied, "Yes . . . burned bodies, it burned children, it burned women. White phosphorous kills indiscriminately. It's a cloud that will, within most cases, to 150 meters of impact, it will disperse and it will burn every human being or animal."[68] The film also included testimony from Muhamad Al-Darraji, who recounted, "A rain of fire fell on the city, the people struck by this multi-colored substance started to burn, we found people dead with strange wounds, the bodies burned but the clothes intact."[69] After the Italian documentary was aired, Al-Darraji was forced to flee Iraq because forces allied with the new government were "liquidating opponent activists and journalists."[70] He relocated to Italy where he finished his PhD and has not since been able to return to his hometown of Fallujah. Today he lives in Austria and teaches at the Karl Franzens University of Graz.

Al-Darraji's testimony was corroborated by others. One Fallujan refugee told independent journalist Dahr Jamail that "they used these weird bombs that first put up smoke in a cloud, and then small pieces fell from the air with long tails of smoke behind them. These exploded on the ground with large fires that burned for half an hour. They used these near the train tracks. When anyone touched those fires, their body burned for hours."[71] There were further reports that white phosphorous projectiles accidentally injured Coalition forces, too.[72]

In another documentary film titled, *Fallujah: A Lost Generation?*, the director Feurat Alani investigated claims that after the second siege corpses had been found with melted skin, albeit with their clothes still intact. The photographic records kept at Fallujah's Martyrs Cemetery show exactly this. Alani's film argues that no weapon other than white phosphorous is capable of burning flesh while not burning clothing. Some have found this argument plausible, arguing that white phosphorous burns when it comes in contact with oxygen and that cloth would not be a source of fuel for phosphorous to burn.

However, many of these attempts to gather evidence of, and seek accountability for, the U.S. military's use of white phosphorus as an offensive weapon in Fallujah have been conflated with the more speculative accusations that it is a toxic weapon, some labeling it a chemical weapon, regardless of how it is used. Such claims were easily dismissed, since white phosphorous munitions are not recognized as a chemical weapon by any international body. Officials seized upon this fact to dismiss the issue altogether. In a broader context, the misuse of white phosphorous in Fallujah was discussed in the mainstream media—along with other singular breaches of international humanitarian law—as isolated, unfortunate, mistakes that ought to be forgiven considering the difficult circumstances of the operation. Whenever there was criticism in the media of the U.S. military's conduct, it was accompanied by the official insistence that the conduct was in accordance with the rule of law and rules of engagement. This of course presupposed the legitimacy of the operation as long as it was conducted within accepted limits defined by the military.

This line of reasoning is disputed by prominent scholar Noam Chomsky, who asserts that any discussion of the particular tactics used during the second siege of Fallujah is irrelevant to their status as a war crime: all U.S.-led military actions in Iraq were part of an aggressive invasion and illegal occupation, and as a consequence no operation could be considered legitimate, no matter how cautiously U.S. forces conducted themselves. Chomsky cites the Nuremberg Tribunal's definition of "aggression" as "the supreme international crime differing only from other war crimes in that it contains within itself the accumulated evil of the whole." According to Chomsky this means that "all the evil in the tortured land of Iraq that flowed from the US and UK invasion" is illegal, and "that includes Abu Ghraib, Falluja, and everything else that happened . . . since the invasion."[73] Chomsky argues that the widespread attention given to the indiscriminate weapons and tactics used during this operation has distracted us from seeing what was wrong with the more conventional tactics and weapons, and with the illegal nature of the operation and occupation as a whole.[74]

Francis Boyle, professor of law at the University of Illinois, has also viewed the operation in the larger context of an illegal invasion and occupation, although he regards the operation in Fallujah as a war crime in and of itself. Boyle maintains that the flagrant brutality with which the operation was conducted deserves focused attention. More generally he argues that the Bush administration's actions in Iraq demonstrate "little if any respect for fundamental considerations of international law, international organizations, and human rights." He adds,

> In international legal terms, the Bush Jr. administration itself should now be viewed as constituting an ongoing criminal conspiracy under international criminal law in violation of the Nuremberg Charter, the Nuremberg Judgment, and the Nuremberg Principles, due to its formulation and undertaking of aggressive war policies that are legally akin to those perpetrated by the Nazi regime. As a consequence, American citizens possess the basic right under international law and the United States domestic law, including the U.S. Constitution, to engage in acts of non-violent civil resistance in order to prevent, impede, thwart, or terminate ongoing criminal activities perpetrated by U.S. government officials in their conduct of foreign affairs policies and military operations purported to relate to defense and counter-terrorism.[75]

On the few occasions when the U.S. military was criticized for using excessive force or violating international norms of warfare in the mainstream press, the U.S. government responded by claiming to *hold itself* accountable to the law. One example of this occurred when an American soldier was caught on camera by embedded journalist Kevin Sites executing a wounded Iraqi in a mosque in Fallujah. Colonel Ballard remarked that this incident soured the "superb relationship" that the U.S. military "had cultivated with the media"; however, the U.S. Marine Corps later found that the soldier's actions were "consistent with the rules of engagement" and did not pursue a court-martial.[76]

On another occasion Sergeant Jose Luis Nazario was brought before a civilian court under charges of voluntary manslaughter, after he had been discharged from the military. Nazario was accused of killing unarmed detainees and was charged under the Military Extraterritorial Jurisdiction Act, a law intended to hold mercenaries hired by the Pentagon accountable for overseas crimes. When Nazario was discharged from the military, he was outside the jurisdiction of the Uniform Code of Military Justice. But under this new law, his case was passed from Navy investigators to the Department of Justice, eventually resulting in his acquittal.[77] In an article in *Foreign Policy in Focus* titled "Fallujah Fall Guy," journalist Aaron Glantz argues that making an example of one soldier "hardly represents justice." He concludes that "the entire operation was a war crime . . . It was a collective punishment delivered to a city, which had refused to accept an American military occupation, which harbored fighters who regularly attacked those soldiers. It was an operation supported by President George W. Bush, John Kerry . . . and military leaders like General John Abizaid and General George W. Casey . . . Rather than being prosecuted, or even reprimanded, these military leaders have been promoted and honored since the siege of Fallujah."[78]

Glantz, Boyle, and Chomsky all maintain that the official rhetoric concerning the legality of the Coalition's tactics, weapons, and rules of engagement avoids any serious questioning of the legitimacy of U.S.-led incursions into Iraq. Although these critical voices were kept at the margins of the national discourse, they have nonetheless challenged conventional wisdoms about Fallujah, placing U.S. military operations in a more historical, ethical, and political context. That said, U.S. strategic communications proved successful in shaping the public narrative around what happened in Iraq and in Fallujah in particular. By ascribing moral virtue, marginalizing dissent, minimizing solidarity, and ensuring impunity for U.S. actions in Iraq, the U.S. political and military leadership could, with the assistance of a compliant media, claim legitimacy where, according to precepts of international law, there was none. This was the deft hand of raw power in action.

"LIBERATED" FALLUJAH ON LOCKDOWN: A CASE OF SOCIOCIDE

On December 14, the Coalition transitioned to "security, stability, reconstruction, and resettlement efforts" in Fallujah.[79] The U.S. 4th Civil Affairs Group began clearing rubble from the streets and coordinating with local authorities on reconstruction projects.[80] Hafid al-Dulaimy, chairman of the Fallujah Compensation Committee, reported that by end of 2004 following the two sieges "almost thirty-six thousand houses [had] been demolished, nine thousand shops, sixty-five mosques, sixty schools, the very valuable heritage library and most of the government offices. The American forces destroyed one of the two bridges in the city, both train stations, the two electricity stations, and three water treatment plants. It also blew up the whole sanitation system and the communication network."[81]

On December 23, civilians began repopulating the city, and as they did so the Coalition logged each resident into a registry using biometric data (fingerprints, iris scan, and digital photograph). Every returnee was issued an ID badge that they were required to wear whenever they left their homes.[82] Additionally, all entrances to and from the city were guarded by Coalition checkpoints, and it became increasingly difficult for individuals to travel outside Fallujah for school, work, or medical care. The blockade of the city led to shortages of basic goods, exacerbating the effects of rapidly increasing inflation, unemployment, and poverty.[83] Unsurprisingly, many of the city's inhabitants likened this level of security to living inside a jail.[84]

Trapped in their city, residents faced rapidly deteriorating public health conditions. Reconstruction efforts proved slow and inadequate, leaving much of the vital infrastructure either unusable or in chronically poor states of repair. Only 10 percent of the population had returned by mid-January 2005, and around 30 percent by the end of March. Sixty percent of the houses and buildings inside the city remained uninhabitable. Many people had no choice but to remain in squalid refugee camps outside the city or pitch makeshift tents or shanties in the rubble of their former homes.[85] In May the Study Centre for Human Rights and Democracy found that there was still no safe drinking water available inside the city.[86] Throughout 2005 electricity and fuel remained scarce, with poor sanitary conditions and a poorly equipped hospital unable to meet the rapidly escalating needs of the city's residents.[87] Consequently illnesses such as diarrhea, scabies, and asthma proliferated.[88] These conditions were further compounded by already high food prices and consequent hunger and malnutrition, resulting mainly from the withdrawal of government food rations that had been available to all Iraqis since 1991.

The security measures imposed on Fallujah made it extremely difficult for independent journalists to enter the city, meaning that little information on the plight of the city's residents reached the outside world. One of the few observers able to obtain information on the situation in Fallujah, Middle East academic and commentator Juan Cole, wrote in March 2005, "I am sorry to say that there is no Fallujah to update. The city appears to be in ruins and perhaps uninhabitable in the near future . . . unlike the victims of the tsunami who were left homeless, the Fallujans have witnessed no outpouring of world sympathy."[89] Other on-the-ground organizations were also able to peer into the city's unfolding tragedy. In May 2006 the NGO Coordination Committee in Iraq noted that a third of Fallujah's residents had still not returned, either because their homes or neighborhoods were completely destroyed or because they expected future military offensives and preferred to settle in other safer places.[90]

The poor conditions in 2006 were a shock even for Staff Sergeant David Bellavia, who returned to Fallujah in June 2006 and witnessed a "broken city."[91] Bellavia recalls, "I zigzagged through desolate neighborhoods full of ruined buildings. Hardly a soul graced the streets. The scars of battle were evident everywhere: broken houses, ruined buildings and bullet-marked walls. The people who remained here lived with these reminders every day. They could not escape the lost families, lost loved ones. Just existing in this half-ghost town required facing these tragedies every day."[92]

In November 2007, Iraqi journalist Ali al-Fadhily reported a "hollow shell of a city," where businesses and cafes remained closed and whose residents were reluctant to talk to the media for fear of being detained by the Iraqi police.[93] Al-Fadhily noted that many neighborhoods remained without running water or electricity. In January 2008, four years after the initial attacks, British journalist Patrick Cockburn found Fallujah devastated and on lockdown. It was, he said, "more difficult to enter . . . than any city in the world," and households were still suffering the most basic privations, including only an hour's electricity each day.[94]

The shocking conditions Fallujah suffered in the years following the 2004 sieges can be captured in the term "sociocide": the destruction of a society, an entire way of life.[95] All aspects of life in Fallujah changed for the worse. The loss of freedom of movement in and out of the city due to checkpoints caused many to lose work, cut family and friends off from each other, curtailed religious life, and disrupted school and university attendance in a society that placed a high value on education. The loss of male relatives thrust wives and sons into new social roles they were not prepared for, as heads of households and bread earners. The disruption of important community rituals such as weddings, religious services, and festivals further fragmented Fallujan society. And the constant threat of violence and insecurity led to widespread trauma and anxiety. During times of violence and chaos the inability to bury the dead according to religious custom caused great and lasting distress to families. Often, only parts of bodies could be buried, ceremonies were hurried and incomplete, and during the attacks in 2004 there were reports of dogs feeding off dead bodies on the street.[96]

Living in a constant siege-like situation for years on end, Fallujah's residents faced the daily reality of suffocating checkpoints, harassment, arrests, detention, and political discrimination. These abnormal and dehumanizing conditions led to the unraveling of the most fundamental aspects of everyday life, compounding the collective trauma of the 2004 attacks.

In an interview in 2006 Muhamad Al-Darraji noted, somewhat prophetically, that "the mood is that people will never forget what was done to them and their city. I don't think we'll see the end of this."[97] He was right.

WAR HEROES AND WAR CRIMINALS

Ross Caputi

My unit returned home from Fallujah to a hero's welcome. The celebration began as soon as our buses rolled onto base. There were crowds of family and friends waiting for us behind a banner that read, "Welcome Home 1st Battalion 8th Marines." After the initial tearful hugs and the solemn gestures to those who did not return, we cracked a few beers. And then a few more, and a few more after that. The celebration continued for several weeks. Parades were thrown in our honor, journalists called us for interviews, free drinks abounded, and everyone thanked us for our service. For a short period of time we were America's favorite heroes—the veterans of the Second Battle of Fallujah. We began our postdeployment leave riding this wave of praise and veneration. We all had a dollar in our pocket from eight months of earning tax-free money in a warzone and a month off to go to our respective hometowns and bask in our glory.

When we returned to base the limelight on us had already faded, but we continued to celebrate. We partied in the barracks every night, reliving the thrill of battle through stories told over beers, booze, and abundant pain meds. This was how we came to terms with Fallujah and the baggage we would carry from that experience forever. We would stuff ourselves into our tiny barracks rooms, fire teams at a time, and exchange near-death experiences, moments of exhilaration, moments of loss, resentments, anger, and grief. Fallujah was such an intense experience that we needed to make sense of it with the only people that we felt fully understood it. We replayed those scenarios over in our heads, which were still so fresh and overwhelming, and recounted them for the feedback of our peers. It helped. The alcohol and drugs helped too. But perhaps more than all of that, it was the story that was told to us—a grand narrative about us and our mission—that helped us to put aside any doubts about the purpose and morality of what we had done.

Most of our experiences in Fallujah made no sense without context. Getting shot at is not itself an insightful event. You need to know who is shooting at you and why. But we shot and got shot at by total strangers. We followed orders without knowing the full battle plan. And we called in air strikes on targets we could barely see. This otherwise fragmented, episodic, and compartmentalized experience was made meaningful to us by our command and the news playing on the TV in the chow hall, which informed us that we were in fact the good guys and the people shooting at us were terrorists. Untroubled by the big picture, we focused on the minuscule—our cherished moments of heroism and bravery.

We were heroes. Everyone in our communities was in agreement about this. Our command told us why we were going into Fallujah—to kill bad guys and liberate civilians. That was why our friends died. That was why we suffered. And the journalists and politicians concurred. Over the course of several months, our sense of triumph and invincibility slowly morphed into thrill seeking and belligerence. As we struggled to transition, our daily emotions volleyed from rage to despair, frustration, and joy. But one thing we never had to feel was shame.

After a year of telling the same Fallujah stories again and again, our command caught wind of what was going on.

On one random Saturday morning they gave a surprise drug test, when many of us were still under the influence from the night before. Of the roughly 120 people in our company, about forty failed the drug test, and almost all of them were discharged. By a stroke of luck, I passed. Over the course of the next several months, I parted ways with several friends. We all moved on from the Marine Corps, scattered across the country, and began new lives that led in very different directions. We tried our best to stay in touch, but in my travels and studies I learned that our mission in Fallujah was not what we were told. In this I was alone and would remain alone because of it.

My relationships with the men from my former unit have soured, because I no longer share in the mythologies that were once so dear to us. There is much at stake in these myths. By denying the narrative given to us by our command, our journalists, our country, I'm taking something away from them—the justification given for the death of our friends and our status as heroes. Many of these men were denied benefits because of their less than honorable discharges, and many have struggled financially and emotionally ever since. For them, these myths are much more than a version of history. Fallujah is the proudest moment of their life. It is what makes their pain bearable.

On the national level, these myths function much the same way. After sixteen years of costly and fruitless war, we are struggling to identify moments to feel good about. The liberation of Fallujah in 2004, as it was told on TV, is one of a few events in our collective memory of the Global War on Terror that is consonant with our national self-image. We want to feel proud, not ashamed. So we are resistant to fact, to the experiences of our victims, to change.

FIGURE 1. Sarah's View, 2004. She was quiet at first. Sarah, age 13, listened intently as we interviewed her family huddled in their hot, stuffy tent at a refugee camp set up on a soccer field in Baghdad. Terrorized by bombing, snipers, and the stench of death all around them, Sarah's family fled Fallujah at the peak of the U.S. onslaught against the town in April 2004. After the interview the children went outside to play. But Sarah remained still and quiet, her round face sullen and thoughtful. Suddenly she blurted out in a loud, defiant voice, "What does America want from us? Why did they destroy our homes?" With tears forming in her eyes she continued. "This is not their home, this is our home. Why did they come here and force us to live like this? The bombing went all day and all night. They made us homeless, they made us wander from house to house to ask if anyone can help us. Why did they come here? I want them to go." She got up and walked away alone.

FIGURE 2. Fallujan children, 2004. These Fallujan children wandered around the dusty field on the outskirts of Baghdad, which was now their home. Sometimes they played together, other times they seemed lost, not knowing what to do in this strange, new environment. Khalid, father to two of the children, invited us into one of the white tents set up on the field. The tent was now home to fifteen members of his family. Khalid explained that his children were forced to flee their homes in Fallujah with nothing but the clothes they were wearing. "What is the sin of these children?" he asked as he pointed to his young son and daughter who sat near him on the plastic floor of the tent. "My daughter has no shoes because we had to leave so quickly we couldn't go back to get them. We ran hard that day. We ran for our lives." He leaned over and gently lifted off his son's shirt to reveal the little boy's back covered with deep, bloody cuts and grazes. "He fell and hurt himself as we climbed over the barbed wire fences," Khalid explained. "But we just had to keep going." The children listened intently to their father talk of violence and death. They sat quietly, sometimes fidgeting, taking it all in. They had endured the terror of bombing, watched their neighbors die, buried relatives in the garden, and fled their home in fear. "What is the future for these children?" Khalid asked. "Even when we go back to Fallujah we have nothing. Our home is destroyed, the town is destroyed. How will we survive?"

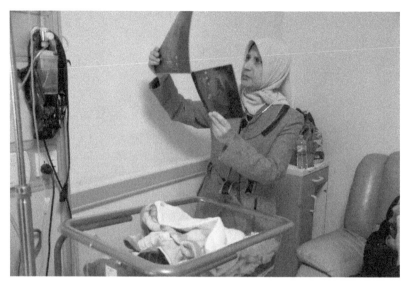
FIGURE 3. Dr. Samira Alaani, Fallujah Hospital, 2013.

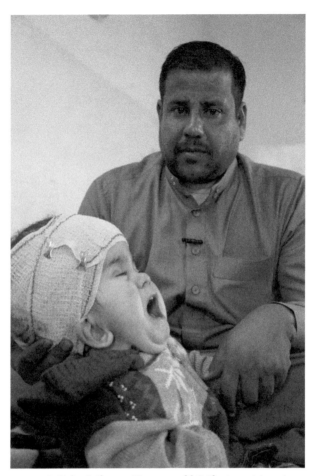

FIGURE 4. Baby Seif, 2013. Two-year-old Seif cries out in pain as his father looks on, helpless. Seif suffered from water on the brain (hence his enlarged head), a damaged spine and nervous system, urinary issues, and partial blindness. He had been in and out of the hospital since birth and endured several operations, until finally the doctors told his parents to "take him home to die." But his family continued to care for him twenty-four hours a day and seek further medical help. His mother became depressed and had to leave the family home, traumatized at seeing her son in a state of constant pain. His father believes Seif's ill health and death—a few months after this photo was taken—were the result of "contamination" caused by weapons used in the 2004 U.S. attacks on Fallujah.

FIGURE 5. The childless couple, 2012. Bashir and Marwan, a young, healthy couple from Fallujah are standing with Donna Mulhearn at the graveside of their baby Mohamed who died five minutes after birth. This is their fourth baby to die: one was stillborn, and three died shortly after birth. Bashir and Marwan always wanted children. After their second baby died, they spent significant time, money, and energy speaking to doctors about possible solutions. Bashir believes their problem stems from the environment being "poisoned by American weapons." Heartbroken, they say they won't try again. "We are sad and angry, but we don't want monetary compensation, we want a solution to our problem." In the meantime, Marwan and Bashir have been forced to give up their dream of having a family.

FIGURE 6. Grieving woman, Martyrs Cemetery, 2012. Fallujah's football field was dug up during the siege in April 2004 to bury the large number of bodies of those killed during the U.S. attacks when the town cemetery quickly filled to capacity. Young men from Fallujah's football team who once played on this very field are now buried here, many were killed when they were not allowed to leave the city when it was under attack. Known as the "Martyrs Cemetery," the site has 3,500–4,000 graves.

FIGURE 7. Baby graves, 2013. A section of the Martyrs Cemetery in Fallujah is specially allocated for infants' graves, some unmarked, others with names or words saying simply "child" or "baby." The babies buried here were often born dead or lived only a short time because of serious birth defects. Like most people buried in the Martyrs Cemetery, the babies' deaths are considered to be connected to the U.S. attacks on the city; thus they died from wounds of a war they never saw. This simple gravestone, typical of many baby graves, says, "Child, Ahmed Waleed, died 12/3/2005."

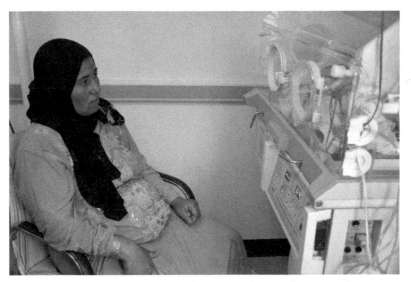

FIGURE 8. Woman in the pink dress, Fallujah Hospital, 2012. This new mother sat motionless, staring intently at her baby girl in the incubator in front of her. The baby was struggling to breathe due to complex congenital heart defects. The woman in the pink dress gazed with loving concentration at her baby, urging her, willing her to live, to take another breath. Her large brown eyes were not angry, more overwhelmed, full of searching questions. The baby, named Dumoa, died later that day.

FIGURE 9. Protests in Ramadi, 2013. Over a twelve-month period hundreds of thousands of Iraqis gathered every Friday on the road just outside Ramadi in peaceful protests, blocking the highway from Baghdad to Jordan. There was little coverage of the protests in the Western media.

FIGURE 10. Dignity and Pride Square, Ramadi, 2013. The protest camp, known as Dignity and Pride Square, became a permanent tent city, with many people taking up residence in the large tents, complete with power and wi-fi. There were meeting spaces, restaurants, cafes, and other amenities. The camp had a peaceful and positive atmosphere with music, children playing, and games of soccer on the road. Every Friday masses from all over Iraq converged on the camp to protest the government's treatment of the Sunni community. The Friday protests included prayers, speeches by clerics and elders, and chanting slogans.

FIGURE 11. Man in prayer, Ramadi protests, 2013.

FIGURE 12. Boy in the crowd, Ramadi protests, 2013.

—Photos and vignettes by Donna Mulhearn.

CHAPTER 6

AFTERMATH

Today, I am here among you as a messenger from Fallujah, or let me say, as a very close witness of the Iraqi Hiroshima. I have decided to tell today the life stories of the mothers in my city: aware of who did what, who encouraged, who kept silent, and who paid. I am a pediatrician, and I have worked in Fallujah since 1997. The story started in 2004 and has continued in a tragic series of events every single day until this moment. The mass use of dirty weapons in a city crowded with people has caused congenital malformations.

—Dr. Samira Alaani, Human Rights Defenders Forum,
The Carter Center, Atlanta, Georgia, 2013

Τhe first siege of Fallujah helped unite various factions of the Iraqi insurgency, most notably the Mahdi Army led by the Shia cleric Muqtada al-Sadr with the Sunni militias. In response, the Coalition took measures to fracture this unity through a number of divide-and-conquer tactics that ultimately fostered sectarian animosity. The sacking of Fallujah in November–December 2004 marked a turning point in the occupation, after which the Coalition gained the upper hand and was able to achieve several of its state-building goals, including holding elections and drafting a new constitution for Iraq.

While Operation Phantom Fury was conducive to these changes, the shaping operations (the al-Zarqawi PSYOP in particular) dovetailed with a broader effort to wage a dirty war that would isolate and weaken the insurgency's primary base of support—the Sunni community. Sectarianism proved to be expedient for a new cast of Iraqi elites and the Coalition alike. While the former sought to capitalize on sectarian fears to build political constituencies and grab power, the Coalition exploited sectarian divisions to split Iraq into manageable enclaves and encourage infighting. To that end, the Coalition portrayed terrorism as a phenomenon originating from the Sunni community, while arming, funding, and training sectarian Shia militias to conduct counterterrorism operations in Sunni localities. The Coalition then went on to secure its neoliberal agenda—most notably the privatization of state-owned industries—by allying itself with sectarian political parties and creating a parliamentary system based on ethnic and sectarian quotas.

Indeed, it was not just Fallujah that, through U.S. propaganda, became associated with Al Qaeda and Islamic terrorism. Commenting on this phenomenon, Nir Rosen observed,

The American view that there was a monolithic group called Sunni Arabs had always been mistaken, just as it was a mistake to identify a Sunni Triangle. The Baath Party was incorrectly viewed as a Sunni regime, since not all Sunnis were loyal to it. Many Sunnis felt they were victims of Saddam, and even Sunni clerics had been executed by the former regime. Some tribes were given privileged status, while others were weakened or marginalized. That there were no obvious Sunni leaders after Saddam was removed was but one sign that his own community had been weakened by his regime. But Sunnis would soon consider themselves the targets of collective punishment. Treated as the enemy, many of them soon became just that, fearing they were about to be exterminated.[1]

The assertion that the Sunni community at large was complicit in the insurgency and ought to be targeted as a whole would guide the thinking of U.S. military leaders in the years to come. For example, a "military source" told Newsweek in January 2005 that "the Sunni population is paying no price for the support it is giving to the terrorists . . . From their point of view, it is cost-free. We have to change that equation."[2] This source was referring to a new operation to defeat the insurgency, which began as a targeted assassination program using paramilitary forces and police commando units under the command of the Ministry of the Interior. The program was headed by U.S. Ambassador to Iraq John Negroponte; the U.S. Drug Enforcement Administration's Steven Casteel, acting as senior advisor to Iraq's ministry of the interior; retired Colonel James Steele, who oversaw the training of these forces[3]; and General David Petraeus. This targeted assassination program quickly grew into a dirty war modeled on Operation Phoenix in Vietnam and the actions of the U.S.-sponsored Contra forces in Central America in the 1980s.[4] A supplementary appropriation to fund this operation was made as early as November 2003.[5]

Fighters were initially selected from Kurdish militias, the Iranian-based Badr Brigade, and CIA-backed secular groups such as the Iraqi National Accord and the Iraqi National Congress.[6] Muqtada al-Sadr's Mahdi Army would later join this operation, which was dubbed "the Salvador Option" in reference to U.S. covert operations in Central America. These combined forces, which peaked at 145,000 men, waged a campaign of state-sponsored terrorism, killing or torturing any Sunni Iraqi who was even suspected of being associated with the insurgency. Men and women were often targeted simply for having Sunni names. Due to the ethnic and religious composition of these forces, Al Qaeda launched reprisal attacks on Shias, Kurds, and other minority groups within Iraq.

While some commentators argue that the U.S.-led occupation oversaw this dirty war,[7] others maintain that the U.S. leadership, due to its own incompetence, or "for the sake of expediency," lost control of the militias under the command of the Ministry of the Interior, "allowing" them to wage a campaign of sectarian-motivated terrorism.[8] John Tirman, principal research scientist and executive director of MIT's Center for International Studies, wrote that the forces within the Ministry of the Interior were "unreliable at best and possibly *genocidaires*."[9]

Much of this was brushed over in the U.S. media, which repeated the Pentagon's characterization of the operation as "preëmptive manhunting," if it was reported at all.[10] On other occasions the violence in Iraq between 2005 and 2007 was characterized as a "civil war" and was explained as being the product of ancient sectarian hatreds. According to this view, two incidents were said to have provoked this war: on September 14, 2005, al-Zarqawi declared war against Shias, and on February 22, 2006, the al-Aksari mosque in Samarra, one of the holiest sites in Shia Islam, was bombed. The campaign of state terrorism initiated by U.S.-backed "death squads" operating from within Iraq's Ministry of the Interior was, however, generally omitted in this narrative.[11]

This dirty war was just one aspect of what Nir Rosen has called the "Lebanonization" of Iraq, in which the occupying powers divided up political power according to sectarian quotas.[12] This was a radical departure from the secular regime of Saddam Hussein. Rosen notes, "The Iraqi Governing Council, a symbolic body created in July 2003 as a concession to Iraqi demands for representation, was established on purely sectarian grounds, as Iraqis were quick to note. Members were chosen for being Sunnis, Shiites, Kurds, or Turkmen, rather than for representing Iraqis. Even the Communist Party member was chosen for being a Shiite rather than for being secular or leftist."[13] In addition to handpicking politicians according to their ethnic and religious identities, the Coalition formed an alliance with Shia political parties with a sectarian agenda, notably the Dawa Party and the Supreme Council for the Islamic Revolution in Iraq (SCIRI), both of which were formerly exiled into Iran under Saddam Hussein's rule, allowing them to take control of key ministries, such as the Ministry of the Interior.[14] These actions were described by Fanar Haddad, scholar and regional expert, as "Shia-centric state building."[15]

It was this state of affairs that allowed Nouri al-Maliki, a member of the Dawa Party, to become prime minster in 2006 and quickly consolidate power to the point that many Iraqis began seeing him as a "Shia Saddam."[16] Marisa Sullivan, a fellow at the U.S.-based Institute for the Study of War, notes that al-Maliki created a number of "extraconstitutional security bodies to bypass the defense and interior ministries," using "an informal chain of command that [ran] directly from his office to the commanders in the field, allowing him to exert direct influence over . . . both the targeting of individuals and the conduct of operations."[17] By the 2010 elections in Iraq, al-Maliki had amassed enough power to retain his position as prime minister, even though he technically lost the election to Ayad Allawi. After the election, al-Maliki took on the positions of interior minister, defense minister, and national security minister to exert control over the "coercive apparatus of the state," often using it for political killings and repression.[18]

These were some of the darkest days Iraq had seen in its previous twenty years of war, sanctions, and occupation. But amidst this chaos and tragedy, the residents of Fallujah faced additional horrors. Within a year after the second siege, the staff at the Fallujah General Hospital began to notice a dramatic increase in the rates of cancers, stillborn births, miscarriages, and birth defects. While the cancers were alarming, the birth defects were truly shocking in both number and kind. But what most concerned the staff was that many children were being born with multiple birth defects. Cases of spina bifida, missing or deformed limbs, severe hydrocephaly, intestines protruding outside the body cavity, and skin or skeletal abnormalities were often combined and compounded with one another. The probability of several cases of compound defects in a single city was beyond a chance occurrence. A number of extreme cases drove this point home—one child was born with two heads, one with a single eye in the center of its forehead, and another with additional limbs. In most of the more extreme cases, the infants died shortly after birth. It was clear to everyone in Fallujah long before the international community took note: the people of Fallujah were experiencing an unprecedented public health crisis.

ECOCIDE

Significant increases in incidents of cancer were observed as early as 2005[19] and unusual birth defects by 2006.[20] Fallujah, however, was closed to the world, and it took years before the public health crisis in the city received any attention from Baghdad or the international community. Journalists could not gain access to the city to investigate the crisis, and Fallujans had few lines of communication with the outside world available to them.

The first report about the snowballing public health crisis in Fallujah did not emerge until 2008.[21] In March of that year, Muhamad Al-Darraji—having just gained a PhD in biology—submitted a report titled "Prohibited Weapons Crisis: The Effects of Pollution on the Public Health in Fallujah" to the seventh session of the UN Human Rights Council. However, the Fallujah hospital's data set was incomplete. With few resources available to him to conduct a proper study, Al-Darraji sourced all the available data, including an array of descriptive statistics gathered by the hospital on rates of illnesses, ranging from leukemia to diarrhea, as well as chilling photos of newborns with birth defects, children with war wounds, and adults with hideous tumors. The report's breadth ended up being its weakness. Al-Darraji's inclusion of both injuries and illnesses painted a general picture of suffering in Fallujah, but the report lacked focus. Also, many of the data used in the report were limited to the period after the sieges of 2004 without a comparable data sample from a healthy population. Further grounds for concern lay in the report's claim that U.S. weapons *caused* these illnesses, without addressing the methodological difficulties of determining causality in scientific studies outside of experimental settings, and without identifying specific weapons as the source of the pollution. A more appropriate response might have been to commission a public health investigation in Fallujah to follow up on Al-Darraji's leads, but instead the report was ignored by the UN Human Rights Council and the media.

It was not until the first major study on the health crisis was published in 2010 that Western audiences learned about cancers and birth defects in Fallujah. This study, led by British scientist and expert on internal ionizing radiation Dr. Chris Busby, titled "Cancer, Infant Mortality and Birth Sex-Ratio in Fallujah, Iraq 2005–2009," was published in 2010 in the *International Journal of Environmental Research and Public Health.*[22] Busby sought to investigate the "anecdotal evidence" presented in earlier reports and establish whether the rates of cancers and infant mortality in Fallujah were indeed higher than what might be expected in a healthy population. Birth defects were not investigated in this study. Nonetheless, the results confirmed that the rates of cancer and infant mortality were alarmingly high after 2005.

The study also revealed that there was a significant drop in the ratio of male to female births after 2005, which suggests a kind of "genetic damage" indicative of radiation exposure. Although Busby's study makes no positive assertions about the direct cause of the genetic damage, it floats the proposition that the most likely culprit is depleted uranium weapons.

Depleted uranium (DU) is a heavy metal, a waste product of the enrichment process used to power nuclear reactors. It is often used in military weapons or armor because of its high density. DU munitions utilize uranium penetrators, which emit low levels of radiation, to punch through tank armor or cement bunkers. While the radiation emitted by an unexploded DU round is too weak to penetrate the skin, the fine particles left over from the explosion can enter the body if inhaled or ingested. Once inside the body, these low levels of radiation become extremely dangerous; the metal particles are also chemically toxic.[23]

By the time of Operation Iraqi Freedom, many Americans had heard of Gulf War syndrome, a cluster of mysterious symptoms suffered by American veterans returning from the 1991 conflict, many of whom had children with birth defects. Some also knew about the United States' use of DU weapons in that conflict, which had similar public health consequences in southern Iraq.[24] The "shock and awe" bombing of Baghdad in 2003 rehashed previous discussions about the dangers of DU weapons. So when Americans first learned about the birth defects in Fallujah, many assumed that DU weapons must have been used in Fallujah too. And when Busby insinuated that DU had caused genetic damage in Fallujah, it fueled the more speculative accusations that were already being thrown around by the war's opponents.

To strengthen his argument, Busby compared the increases in incidents of cancer and the drop in the rate of male births relative to female births in Fallujah with the rates in Hiroshima, Japan, after the dropping of the atomic bomb, showing that the rates in Fallujah were, in fact, higher. Busby later expanded on this comparison in an interview, stating that what his team found in Fallujah was "like nothing that you have ever found in any epidemiological study anywhere, ever. This is like the highest rate of genetic damage in any population ever studied. It's worse than Hiroshima."[25]

Inevitably, such dramatic statements made headlines and grabbed the public's attention. In July 2010, Patrick Cockburn of London's *Independent* published the first mainstream news article on the public health crisis in Fallujah titled "Toxic Legacy of US Assault on Fallujah 'Worse Than Hiroshima.'"[26] The article went viral, and assertions about the use of

DU in Fallujah quickly became a conventional wisdom in activist online communities. Now in the public eye, Busby's study brought international attention to the situation in Fallujah but also encouraged some activist groups to echo his speculations as fact, giving rise to a highly politicized debate based on inconclusive evidence. In fact, evidence of the use of DU in Fallujah was not made publicly available until 2016.[27]

Complicating matters further, Busby's persona is difficult to separate from his science. He is known as much for wearing his signature black beret and his willingness to bring politics and values into science as he is for his research on low-dose ionizing radiation. While some have faulted him for not placing scientific impartiality above humanitarian concerns—some even accusing him of peddling junk science[28]—others have applauded him for his willingness to research controversial topics and defend his findings in the face of political pressures. His study was also criticized for a number of methodological flaws, which gave many of his detractors an opportunity to dismiss Fallujah's public health crisis out of hand. Others, however, maintained that the flaws in Busby's study should not cast doubt over the seriousness of the situation in Fallujah but recognized the need for further corroborative studies.[29]

In 2011, Busby and others published a second paper that would eclipse the first in terms of controversy. This time, however, Busby took a back seat, and Dr. Samira Alaani, a pediatrician at the Fallujah General Hospital, was lead author. Her paper sought to investigate the most controversial of Busby's claims—the cause of Fallujah's birth defects. Many scientists would scoff at the study's attempt to identify causal relationships outside of experimental settings, where variables are minimized and controlled. But Dr. Alaani's team collected hair, soil, and water samples from Fallujah and looked for the presence of known teratogens, carcinogens, and fetotoxins. They found "unusually high levels" of lead, iron, aluminum, manganese, strontium, barium, bismuth, mercury, and uranium. But the uranium was not depleted, as expected, nor was it natural uranium. Test results showed "slightly enriched" uranium.[30]

Conspiracy theorists and critics alike seized on the study's findings. But a handful of researchers pointed to a growing body of evidence that shows traces of slightly enriched uranium showing up on battlefields throughout the greater Middle East. Dai Williams, an independent weapons researcher, compiled these findings and posited the existence of "third-generation uranium weapons." The first generation of uranium weapons—commonly referred to as nuclear weapons, he argues, "exploited the fission potential of the U-235 isotope in enriched uranium."[31] Second-generation uranium weapons (i.e., DU) exploit the "nonfission properties" of uranium, namely its density.[32] The third generation of uranium weapons, however, which might range from shape charges to thermobaric weapons, uses uranium for its "incendiary" and "pyrophoric" properties (uranium burns at very high temperatures).[33]

Thermobaric weapons are a new powerful class of explosives that combine high heat with high pressure blasts. A number of thermobarics came into popular usage during the Global War on Terror, such as the Hellfire missile. Williams believes that thermobaric weapons could use "uranium alloys" in either the casings or ballasts of these weapons. Williams's evidence, however, is circumstantial. He points to just a few cases in which slightly enriched uranium was found in the bodies of civilians in conflict zones or on the actual battlefield. Williams also notes the ambiguous language in a number of patents for thermobaric weapon systems, which vaguely state that a "heavy metal" is used, suggesting that weapons manufacturers are intentionally obscuring the use of uranium.[34]

Dr. Alaani and her team point to further circumstantial evidence, noting that U.S. forces combat tested "at least two" new thermobaric weapons in Fallujah during the second siege—the AGM-114N Hellfire missile and the SMAW-NE.[35] The evidence presented in these studies, although intriguing, was often mistaken for conclusions, and the preliminary nature of these investigations and their sensational results—as well as the proliferation of misinformation on the topic—has led to heated debates between the war's supporters and its critics. In this shrill environment, scientific research and documented evidence have become increasingly difficult to distinguish from mere conjecture. And the sense of deadlock on this issue has only added to the suffering of the Iraqi people as they grapple with the tangible, lived effects of war. Some observers, though, have sought to break this spell by speaking openly and unequivocally about what has unfolded throughout Iraq and particularly in cities such as Fallujah.

EVERYDAY HEROICS

Dr. Alaani is a middle-age woman—small but determined, kind but serious. In June of 2013, she addressed an international audience at the Carter Center in Atlanta, Georgia, for the Human Rights Defenders Forum. She began with a traditional Islamic greeting, "*salamu alaykum wa rahmatullahi wa barakatuh*" (peace be upon you with God's mercy and blessing), but then got right to the point: "the Iraqi Hiroshima" is not a medical puzzle of pedantic interest, nor is it an esoteric question of variables and correlations; it is a war crime committed in the context of an illegal occupation, which global governing institutions have failed to prevent, palliate, or punish.

> Ladies and gentlemen, this year, 2013, marks the 10th anniversary of the 2003 Iraq war. Since the invasion, the occupying U.S.–U.K.-led coalition forces and the Iraqi authorities have failed to fulfill their obligation to protect people's right to life and health, with devastating results for Iraq's people. Grave human rights violations, against international law, have been reported during and after the Iraq war. Most of the alleged violations have not been properly investigated, nor have their perpetrators been brought to justice.
>
> As a consequence of the use of inhuman, indiscriminate, and toxic weapons, many people have been killed, and many are still suffering physical harm without any reparations.[36]

Dr. Alaani broke from the scientific pretensions of impartiality and urged her audience to look at the data on Fallujah's public health crisis in its human and political context. She implored them to consider what this public health crisis has meant for families in Fallujah: in 2013, 14 percent of all newborns in Fallujah were born with congenital malformations and 5 percent would die before they reached the age of one.[37] There is far more riding on these scientific questions than treatment options, and cautionary attitudes about scientific skepticism must be balanced with the urgent need for environmental cleanup and political accountability.

This tragedy is not abstract, it is ongoing, and its causes must be studied if something is to be done about it.

We met Dr. Alaani at the Fallujah hospital that same year when it was still possible to conduct epidemiological studies or make public health interventions—before the Iraqi government laid siege to Fallujah again, before the Islamic State arrived, and before the city's entire population was displaced again. In our conversations with Dr. Alaani, she brought with her the same balance of scientific skepticism, political awareness, and humanitarian urgency that has characterized her work.

At the time of the invasion in 2003, she was working as chief of the Pediatrics Department at the Fallujah hospital. Following the sieges of 2004, Dr. Alaani oversaw the collection of data on birth defects that occurred in babies born at the hospital. This was a significant intervention, since until that point, no records had been kept in the hospital on cases of birth defects. The health crisis emerged gradually, and it was only once the urgency of the situation became apparent that Dr. Alaani took on the responsibility of diagnosing the defects and cataloguing the data. But the hardships of life under occupation made it difficult to keep a formal register. This informal data log, consisting only of the entries made on her shifts, would later become vital to attracting Western attention and support. Many births went unreported, and a formal register, although still imperfect, was not created until 2009. Given this, it is probable that the rates of birth defects in Fallujah are even higher than has been presented in the scientific literature.

Dr. Alaani bears an enormous burden in both treating and searching for a solution to this public health crisis. In addition to her work in the Pediatrics Department, she has taken on a newly created position as head of the Department of Congenital Malformation. Dr. Alaani also coordinates with aid organizations, organizes media interviews, conducts research, and publishes papers in medical journals. But the most difficult part of her job, she tells us, is interacting with the families. "Will my baby survive? Will he be normal? Will the next one live? These are the questions I get every day," she says. "I struggle to keep the tears inside because I have no answers and we have no facilities for good postbirth care, so often the baby will die, not like in the U.K. or U.S. where babies with similar conditions have a chance to survive." Such encounters are most taxing on Dr. Alaani, but they are also what drives her. On her laptop and on the walls of her office are three enlarged photographs of babies suffering typical deformities: one with a cleft palate, another with an enlarged head, one with the intestines protruding outside its body. She never looks away.

The hospital staff are witnessing a range of defects, Dr. Alaani tells us, "a strange collection," some of which "have not been seen by many doctors in the world." But the most common of these, she says, are heart defects. These are often "hidden defects" that the staff are not able to detect with their limited equipment. Most of the children with such defects die within a year.

The health crisis has also affected Dr. Alaani's own family. Her brother and sister-in-law had two children, both with birth defects. Neither survived. This led Dr. Alaani to offer drastic advice: "I asked my brother's wife to stop having any more babies until we have a solution, but she is now thirty-three years old, and I'm not sure when the solution will be available and if it will ever be available or not." Her advice to all women in Fallujah is the same: "I advise them not to fall pregnant," she says. Of course, for many families this is no solution at all, and the implications for the future of the city are dire. But without adequate medical equipment to detect congenital malformations in utero and to treat newborns, and bereft of properly funded epidemiological and environmental studies, and with no real attempt to decontaminate the city, mothers trying to conceive and bear children run a great risk for their yet unborn children.

"We need equipment that will help to save the life of the child at birth," Dr. Alaani says. "We need to investigate what is going on, we have to check for environmental contaminants and we have to check the DNA; if DNA has changed this is a disaster. We have no facilities or no laboratories in Iraq to do that kind of test or investigations so we need help from outside. We ask the honest person, the honest scientist everywhere to try to help us as much as they can." But the international community has not rushed to the aid of Fallujah. The Fallujah General Hospital's relationship with the Iraqi Ministry of Health is fraught, and the U.S. government has refused to recognize that there is a public health crisis throughout

Iraq, with severe clusters in places like Fallujah, Basra, Hawija, and elsewhere. This is unsurprising. But perhaps most disappointing is the lack of response from the United Nations and the World Health Organization (WHO). "We saw nothing [from them]," she said. "It is now nine years."

A summary of the WHO's collaborative study with the Iraqi Ministry of Health would come out later in 2013, declaring that no such public health crisis existed.

Dr. Alaani is acutely aware of all the potential contributing factors to these birth defects. But she notes that as much as this may include "factors relating to the mother, the nutrition of the mother, drugs taken by the mother, and stress that the mother may have been exposed to during her pregnancy, there are also factors relating to the environment, like pollution." Indeed, Iraqis have been under extreme stress for decades, living under a brutal dictator, surviving three (now four) Gulf wars, and a devastating period of sanctions that malnourished the entire nation. Without a comprehensive study of birth defects and the spike in cancers, it is not possible at this juncture to draw any firm conclusions as to the precise causes of this situation. That said, environmental factors must surely have played a key role in the sudden emergence of these symptoms in 2005: the coincidence of an enormous environmental disruption, like Operation Phantom Fury, followed by the outbreak of a public health crisis is too apparent to be dismissed. As uncomfortable as many scientists are with trying to determine causal relationships outside of experimental settings, Dr. Alaani insists that this is the most urgent question for Fallujans: "Our job as doctors, our first job and our urgent need is to investigate possible causes and to decontaminate the environment. This is the most important."

If Dr. Chris Busby's hypothesis about genetic damage is correct, the options left to Fallujans are very few. Whether the environment can or cannot be decontaminated, and whether Fallujans are able or willing to relocate, become moot. Genetic damage might be irreparable. But there is still more that can be done—at least more than simply assigning blame for this tragedy in Fallujah and elsewhere in Iraq. "We are not looking for compensation," Dr. Alaani says, arguing that her country is in fact rich and ought to be supporting the Fallujah hospital. More urgently, she insists, "We need the scientific community and research community to listen to this and to support research in Fallujah . . . by providing facilities like machines, material, training, all that is very important."

THE POLITICS OF SCIENCE

In addition to investigations by Chris Busby and Samira Alaani, there have been other studies focused on the increased levels of toxic heavy metals in Fallujah and other Iraqi cities. In a 2012 study, a team of international epidemiolocal researchers compared the levels of lead and mercury in hair, nail, and teeth samples from Fallujah and Basra.[38] The study found that the population in Fallujah had been exposed to high levels of "two well-known neurotoxic metals," lead and mercury.[39] The authors of this study observed, "Toxic metals such as mercury (Hg) and lead (Pb) are an integral part of war ammunitions and are extensively used in the making of bullets and bombs . . . the bombardment of al-Basrah and Fallujah may have exacerbated public exposure to metals, possibly culminating in the current epidemic of birth defects."[40] In Basra, the authors found even higher levels of lead exposure than in Fallujah. Basra, in fact, has the highest ever reported level of neural tube defects, and the numbers continue to climb each year.

Lead and mercury are designated by the WHO as among the top ten chemicals of major public health concern. Their adverse toxicity effects, particularly for fetuses and children, are well documented.[41] Absorption of lead into the body can lead to a range of negative effects, including neurological damage, kidney damage, miscarriage, premature birth, and death. Mercury is known to cause impairment of neurological development, particularly in fetuses and infants, has toxic effects on the immune and digestive systems, and is a possible human carcinogen.[42]

Another study, led by independent researcher Dr. Mozhgan Savabieasfahani, looked into another source of environmental pollution and harm to public health. What went by the name of "burn pits" at Coalition military bases were man-made pits used for the disposal and incineration of everything from human waste to electronics, plastics, and batteries, creating toxic smoke that could potentially carry pollution downwind to communities, farmlands, and waterways. Savabieasfahani's study investigated the public health effects of one burn pit near the Iraqi city of Hawija, where her team found elevated levels of magnesium and titanium in the bodies of Iraqi adults who, after exposure to smoke from the burn pits, bore children suffering from neurodevelopmental disorders. These findings mirrored the results of previous studies about the composition of dust found in the lungs of the American soldiers. The study argues that the common profile of toxic metals suggests a common source of exposure—the burn pits. The study also argued that what we know about the heavy metal pollution originating from burn pits and exposure in places like Hawija could likely explain the rates of birth defects in Fallujah, where children showed levels of lead in their body 3.7 times higher than their peers in Hawija and levels of mercury twelve times higher.[43]

With each new study an increasingly complicated picture begins to emerge of multiple sources of environmental contamination and allied health problems. Taken together, these studies provide a body of evidence that suggests that the most likely explanation for the public health crisis in Fallujah is environmental contamination originating from weapons used during the sieges of 2004.[44] However, all these studies suffer from methodological constraints imposed by the difficulties of conducting research in a war zone, and they have all come up against harsh criticism and political pressure. Critics of these studies are correct on two points: first, causal relationships simply cannot be demonstrated outside of experimental settings and, second, there is no way to prove that the source of any particular type of contamination was an American weapon, even if more evidence were available. Instead, the most that researchers can confidently state is that it is *likely* that the environmental contamination is linked with the public health crisis in Fallujah. Articulated so generally, the Pentagon is able to dismiss the issue and avoid accountability.

Still, the studies cited above raised enough awareness to pressure the WHO into conducting its own study in collaboration with the Iraqi Ministry of Health. Focused on the rates of birth defects in various Iraqi provinces, the study was originally scheduled for publication in

November 2012 but was delayed for several months. Finally, in September 2013, after much pressure from Iraqi doctors, public health researchers, and activists, the Iraqi Ministry of Health released just a summary of their results, which stated, "The rates for spontaneous abortion, stillbirths and congenital birth defects found in the study are consistent with or even lower than international estimates. The study provides no clear evidence to suggest an unusually high rate of congenital birth defects in Iraq."[45] The findings of the summary document came as a shock to many, contrasting starkly with those from earlier studies and even contradicting previous statements by Ministry of Health officials about their preliminary conclusions. Several independent experts, including former UN and WHO officials, along with the respected medical journal, the *Lancet*, questioned the validity of the report. They argued that the study's methodology and peer-review process were inadequate and that the conclusions may have been influenced by political pressure.[46]

In an article for the *Huffington Post*, Neel Mani, the WHO's Iraq director between 2001 and 2003, claimed there is a history of political interference in public health research in Iraq. He believed that the Ministry of Health's most recent study was yet another example of such interference.[47] Mani had direct experience of such practices in health research during his tenure when members of the UN Security Council repeatedly blocked his attempts to fund research into rates of cancers and birth defects in Iraq. "Any project that proposed to investigate abnormal rates of birth defects in southern Iraq and their relation, if any, to environmental contamination, never got through the Security Council's approval process," he wrote. "Political sensitivity over the legacy of the use of depleted uranium munitions may have helped catalyse Security Council objections to the research into the public health legacy of the conflict."

Former long-standing WHO expert on radiation and health, Dr. Keith Bavistock of the Department of Environmental Science, University of Eastern Finland, also questioned the study's methodology, telling the *Guardian* that the report "is not of scientific quality. It wouldn't pass peer review in one of the worst journals."[48] He pointed out that, of the many methodological problems with the study, the most significant was that it failed to examine medical records kept by doctors in Iraqi hospitals. "The way this document has been produced is extremely suspicious," he said. "There are question marks about the role of the US and UK, who have a conflict of interest in this sort of study due to compensation issues that might arise from findings determining a link between higher birth defects and DU."

A third UN official, the former UN assistant secretary general and UN humanitarian coordinator for Iraq, Hans von Sponeck, also criticized the report, pointing out that when one looks "at the stark difference between previous descriptions of the WHO study's findings and this new report, it seems that someone, somewhere clumsily decided that they would not release these damning findings, but instead obscure them."[49]

These allegations of political interference suggest the extent to which the international deck is stacked against Fallujah. But far more is at stake here than "compensation" claims. If the United States were to be deemed responsible for this atrocity and held accountable, it would suffer damage to its global image, leaders of the Iraq war effort could be tried as war criminals, and, if international conventions are passed to ban the use of uranium weapons, the U.S. military would lose valuable munitions in its arsenal.

The stakes for all these parties are high, but none are higher than for those most impacted: Fallujans. For them, the cause of this public health crisis is not just a political question, but a pressing humanitarian concern, touching deep at the heart of family life. "I can't only be a doctor," Dr. Alaani says. "When [patients] come holding the baby with the defects they were always crying. Not only the mothers; I saw the tears of many fathers. Most of the time I cried with them. They didn't know why this happened with them specifically. They didn't know what will be the fate of this baby, if he is going to survive. They are not blaming but they are always asking us the doctors 'why is this happening'? We don't have answers because we have no document, no proof."

Family life is central to Iraqi culture, and the inability to have healthy children has been devastating for many Fallujan families. Couples also suffer from the stigma attached to miscarriage, stillborn births, and infant death. And then many parents struggle with caring for their disabled child, since few services are available to offer support. Young women are fearful that they may never become pregnant and give birth to a healthy child, and many couples have chosen to move out of the city and start families elsewhere.[50] These radical changes in interfamilial dynamics are just one component of the sociocide that resulted from the U.S. operations. For several years after the sieges, the United States successfully stifled critical inquiry into the public health consequences of American military operations and went on to use the very same, potentially toxic and radioactive weapons in other war zones. But while U.S. officials were protecting their image and arsenal, Fallujans continued to bury babies in tiny graves at the Martyrs Cemetery, and the international community looked away.

THE CHILDREN OF FALLUJAH

Donna Mulhearn

I've never seen a face as sad as a mother watching her new baby die. I saw it several times during my time spent in Fallujah Hospital in 2012–13, but the most heartbreaking was the round, brown face of the woman in the pink dress. I entered the room in which she sat motionless, staring intently at her baby in the incubator in front of her. She did not turn to look at me, despite my odd appearance—a white girl in an oversized, black abaya and untidy hijab, juggling a camera and notebook. I attracted stares throughout the hospital, but the woman in the pink dress was too engaged with her baby to notice.

Her baby girl was struggling to breathe due to complex congenital heart defects, like so many babies born in Fallujah. The woman in the pink dress gazed with loving concentration at her baby, urging her, willing her to live, to take another breath. Her large brown eyes were not angry, more overwhelmed, full of searching questions. I saw the baby's eyes as she stared back at her mother, only innocence there too.

I dropped my camera bag to the floor and just stood there sharing the sacred, painful space between life and death, between love, yearning, and grief, and so many questions. In that small room in the Fallujah Hospital I stood for a while in sad, silent solidarity with the woman in the pink dress and her baby. At one point the mother looked up at me, we held a gaze, and in a wordless gesture I said I was sorry. She nodded. I motioned to ask if I could take her photo and she nodded. I left feeling gutted, tears stinging my eyes, my mind haunted by her face. An hour later I heard the baby died. Her name was Dumoa.

Like Dumoa, so many of Fallujah's children end up in the Martyrs Cemetery, which was once the city's football stadium. Residents were forced to dig up the playing field in haste to bury the large number of bodies from the U.S. attacks in 2004. The site has 3,500 to 4,000 graves with a special section allocated for infants' graves, some unmarked, others with names or words saying simply "child" or "baby." The babies buried here were often born dead or lived just a few minutes because of birth defects.

I was also able to spend time with some of the survivors. I sat in the homes of children with birth defects and listened to their families' experiences dealing with the challenges of raising a child with a disability or serious health problem. Fallujah has no services for children with disabilities, special schools, or day care centers, so families are left to cope with raising the child more or less on their own. Access to specialist medical care is a particular challenge and financial burden, which often means families are required to take their children to a neighboring country, such as Jordan or Turkey, for operations.

One night I visited the home of the al-Bakr family to hear about their struggle to care for their son, Azraq, who is suffering from congenital heart defects. It was a hot night. We sat on a mattress on the floor to talk. A ceiling fan rotated, circulating the warm air. Marwa, the young mother of Azraq, wore full black niqab—a veil that leaves only her shiny brown eyes, curious and engaging, uncovered. Azraq, two and a half years old, sat on her lap. His big brown eyes were tired and a little sad, but they were still the eyes of a little boy, looking around and up at his parents; watching, fiddling, yawning; a plastic pacifier in his mouth. His face and hands were tinged with blue.

Azraq was born with a serious heart defect. His father, Hamid, told me he had a gap in his heart and that some of his blood vessels and valves were closed. Hamid said they became aware of Azraq's problems immediately at birth. Their other son, age four, had no health problems, so they were surprised at Azraq's serious heart condition. Azraq was treated first in Fallujah, but it soon became clear that the Fallujah Hospital was not equipped to cope with his condition. He was then taken to a hospital in Baghdad, and then another—neither could help. Unable to gain access to the required medical procedures in Iraq, Azraq was taken to Turkey and underwent surgery in Istanbul. It was a failure. He then underwent a second surgery to open his heart valves. That was a year ago.

Hamid said they are now waiting for the next surgery. They went to Baghdad many times, but surgery was repeatedly delayed because there were so many patients waiting for treatment. Mindful of this situation, the Iraq Ministry of Health and international NGOs developed a program to send some patients outside Iraq. Azraq's parents applied to join this program, hoping that he might have another round of surgery in Turkey. They don't know if and when he will go. "We are waiting," Hamid explained.

The whole family is affected by Azraq's condition. "When he's suffering no one is comfortable," Marwa said. She described Azraq's current health as "one day good, another day not good." When Azraq is "not good" he is tired, his skin is blue, and can be too weak to walk. Most days he is sad and withdrawn. Marwa said Azraq needs two kinds of special medication daily, which are very expensive, especially on Hamid's wage as a construction worker. They brought some medication back from Turkey, but their supply will soon run out.

Hamid and Marwa believe the reason Azraq is sick is connected to the U.S. attacks on Fallujah in 2004. Hamid said he was able to escape the first attack but could not get out before the November attack and was trapped, hiding in his house for ten days during the bombardment.

"It was a heavy attack on the city," he said, "I was afraid to leave the house." When he tried to leave, U.S. troops turned him back at a checkpoint. He thought about trying to swim across the Euphrates, but he witnessed U.S. helicopters firing on others as they tried to cross the river. "I tried to get out but was trapped," he insisted, "I wasn't a fighter." Terrified, he endured the daily bombing and shooting in his home, even though it was damaged by tank shells. "When the bombing finished, the U.S. troops used a loud speaker to call people to come out of their houses," he told me. "I carried a white cloth and told them I am civilian and peaceful. The translator said not to be afraid and just come out." But when he came out of the house, U.S. troops detained him, searched his house, and took him to a military base. After five days of interrogation he was released.

Hamid became agitated by these memories, and he blames Fallujah's health crisis on the 2004 sieges. "Azraq's problem comes from U.S. weapons," he asserted. "Before the attack the city was never suffering these problems, but after, many people suffer from these cases. These problems always remind us about what happened in 2004, so we can never forget. They are responsible for what happened so they have to give medical support and try to improve the soil and water. We want justice, for people outside Iraq to care about Iraqis, and the U.S. to be punished. I don't believe I'll see it, I want it, but there is no justice."

Marwa and Hamid wish they could have more children, but they think it imprudent. "Azraq takes all our time so we have no time for another child; also the doctors don't recommend another," Marwa said. They would also like to leave Fallujah but cannot afford to relocate. "Fallujah has no future because of these things," she said.

CHAPTER 7
THE THIRD SIEGE OF FALLUJAH

The fighting from 2004 never stopped. We simply switched from
fighting the Americans to fighting Maliki and his injustice and
corruption.

—Sheikh Khaled Hamoud Al-Jumaili, a leader
of the Iraqi Spring Uprising

As the last American combat soldiers prepared to withdraw
from Iraq, in December 2011, ending the Coalition's formal occupation of the country, President Barack Obama
addressed an audience at Fort Bragg, North Carolina,
calling the completion of the U.S. mission in Iraq "an extraordinary
achievement." President Obama went on to say to the men and women of
Fort Bragg, "Because of you, because you sacrificed so much for a people
that you had never met, Iraqis have a chance to forge their own destiny."[1]
Of course, not all Iraqis shared President Obama's appraisal of the U.S.
mission in their country, and most would argue that the damage inflicted
by the U.S.-led occupation would ensure conflict and corruption in Iraq
for years to come. By the time of the United States' withdrawal, nearly all
Iraqis from all sects and ethnic groups were deeply dissatisfied with the
new Iraq and its lack of democracy, disregard for human rights, inequita-
ble economy, and poor public health conditions. Sunnis felt particularly
disenfranchised and aggrieved, and Prime Minister al-Maliki's failure to
incorporate the Sahwa militias—Sunni tribal militias that accepted U.S.

arms and funding to fight Al Qaeda—into the Iraqi military added to their feelings of frustration and betrayal.[2]

This led to the nonviolent Iraqi Spring protest movement that began in December 2012. The movement enjoyed widespread support throughout Sunni provinces, as well as sections of the Shia community.[3] In Fallujah and Ramadi, protesters set up camps modeled on the Arab Spring and Occupy Wall Street protests. Weekly large-scale, nonviolent demonstrations were held calling for reform.

The protesters articulated a set of demands that addressed sectarianism, corruption, and abuses of power by the new Iraqi government, including calls for the release of political prisoners and for an end to the labeling of political dissent as terrorism.[4] The protesters' grievances were explained by Sheikh Khaled Hamoud Al-Jumaili, a leader of the protest camp in Fallujah, who told Al Jazeera, "We demand an end to checkpoints surrounding Fallujah, we demand they allow in the press, we demand they end their unlawful home raids and detentions, we demand an end to federalism and gangsters and secret prisons."[5]

For a year al-Maliki ignored the protesters' demands and sent troops to attack them repeatedly.[6] Despite this violent suppression, the protesters remained nonviolent and steadfast in their aim of rolling back the political legacy of the occupation. However, on December 1, 2013, the violence suddenly escalated. On that day Sheikh Khaled Hamoud Al-Jumaili was driving with his son when they stopped in front of a car that was blocking the road. Two men armed with Kalashnikovs exited the car in front of them and proceeded to fire, killing the sheikh and his son. The men who killed them were from Hamas al-Iraq, a militia group tied to the Muslim Brotherhood and the al-Maliki government.[7]

On December 30, the Iraqi government sent security forces to clear the protest camps—first in Ramadi and then in Fallujah—under the pretext that the protests had been infiltrated by ISIS, the Islamic State of Iraq and al-Sham (greater Syria), a group formerly affiliated with Al Qaeda.[8] The next day, on December 31, a convoy of ISIS fighters arrived in Fallujah, but after consulting with tribal leaders they agreed to position themselves on the outskirts of the city.[9] After the protesters were dispersed by military force, many gave up hope that the tactic of nonviolence could bring about political change and picked up arms against the Iraqi security forces.[10] The uprising quickly organized itself according to tribal, neighborhood, and other local affiliations, which eventually led to sustained localized skirmishes with Iraqi security forces.[11]

On January 2, the Iraqi Ministry of the Interior reported to the press that half of Fallujah had "fallen" to ISIS.[12] This claim was false, but the media quoted it repeatedly until it became conventional wisdom that Fallujah had indeed succumbed to the terrorists. Again, the Western media framed the violence as an ethnosectarian dispute between Sunni extremists and the Shia-led government in Baghdad. In response to this, the United States increased its level of military support to Iraq, promising to send fresh shipments of Hellfire missiles and Apache attack helicopters to "help" the Iraqi military "in the battle to uproot Islamic fighters from Ramadi and Fallujah."[13]

The Iraqi government's justification for its assault on Fallujah paralleled its justification of the U.S.-led sieges in 2004. Once again it was falsely claimed that Al Qaeda (or an affiliate) had taken over Fallujah and that a heavy-handed military response was needed to "take back" the city. The media amplified these assertions by focusing on radical Islam, or conflicts between competing sects of Islam, as the main explanatory factors for the violence.[14] In reality, it was a government attack that turned a nonviolent movement into an armed insurrection. The mainstream U.S. media repeatedly characterized Fallujah as an epicenter of extremism, and again the residents of Fallujah were denied the opportunity to speak for themselves or to articulate their own reasons for turning to armed resistance.

Many Western analysts and commentators posited a link between ISIS and the group allegedly led by Abu Musab al-Zarqawi, al-Tawhid wal-Jihad, thereby implying that the reemergence of an Al Qaeda–linked group in Fallujah was evidence that the U.S. withdrawal from Iraq in 2011 had been a misguided decision that squandered the sacrifices of American soldiers in 2004. Further military action would be needed, they argued, to eradicate terrorists from the city once and for all.[15]

The alleged connection between ISIS and al-Tawhid wal-Jihad and their unified presence in Fallujah is, at best, tenuous. In 2006 al-Tawhid wal-Jihad merged with a group known as the Islamic State of Iraq (ISI) and took on the latter's name.[16] However, by 2007 ISI was forced out of its strongholds in Anbar province by the Sahwa militias and became ostracized in Iraq due to its sectarianism and its acts of terrorism.[17] The group remained at the margins of Iraqi society for several years until the Syrian uprising of 2011, when it seized the moment to join a growing insurgency and rebuild itself as a military force. ISI's leadership helped to found Jabhat al-Nusra, which became one of the strongest Islamist groups in the insurgency against the regime of Bashar al-Assad and one of its best funded due to Al Qaeda's sponsorship and capture of oil fields in Syria.[18] However, two years later ISI disassociated itself from Jabhat al-Nusra when the latter refused an official merger with its progenitor. ISI disregarded al-Nusra's autonomous stance, changed its name to the Islamic State of Iraq and al-Sham[19] (ISIS), and then moved into al-Nusra's territory, absorbing much of its membership and its sources of funding, including oil.[20] ISIS expanded rapidly in Syria but remained concentrated there until an opportunity to overcome its past unpopularity in Iraq presented itself. That opportunity was the third siege of Fallujah.

Importantly, it was local fighters from Fallujah who took the lead in the fight against the Iraqi government. ISIS arrived after the fight had already begun, attempting to piggyback on the success of the local fighters. The Fallujah-based groups formed an allegiance with ISIS, in what the International Crisis Group called a "Faustian bargain,"[21] and agreed to let ISIS play an ancillary role in the fighting. But ISIS soon began attempting to raise its flag over neighborhoods cleared of government forces.[22] This move was reported by the Western media as a sign of ISIS's power in Fallujah. However, ISIS took the flag down shortly after being ordered to by tribal leaders.[23]

In fact, a command structure was established in Fallujah during the first weeks of fighting. It consisted primarily of tribal leaders and former Baathist army officers and went by the name of the General Military Council for Iraqi Revolutionaries (GMCIR).[24] This Council was led by Sheikh Abdullah al-Janabi, who led the Shura Council of Mujahideen back in 2004. After the second U.S.-led assault on Fallujah, al-Janabi fled to Syria. He returned to Fallujah in 2011. His calls for cooperation

between the various militant factions in Fallujah were a significant uni-
fying factor in the resistance.[25] Initially ISIS was cooperating with the
GMCIR. But over the course of several months of fighting with the government, ISIS grew in size and strength. Divisions and power struggles
began to emerge between the various rebel factions fighting against the
al-Maliki government.[26] Yet despite all the glaring factional differences
in Fallujah, the Iraqi government refused to acknowledge the legitimacy
of any Sunni militia. As one government official put it to *Reuters,* "If anyone insists on fighting our forces, he will be considered an [ISIS] militant
whether he is or not."[27]

The first two weeks of fighting between the resistance and Iraqi government forces were fierce and led to many losses on both sides. The
rebellion quickly spread to other cities in Anbar province, and the rebel
fighters began calling the uprising a "revolution." Faced with fierce resistance, the Iraqi military stopped trying to penetrate into Fallujah and
instead sealed off all entry and exit points to and from the city. This was
quickly followed by a campaign of indiscriminate bombing and artillery shelling from the outskirts of Fallujah, safely outside of the range
of the rebels' weapons. Civilian structures in Fallujah and elsewhere
were repeatedly shelled and bombed, including hospitals, with civilians
wounded and killed on a daily basis. Over the following two years, more
than 3,521 civilians would be killed in Fallujah (including 343 women and
548 children) and over 5,966 wounded (including 840 women and 1,013
children).[28] On February 25, Struan Stevenson, president of European
Parliament's Delegation for Relations with Iraq, wrote an open letter
calling the Iraqi government's operation "genocidal."[29] The Geneva International Centre for Justice issued a number of appeals and various letters
to the UN High Commissioner on Human Rights, UN Special Procedures, and other UN bodies, arguing that the assault on Fallujah, and all
of Anbar province, met the legal definition of genocide.[30]

On March 26, an electrical plant in Fallujah was bombed, leaving
much of the city without power. On March 27, the HVAC system at the
Fallujah Teaching Hospital was shelled, affecting the entire hospital's
ability to heat and refrigerate—essential functions for any hospital.
Iraqi security forces would go on to bomb or shell the Fallujah Teaching

Hospital on more than forty separate occasions over the next two years.[31] Through social media, Dr. Ahmed Shami Jassem, media spokesperson for the Fallujah Teaching Hospital, released daily casualty figures and reports about attacks on the hospital. Dr. Muhamad Al-Darraji detailed many of these crimes in a report submitted to the International Criminal Court.[32] And the Tokyo-based NGO Human Rights Now backed up many of these accusations through their own interviews in Fallujah.[33]

During this time, Fallujah was encircled and sealed off by government forces, placing the city under siege. Naji Haraj, a Fallujah native and now the executive secretary of the Geneva International Centre for Justice, told us in an email correspondence that for several months after January 6, no humanitarian aid was allowed to enter Fallujah. He added that "there was an attempt to send aid collected by individuals but it [the shipment] was attacked by the government troops." By May 4, Human Rights Watch released a report revealing that Iraqi security forces were still "impeding" aid from entering Fallujah, in addition to "hindering" residents from fleeing areas where fighting was taking place.[34]

This campaign was initiated by Prime Minister Nouri al-Maliki, who managed to hang on to power again in the parliamentary elections of April 30, 2014, even though the elections were mired in allegations of fraud and intimidation. A few weeks prior, the electoral commission threatened to resign due to "alleged parliamentary and judicial interference."[35] There were also many complaints relating to voter privacy and transparency during the electoral process. Reportedly, a new electronic voting system failed on many occasions, and some observers claimed that members of the Iraqi army and police force were allowed to vote twice.[36] Some also expressed concerns that voters' identities were being recorded along with their vote, giving people reason to fear reprisals if they voted against al-Maliki.[37] It is no surprise then that al-Maliki's Islamic Dawa Party won more seats than any other political block, securing continued dominance over the political establishment in Iraq.

Flush with electoral success, al-Maliki increased the intensity of the air assault on Fallujah. On May 4, five civilians were wounded and fifteen were killed as a result of bombing and shelling. On May 5, nine civilians were wounded and four killed. The next day nine more civilians were wounded and four more killed. The following day, forty-five civilians were wounded and seven killed. And so it went on. Day after day the killings continued, and reports emerged of new experimental "barrel bombs" being dropped from Iraqi Air Force M18 helicopters in residential areas of Fallujah.[38]

Predictably, the assault on Fallujah and other cities in Anbar province created another wave of refugees, compounding an already dire situation. In February 2014, the UN estimated that 62,679 families had been displaced, or roughly 370,000 people from Anbar province.[39] That number continued to grow over the next three years. Even Dr. Samira Alaani was forced to flee her home. "I am a refugee now," she told us. "In the place where I am now, there are more than 1,500 families living in very hard conditions. Some are living in unfinished buildings, shops, and kindergartens. We are five families living in three small rooms with few beds and no furniture. . . . It seems that there is no hope. I wonder if we are ever going to be able to live like other people."

FAILED STATES

Just when it seemed as if the government and the insurgency in Fallujah were locked in an indefinite stalemate—steadily killing off or starving the population of Fallujah—ISIS and several other militias launched a blitzkrieg assault that captured the city of Mosul, Iraq's second largest city. On June 10 the Western media reported that Mosul "fell" to the terrorist organization known as ISIS and 500,000 residents fled their homes in fear.[40] Again, ISIS was portrayed as a lone actor that was conquering territory through extreme violence and intimidation.[41] In reality ISIS, in collaboration with tribal and Baathist militias, launched a joint operation to take Mosul, and it faced little opposition from the Iraqi army, which threw down its weapons and deserted en masse.[42] Over 500,000 Mosul residents fled their homes, but not out of fear of ISIS's Sharia courts. Rather, they fled because they feared that al-Maliki's reprisal would make their city "another Fallujah."[43]

The uprising, which started in Fallujah and slowly spread to other cities in Anbar province, suddenly attracted international headlines and the watchful eye of Washington and Tehran. The loose coalition of rebel militias, including ISIS, went on to capture—or "liberate"—other cities north of Baghdad, including Tikrit, and Tel Afar, as well as one of Iraq's largest oil refineries at Baiji.[44] Their encroachment on Baghdad provoked Ayatollah Ali al-Sistani, the highest Shia cleric in Iraq, to issue a *fatwa*—a religious declaration—calling for the formation of citizen militias, which would come to be known as al-Hashd al-Shaabi, or the Popular Mobilization Units (PMUs), to help fight ISIS. In an affirmative response, Shia cleric Muqtada al-Sadr recalled his Mahdi Army and rebranded them "the Peace brigades."[45] Opposition to the government, however, was not divided along sectarian lines, as the Western media so often claimed. Some predominantly Shia organizations, such as the Unified Confederation of Tribes of the South and Middle Euphrates and the Popular Movement for the Salvation of Iraq, announced their support for a nationalist uprising against the political establishment in Baghdad (although not one that includes ISIS).[46] Some Shia religious leaders announced their support as well.[47]

It is important to note that ISIS's emergence and growth as a powerful military organization, and its various military successes, are not evidence of its popularity among Sunnis, as the media often seems to insinuate. ISIS attached itself parasitically to both the Syrian and Iraqi uprisings, riding the coattails of Sunni discontent to advance their own political, religious, and military goals. The alliance of nationalist, tribal, neighborhood, Baathist, and other militias with ISIS was pragmatic and intended to be temporary. However, ISIS's capture of U.S. military equipment in Mosul—including arms and armored vehicles gifted to the Iraqi army—and the oil refineries at Baiji helped make them one of the most powerful military forces in the region. No longer needing to follow the lead of the GMCIR, ISIS attempted to coopt the uprising as it had done in Syria.

In July 2014, ISIS changed its name from the Islamic State of Iraq and al-Sham to just the Islamic State (IS). It also announced that its military leader Abu Bakr al-Baghdadi was now also the caliph of their fledgling theocracy.[48] That same month, reports began to emerge of IS threatening the military leadership in Fallujah, demanding that they swear an oath of allegiance to Abu Bakr al-Baghdadi.[49] Yet by the end of August, eight months after the media declared that Fallujah had "fallen" to ISIS, groups from within Fallujah continued to resist ISIS's attempts to dominate them. A member of a local militia in Fallujah told *Niqash,* "We are against the things that the IS group do . . . We don't support their acts. But we do have a common enemy: the Iraqi army, who are trying to kill us all with any means available to them."[50]

The rebels' gains that summer prompted both the U.S. and Iranian governments to intervene more directly. U.S. president Barack Obama initially promised to send three hundred "advisers" to aid the Iraqi military, but by the summer of 2016 that number reached 4,700 and would include military advisors, trainers, special forces, and air support.[51] Iranian intervention is believed to have begun in June of 2014[52] and would eventually include the deployment of Iran's Quds Force teams[53]—elite units of the Iranian Revolutionary Guard led by the controversial general Qassem Suleimani[54]—as well as air support, intelligence support, and a tank division.[55] Iran also worked closely with the PMUs but is said to have commanded several "core" militias within the PMUs that had received Iranian sponsorship and training for years and that enjoyed "considerable autonomy from the Iraqi state."[56]

That summer the Iraqi army expanded its campaign to rebel-held territory in western, central, and northern Iraq, while maintaining the siege on Fallujah. Violence escalated further when the IS's territorial gains began to encroach upon Kurdish territory, and particularly when IS began killing and evicting religious minorities from captured areas.[57] When IS trapped tens of thousands of Yazidis (neither Christians nor Muslims and, therefore, apostates in the eyes of IS) on top of Mount Sinjar and threatened genocide against them, the Obama administration ordered air strikes on Iraq.[58]

In an address to the nation on August 7, 2014, President Obama identified the beginning of IS's "advance across Iraq" as starting in June with the capture of Mosul, omitting the six months prior when IS was gaining strength and momentum by supporting militant groups in Fallujah in their fight against the Iraqi government. President Obama also omitted the United States' role in creating the conditions that allowed IS to grow and thrive by arming the al-Maliki government and facilitating what many considered a genocidal campaign against the Sunni population in Anbar province. Instead, President Obama claimed that the United States was just at that moment choosing to intervene in Iraq against a terrorist threat that appeared out of nowhere to "prevent a potential act of genocide."[59]

This framing of events was used to justify Operation Inherent Resolve, which began in September 2014 as a joint operation conducted by an Iraqi-led coalition of nations against the IS and the Sunni uprising (the latter being conflated with the former).[60] History was being actively rewritten. According to the operation's official website the "invaders," referring to IS, "attacked across the Syrian-Iraqi borders" in "the summer of 2014."[61] While the United States has been unwilling to publicly acknowledge how its occupation of Iraq and its support for the al-Maliki government contributed to IS's success, in internal discussions, however, several officials have stressed the importance of "addressing the underlying political roots of [IS] in Iraq," which they attribute to "Sunni Arab disfranchisement."[62]

Not that such acknowledgments influenced the U.S. military's approach to the deteriorating situation in Iraq. As one of nine "lines of effort" in Operation Inherent Resolve, U.S. forces launched a propaganda campaign aimed at countering IS's "ideology."[63] This gave rise to two conflicting discourses about IS: one public, that presupposed IS's "ideology" constituted a danger and that assumed that "Syria and Iraq are unstable because of [IS]" and the other circulating among experts and insiders that viewed IS as "a symptom of pre-existing conflicts and instability in Iraq and Syria."[64]

Such differences reflect the contradictory orientations of Operation Inherent Resolve. On the one hand, the United States made efforts— although superficial and ineffectual in nature—to address the political roots of the conflict and to pressure the Iraqi government to engender reforms. On the other hand, the United States assisted a violent military campaign, consisting of a series of clear-and-hold operations by the Iraqi army and the PMUs with Iranian support, which has only exacerbated the sectarianism driving the conflict.

The belief that propaganda could win over the Sunni Muslim world by delegitimizing IS along ideological lines, despite the outrages of the operation's ground campaign, inspired an information campaign designed to sway Sunnis away from fundamentalist or extremist ideas (as they are understood in the West) and toward a "moderate" Islam perceived as being more compatible with Western culture and economic priorities. In addition to launching cyberattacks on IS,[65] U.S. forces focused an information war on countering IS's propaganda and its recruitment efforts on social media.[66] The campaign even reached out to Hollywood film studios for help to counter IS's "narrative."[67]

Leaving aside whether Muslims in Iraq found this campaign persuasive or not, it appears to have successfully conveyed to the non-Muslim world that the motives of IS fighters were largely ideological and ahistorical, not political, and therefore they and their ideas had to be eradicated. In effect, the campaign produced a moralistic tirade of anti-ISIS jingoism and a consensus of uncritical approval for military action against IS.

In reality, it is difficult to understand what constitutes IS's ideology or even if it has a coherent one.[68] Tim Jacoby, professor of international relations at the University of Manchester, argues that IS rejects "almost all contemporary Islamic scholarship," including those scholars thought to inspire radical Jihadist movements. Tellingly, IS's publication *Dabiq* has instead relied on "in-house *fatawa* [religious rulings] from current and deceased members of the Iraqi resistance like Abu-Mus'ab al-Zarqawi and Abu Muhammad al-Adnani (neither of whom had any formal religious training)."[69] Jacoby adds, "Eschewing clerical input, then, the writers of *Dabiq* generally prefer to approach exegetic sources directly in order to present an action-orientated discourse in which the ends— the establishment of a Sunni homeland—justify the means . . . [ISIS] is, in other words, not principally mobilised by any particular branch/ distortion of Islam. Neither Wahhabi nor *salafi,* it is driven forward by the quintessentially *political* objective of state-building."[70]

Indeed, it appears the local support for ISIS prior to its capture of Mosul was based on pragmatic political and military goals rather than on a commitment to any shared religious ideology. Many Iraqis who came to tolerate, support, or ally themselves with IS were former nonviolent protesters in the Iraqi Spring movement, which explicitly opposed federalism and sectarianism. They were willing to overlook IS's sectarian rhetoric and its goal of dividing Iraq out of desperation to overthrow the al-Maliki government.[71]

In spite of their public rhetoric that blamed IS for the violence in Iraq, the U.S. State Department and the Pentagon understood well that the Maliki regime's violent internal repression was fueling the conflict. By the summer of 2014, the crimes committed by al-Maliki's administration had become so egregious that Washington finally started taking seriously calls for Nouri al-Maliki to resign. The Obama administration pressured al-Maliki to step down from his prime ministership and called for his successor to create a more inclusive government.[72] In response, the Iraqi president, Fouad Massoum, appointed Haider al-Abadi to take al-Maliki's place. However, a new "presidential structure" was created to allow for three vice presidents, and one of those positions was given to Nouri al-Maliki.[73]

Furthermore, the new prime minister was a member of the same sectarian political party as al-Maliki.[74] Skeptical of these reforms, the GMCIR called for a criminal investigation into al-Maliki's assault on Anbar province as a prerequisite for its cooperation with the new government.[75] No investigation ever took place. Shortly after Abadi's cabinet was formed, the Sunni community's suspicions that the new government would continue its predecessor's policies were proven true. On September 13, 2014, Prime Minister Abadi promised to end all attacks on civilian areas. However, the very next day Fallujah was bombed and shelled.[76] Six civilians were killed, and twenty-two were wounded. On September 15, Fallujah was bombed again. Two civilians were killed and fourteen injured. On September 16, three civilians were killed and nineteen wounded.[77] In short, the bombing and shelling of Fallujah continued on a nearly daily basis under the new Abadi government.

Despite these atrocities, Western media coverage of the conflict continued to depict IS as being uniquely violent and barbaric. Jacoby notes that in addition to portraying the organization as being "principally mobilised by faith" and "ancient sectarian hatreds," the news media has constantly fed the idea that IS had "deployed an exceptional . . . level of brutality."[78] This is not to suggest that IS's violence was anything less than horrifying. It was in fact the only actor in this conflict that did not seek to conceal its atrocities; instead, it promoted them brazenly on social media, releasing videos of executions, corporal punishment, and mass killing to instill fear in its enemies and to attract recruits. However, the official line being peddled in Washington and repeated by the mainstream media tended to presume that the violence of the Iraqi-led coalition was purely responsive to, and certainly more moral than, the violence being perpetrated by IS. The result has been a differentiated response to the atrocities committed in this conflict, with the anti-IS coalition enjoying near impunity for its use of violence.

Operation Inherent Resolve went on to "liberate" villages and major cities, including Tikrit and Ramadi, and to slowly roll back IS's territorial gains over the next two years. However, every victory against IS was mired in accusations against the PMUs of war crimes and ethnic cleansing. Human Rights Watch documented the looting and destruction of Sunni villages and the abduction of Sunni residents around Amerli in Salah al-Din and Kirkuk provinces by both government forces and the PMUs "as a combination of revenge attacks against civilians believed to have collaborated with ISIS, and collective punishment against Sunnis and other minorities on the basis of their sect."[79] They also documented "possible war crimes" including "unlawful destruction of property, collective punishment, and forced displacement" in the primarily Sunni Tikrit and surrounding areas by the PMUs.[80] Additionally, Amnesty International released a report in October 2014 titled "Absolute Impunity: Militia Rule in Iraq," detailing persistent abductions, killings, and kidnappings committed by the PMUs, for which it also held the Iraqi government responsible.[81] Despite the international outrage elicited by these reports, Prime Minister Abadi failed to bring the PMUs under control, even after they were officially made a permanent "independent military formation" parallel to the Iraqi army in February of 2016.[82]

However, to avoid further controversies and divisions, Abadi ordered that the PMUs not take part in the operation to recapture Ramadi, beginning in October 2015 and lasting until late December.[83] In fact, newly formed Sunni militias—of a tribal composition similar to the Sahwa militias[84]—participated in the fighting under the precondition that the PMUs would not be included in the operation.[85] Although the recapture of Ramadi was a political victory, the operation came at a high cost, leaving the regional capital of Anbar province, once home to 500,000 people, almost completely destroyed. Lise Grande, the UN's humanitarian coordinator in Iraq, remarked to Al Jazeera that the destruction in Ramadi was "worse than in any other part of Iraq."[86]

After Ramadi was recaptured, IS held only two other major cities in Iraq: Mosul and Fallujah. In anticipation of the coming assault on Fallujah, Iraqi forces tightened their siege of the city and IS forbade civilians from fleeing, trapping them as human shields and shooting anyone who tried to escape. Early estimates claimed that fifty thousand civilians remained trapped in the city.[87] In addition to using the population as human shields, IS's control over the city had become a full-fledged occupation that imposed a ruthless social order. Strict codes of dress and social conduct were imposed by force, and women were often raped or forced into marriages with IS fighters.[88]

By January of 2016, reports began to emerge that residents within Fallujah were facing starvation.[89] As the siege tightened, deteriorating conditions in the city led to massive hikes in food prices. One resident reported to Human Rights Watch that a 50-kilogram sack of flour had risen from the equivalent of $15 to $750 and a bag of sugar from $40 to $500.[90] On March 23, a dramatic video was circulated on social media showing a woman from Fallujah who had drowned herself and her two children in the Euphrates River to escape starvation.[91] Many residents resorted to eating patties made from ground date seeds or soups made from grass. By April, residents reported that 140 people had died from lack of food or medicine.

Much of this violence and privation was eclipsed by the media's focus on Prime Minister Abadi's efforts to answer the most recent of Grand Ayatollah Ali al-Sistani's rare injunctions on Iraqi politics, calling for reform and accountability.[92] When Abadi's efforts to reshuffle his cabinet were stalled by parliament, Muqtada al-Sadr revived a protest movement, staging sit-ins and ultimately storming parliament on April 30.[93] The political stalemate in Baghdad delayed the early efforts of the operation to retake Mosul.[94] The Coalition then shifted focus to Fallujah, beginning Operation Breaking Terrorism to "liberate" the city on May 23.

Just as in Ramadi, it was promised that the controversial PMUs would not enter Fallujah proper and would only participate in operations around the city.[95] But when the commander of the PMUs, Iranian General Qassem Suleimani, appeared in photos with his planners just outside Fallujah, many feared the operation would lead to more sectarian violence.[96] These concerns proved true. Reports soon emerged that the PMUs and federal police units were "disappearing" hundreds of civilians from Fallujah and its surrounding towns.[97] The PMUs entered the city center of Fallujah and have been accused of arson, destruction of property, demolition of homes, and looting.[98]

On June 7, the Geneva International Centre for Justice sent an urgent appeal to the UN High Commissioner of Human Rights regarding the abuses of the PMUs in Fallujah and the "growing number of civilian casualties." The organization claimed the number of civilians remaining in the city was much higher than the early estimates of fifty thousand and that the artillery and air campaigns conducted by Iraqi security forces were taking a heavy toll on civilians. It also reported that the PMUs had beaten, tortured, and executed civilians trying to flee the city.[99] The group released a more detailed report a week later, accusing the Risaliyon militia and the Badr Brigade of intercepting refugees and killing them, the latter group marching its victims single file to a location where they were tortured and executed.[100] Human Rights Watch gathered similar testimony from civilians who fled Fallujah and witnessed the federal police and the PMUs committing war crimes.[101] Additionally, the UN human rights chief Zeid Ra'ad al-Hussein said there was strong evidence that one unit within the PMUs had "perpetrated atrocities," including executions, torture, and beheadings.[102] Prime Minister Abadi commissioned an in-house investigation into these allegations. However, Human Rights Watch released a statement denouncing the secrecy of this investigation.[103] So far, the Iraqi government's investigation has found only one soldier guilty of "terrorism offenses," claiming that he shot dead seventeen civilians fleeing Fallujah. It found "no evidence of systematic abuse" by the PMUs.[104]

This was not the end of the horrors endured by civilians in Fallujah. Shortly after the operation began, the Coalition attempted to create "safe corridors" in the city to allow civilians to flee. Those unable to reach the safe corridors attempted to swim across the Euphrates or pay smugglers to help them cross the booby-trapped perimeter of the city.[105] Those who made it out safely were escorted to refugee camps where the humanitarian efforts were drastically underfunded and disorganized.[106] Karl Schembri of the Norwegian Refugee Council called conditions in the refugee camps "apocalyptic." "I've never seen anything like this," he wrote. "This is hell on earth."[107] The UN High Commissioner for Refugees estimated that eighty-seven thousand civilians poured into the camps surrounding the city in the blazing summer heat only to find insufficient quantities of tents, bathrooms, food, water, and medicine.[108] Many families were left exposed to the elements, and the World Health Organisation was so concerned about the poor hygiene conditions in the camp that it warned of the possibility of disease outbreaks.[109]

While the conditions in the refugee camps were appalling, Fallujah itself was destroyed yet again and left completely uninhabitable. When the operation officially concluded on June 26, Iraqi officials stated that the city had been "laid to waste." Preliminary reports claimed that Fallujah's basic infrastructure was "almost completely destroyed" and that 400 educational facilities, 238 health centers, 44 residential compounds, 7,000 homes, and 6,000 shops were heavily damaged, many beyond repair.[110]

Reconstruction in Fallujah would not begin for another seven months, leaving nearly its entire population displaced, traumatized, and fearful of what the future had in store for them next. One woman living in the camps, identified as Umm, told her harrowing story to *AFP* and the *Daily Mail*. She spent nearly two years living under IS occupation, with her family reaching the brink of starvation. Her five-year-old son got so hungry he begged for death. Umm was expecting twins. But due to the fear, stress, and malnutrition, she miscarried. "I don't want to go back," she said. "[Fallujah] has been through so much—the Americans, Al Qaeda, Daesh (ISIS), starvation . . . And I don't know what's next but this city is cursed, I'm not going back."[111]

SAMI

PART II

Kali Rubaii

Sami and his family lived in Saqlawiya several years into the occupation, until Coalition forces came and displaced many families to the outskirts of the town. Sami remembers hearing British and Australian accents, and seeing tanks with crosses hanging on the mirrors. He began to suspect this was a holy war, instead of an ordinary imperial occupation like the ones his grandfather told of the British and his ancestors told of the Ottoman Turks.

In the later years of the occupation and after, more and more people from Anbar province fled urban centers to join relatives in rural villages, relying more on local food sources, family networks, and tribal governance and less on state institutions like hospitals, public employment, and (now destroyed) highway systems. As people encroached on the rural communities, they built hastily constructed cheap dwellings on relatives' land, and the rural rings outlying the cities in Anbar became urbanized. Small construction jobs were common. Sami, a teenager by 2012, dropped out of school to work on construction projects and support his mother and sister. He was the male head of his household. When I initially asked for an interview with him, his response reflected a sense of rage and frustration with the American-made context in which he was forced to assume this role at too young an age:

"What can I tell you?! That I dropped out of school when I was only twelve? That I can't read because Americans took my education? That I will never marry because I cannot afford to feed even my own family? That I am responsible for my entire kin, for feeding and clothing my siblings, my mother? That I am making man decisions at the age of a child? That I watched all the men die? That the only way out of this is to become like them? That I fear for my life every time I move? That I have no future?"

His anger flashed across his face, and he waved his arms at me. Sami has clear amber eyes that show the exhaustion and intelligence of an adult. He is among so many young men and women who share the common experience of assuming leadership roles in their families in the absence of social and institutional structures that make adult life possible in the way they imagined. Many young men and women I met during fieldwork asked me for books and reading lessons, aware of the falling rate of literacy in Iraq, once the highest in the region, especially among women. They expressed an urgent concern about missed exams and talked about discrimination against Anbaris, whose exam scores were erased or marked as failing by the Iraqi government, presumably because they are Sunni. They described a world in which sectarianism had become a stand-in for broader regional and geographic cleavages that come with state breaking and a future in which the place called Iraq no longer exists. While the first and second sieges of Fallujah are straightforward in their horror, it is the cascading chaos such battles unleashed that captures the attention and emotion of young interlocutors.

"With Maliki, we did not gain our independence from the occupation. They brought in people from outside, people we did not know, not Iraqi people at all. These people they made into the government. They are very bad. Who is left in power that is good? And they are owned by outside, by Iran. And now they are trying to kill us. We lived this for a long time, many years. And we continued to resist. We had Anbari tribal militias, and we fought the government this way. And then the sheiks said, Let us try nonviolent protest like the Occupy [Wall Street] people. There were thousands of people there every day in Fallujah, on the highway, we came into the city to do it. Men and women and children, sitting with no weapons, just with signs demanding our rights. The sheiks had a list of demands for the Sunni people, for fair treatment.

"It lasted for a long time, months! Maliki came, clever idea, and took all the women only. Arrested all the women and kept them for a long time. The protests changed, and we were asking the government to give back the women. They did not give back the women, so the men decided to fight with weapons again. It did not work, this protest way. Same thing. We never know what will come. Ordinary day in the protest, and one of those ordinary days, they took all our women. You cannot expect it unless you are keeping your mind to imagine all the possibilities of the enemy. You will go mad if you do this. So you have to stop imagining the future at all, because the future is too much chaos. You cannot know anything, you cannot even dream about anything, because there are so many possibilities and no way to imagine the one possibility that comes to you.

"Even this we lived with. But then, for revenge, the government, Maliki started to drop bombs everywhere. On hospitals. On schools. No more snipers, now we had big bombs that are everywhere. We never know if our house is going to be hit next. Many people died. Many people were being killed. It was real chaos. Even in the war in Fallujah, we could say, okay, our house is a safe place to hide. It is broken, but we can keep my brother there sick and moaning and we could wash my sister's body. Now the house is a bomb too. We never know if it is safer outside, sleeping outside, or in the house? We slept some nights in the fields like animals where my uncle still had some crops growing. Then it got too close to us, and all of us saw bombs. They said on the news we were terrorists, and we were Al Qaeda, and we were

Daesh [ISIS]. They said this to get American support. Maliki will say anything to get American support to kill us. It is a sectarian thing."

It was the government bombing in 2014 that finally displaced Sami from Anbar province altogether. Sami describes how he and his mother and little sister crawled on hands and knees through an orchard of almonds and figs to escape bombing. Sami insisted that he take his family east toward Mosul, where he knew there were hospitals and intact infrastructure not being targeted like Anbar province was. His immediate family made it across northern Iraq and into Kurdish territory. He found himself in Shaqlawa, where I met him. He arrived in a rare window, just before Kurdistan locked down internal borders to Anbari refugees.

Sami's uncle took his immediate family another way. Sami remembers turning to see their shoulders moving as they shuffled away through the dried-out aqueduct in the orchard. They made it to another village [name indistinguishable], which was later seized by Daesh. They lived with limited internet and phone communication, and the last opportunity I had to ask Sami about them, they were alive but living primarily inside the bottom floor of a relative's house.

Sami [a pseudonym] works for a hotel in Shaqlawa and now reads at a third-grade level. His goals are to become literate and to support his sister in completing high school.

CONCLUSION

The official story of Fallujah, as told by the mainstream media, recounts the heroic efforts of U.S. soldiers to vanquish an evil enemy and liberate helpless civilians. But as we have argued, this narrative was constructed as propaganda, largely to pacify Western—and particularly U.S.—audiences so that Coalition forces could crush the resistance movement in Fallujah, unencumbered by the constraints of the Geneva Conventions. What then is the true story of Fallujah? And what should we do with this history?

The revisionist account presented in this book should not be mistaken for an attempt to sully the intentions of U.S. lower-enlisted soldiers—who were misled by their leaders—or minimize their suffering. We contend, however, that any history of this conflict must include the experiences of ordinary Fallujans. Each and every family in Fallujah has suffered tremendous loss and hardship as a result of these operations; and the collective trauma, which is now engrained in the psyches of all Fallujans and woven into the social and cultural fabric of the city, will endure for generations to come. Any attempt to ignore or obscure this fact is as disingenuous as it is violent. It is precisely because Fallujans were silenced by embedded journalists and U.S. military historians that the assaults on Fallujah were possible. U.S. strategic communications understands well the power of disseminating legitimizing stories in the media. Foreign wars have little impact on the American public, who—except for a small percentage of the population that volunteers to fight these wars—can choose to casually follow along with the daily media reports, or not. The choreographed stories and sanitized images provided by U.S. strategic communications are enough to ensure an information-poor and disengaged public, insulated from the discomforting realities experienced by our war victims.

As Fallujans languished in refugee camps, their city in ruins, Americans flocked to the cinema to enjoy *War Dogs*, a satire about Pentagon weapons contracting during the early years of the Global War on Terror. The timing was surely a coincidence, but the juxtaposition of these two experiences—one of terrible suffering, the other of privilege and leisure—laid bare the ways in which stories of Middle Eastern conflicts are consumed in the West. *War Dogs* tells the story of two young and rapacious entrepreneurs, David and Efraim, played by Miles Teller and Jonah Hill, respectively, who get rich quick by conning their way into the defense contracting industry. The film enjoyed considerable success, pulling in $86.2 million at the box office. Any suggested criticisms of the Pentagon's outsourcing practices were eclipsed by the story of David and Efraim's bromance, which inevitably falls apart amidst scandal and betrayal.

To work around a shipping embargo on Iraq, David and Efraim hire a driver in Amman, Jordan, to take them and their cargo of firearms to Baghdad without a security escort. Along the way, they stop for gas on a desert highway. But when Iraqi insurgents appear on the horizon, they are forced to flee.

"Go! Go! Fallujah bad! Fallujah bad!" their driver screams, to which David replies, "Are you kidding me? We stopped for gas in FALLUJAH!?"[1]

When David and Efraim arrive in Baghdad, they are shocked to learn that they had just driven through the "triangle of death," which they recognize by name and seem to understand is a dangerous place for Americans, even though they were unaware that the road from Amman to Baghdad took them through its center. For these young contractors, "Fallujah" and the "triangle of death" are familiar references, no doubt gleaned from media headlines, but devoid of historical or geopolitical meaning. Similarly, for many audiences around the world in 2016,

Fallujah was equated with terrorism and violence, a place composed of barbarians intent on death and destruction and, according to some, a place beyond salvation. Indeed, Fallujah had become notorious in a way that other sites of resistance in Iraq had not, and audiences watching *War Dogs* knew that David and Efraim *should* be afraid when they learned that they were in Fallujah. Interestingly, there is no city in sight when David and Efraim stop for gas, only a place name and some shadowy, menacing insurgents. The city was thus rendered a violent abstraction; its symbolic meaning and historical relevance usurped by media myths that included the presence of sadistic Islamic extremists who, supposedly, ruled the city by fear. Apparently, it is enough to make Fallujah intelligible in *War Dogs* by showing scenes of militants lurking in the distance.

For U.S. audiences, Fallujah became a fearful place, forbidding and yet unknown. The images that continue to dominate the collective memory of this conflict are of Islamic militants, not families or neighborhoods, not the city itself, not even the Euphrates River or the blue-domed Omar Bin Khattab Mosque. Similarly, in the mind's eye of the mainstream U.S. media, Fallujah became less a place of city dwellers than a site of unmitigated and pointless violence. When Fallujans did enter the narrative, they were depicted as hapless victims, constantly in need of rescue from Islamic extremists, who for over fifteen years insisted on making Fallujah their safe haven. The representation of Fallujans as the aberrant "other" has had far-reaching, tragic consequences. So when the news media first showed images of an Islamic State convoy rolling into Fallujah in January 2014, this was enough to provoke calls for urgent military intervention. The exact details of these events and the historical context mattered little, the thoughts and wishes of Fallujans least of all. As if following a familiar script, U.S. political and military elites looked to military solutions for a complex political problem and began assisting a third siege of Fallujah.

After the "liberation" of Fallujah in June 2016, the mainstream media quickly shifted its attention to the pending operation to recapture Mosul. The operation began on October 17, and on July 9, 2017, culminated in the Islamic State being forced out of its last stronghold in Iraq. Predictably, the victory came at a heavy price. Amnesty International estimated that 600,000 residents were displaced from Mosul.[2] According to an investigation by the Associated Press, the total civilian death toll from the operation is estimated to be between 9,000 and 11,000.[3] The numbers are potentially much higher, however. And numerous reports continued to emerge months after Prime Minister Abadi declared victory, accusing the Popular Mobilization Units (PMUs) and Iraqi military of acts of extrajudicial executions and collective punishment.[4] While U.S. ground troops played a limited role in the operation, the nonprofit organization Airwars estimated that between 900 and 1,200 civilians were killed as a result of Coalition air strikes.[5] Airwars also noted that civilian casualties from Coalition air strikes increased dramatically after President Trump took office, with "at least" 2,300 civilian deaths in both Iraq and Syria within the first seven months of his presidency.[6] The documentation collected by Airwars reveals the reckless nature of the U.S. air campaign. This was powerfully illustrated by a story in the *New York Times* that reveals the carnage caused by an air strike the United States claimed had taken out a VBIED (vehicle-borne improvised explosive device) facility but that actually killed four members of a single family as they slept in their beds.[7] On another occasion, a series of U.S. air strikes in the Jadida neighborhood of Mosul killed up to 150 civilians in a single day.[8]

During the course of the Mosul operation, reconstruction efforts stalled in Fallujah. Eissa al-Sayer, the city's mayor, reported that it would cost $2 billion to rebuild the city.[9] The Iraqi government had largely been "outsourcing" reconstruction costs, leaving most of the financial burden to fall to the UN and other states.[10] In Mosul, reconstruction funding was handled much like an "auction," with the Iraqi government eliciting bids from other countries.[11] The Iraqi administration even organized a fundraising conference in Kuwait to attract donations from its allies to help cover its total reconstruction bill, estimated at $88 billion.[12]

Seven months after Operation Breaking Terrorism, on February 26, 2017, the Iraqi government finally announced that it would begin reconstruction work in Fallujah. Progress has been grindingly slow, with residents gradually returning from camps in western and northern Iraq. Many Fallujans, however, expressed concern that the booby traps set by the Islamic State around the city had not been cleared.[13] Others found it more economically viable to remain in the camps and work as laborers and fruit vendors than to return to Fallujah where the economy was smothered by harsh security measures.[14] A year later, the Iraqi government, eager to demonstrate that it was making headway, began forcing refugees out of the camps and back to Fallujah.[15]

But many residents were reluctant to return out of fear of the PMUs, who opened an office in Fallujah and remain ever present the city.[16] The stigmatization of Fallujah within Iraq has only increased since ISIS occupied the city, and with the PMUs in the city, residents are living in an atmosphere of open discrimination. After Operation Breaking Terrorism concluded, Iraqi government security forces and the PMUs made their control of the city visible to all by raising banners with the emblems of the various PMU militias from buildings and spray-painting slogans denouncing the Islamic State and proclaiming loyalty to Shia holy figures. The point was to intimidate Fallujans into cooperation with the government and the PMUs. One militia leader stated plainly his prejudice against Fallujans: "The mind-set of the people here is a bit different from the rest of the country, dogmatically, ideologically, religiously," he said. "[Fallujah] is the center of terrorism in all of Iraq. We need to vet the communities again." Others spoke plainly about their intentions to persecute Fallujans. A junior officer told the *Guardian* that "the people who allowed ISIS to come here need to explain themselves. They need to answer why they should have a future here."[17] Some Iraqi politicians have called for the construction of a "security trench" around the city, claiming that it is a breeding ground for terrorists.[18] And again, the Iraqi government has proposed placing Fallujans under constant surveillance by issuing all residents special electronic IDs that would enable them to pass in and out of the city through a single checkpoint. Overall, life in Fallujah is looking much like it did after the second U.S.-led siege in 2004, with residents living in constant fear and under oppressive security measures.

Additionally, the Iraqi government has established a "deradicalization" program to address the "religious psychology of post–Islamic State Fallujah."[19] This is just one of several ways in which Sunni Iraqis are, in effect, being blamed for a complex social and political phenomenon like ISIS. In the wake of the war, discriminatory attitudes toward Sunni Iraqis, who are often accused of collaborating with the Islamic State, have become even more pronounced.[20] In some cases, this has led to acts of collective punishment by the authorities. For example, in mid-July 2017 shocking photographs emerged showing Sunni men accused of fighting for the Islamic State crowded into filthy prison facilities, starved, beaten, and tortured.[21] Anti-Sunni sentiments have led to the hounding, including arrest and imprisonment, of anyone with any traceable ties, no matter how vague, to the Islamic State. In one incident, Iraqi forces "forcibly displaced at least 125 families" who were accused of having "family ties to affiliates of the Islamic State."[22]

Clearly, military victories against the Islamic State have not easily translated into national reconciliation.[23] In the lands and cities "liberated" from the Islamic State, ordinary Iraqi families are reeling from the destruction and internal displacement. Meanwhile, government corruption, sectarianism, and crimes committed against the Sunni population continue unabated. In short, the conditions that gave rise to the Sunni uprising in 2014 still exist.

Even the parliamentary elections of May 2018, which promised change with the unexpected victory of the Sairun Coalition, headed by Muqtada al-Sadr and members of the Iraqi Communist Party, proved a disappointment.[24] Two months after the election, little had changed and Iraqis from Basra and other southern cities took to the streets in what has been "the single largest protest since the Shaabaniyah uprisings against Saddam Hussein in 1991."[25] These protests were prompted mostly by severe shortages of water and electricity, which are potentially dangerous in Iraq's summer heat, and long-standing complaints about corruption, sectarianism, and high rates of unemployment. The government's response was, as usual, to crack down on the protests. At the time of writing, eleven protesters have been killed and nearly eight hundred wounded.[26] Iraqi security forces have even been accused of blocking the internet to hide their attack on the protesters, who use Twitter to document human rights violations.[27]

Many commentators, however, have been dismissive of the uprising, arguing that the latest round of protests is not unlike past protests, when the summer heat has brought a frustrated public to the streets. Fanar Haddad argues that what differentiates these protests from past "summer protests" is that the Iraqi public has yet to see a "peace dividend" following the war with ISIS. He notes, "There has been incessant talk of political reform since at least 2014, but it continues to be business-as-usual for Iraq's political class. The supposedly game-changing "post-ISIL" election has come and gone, but brought no change. The ever more distant, unresponsive, self-interested and thoroughly rotten political elites are still enriching themselves, while ordinary Iraqis struggle to make ends meet . . . In other words, even if the grievances of the Iraqi public are the same, their hopes, expectations and tolerance for the status quo are not."[28] Protest has been a regular feature of Iraqi society since the occupation ended, with major protest movements in 2011, 2013, and now 2018. But, as journalist Nazli Tarzi puts it, "What is beginning to crystallise is a political street movement, whose aspirations have been plundered alongside the nation's wealth."[29] However, sectarianism remains a major dividing factor. Many Sunnis have been reluctant to join these protests after their experiences during the Iraqi Spring protests of 2013. Also, many fear that any expression of political dissent could invite accusations of being ISIS collaborators.[30]

As residents of Fallujah enter a new phase of life, ready to rebuild and recover, this moment of "peace" looks more like a lull in a long-term struggle against the powers that were entrenched by the U.S.-led invasion and occupation. If Iraqi security forces continue to frustrate legitimate protest movements, they might make insurgency—as they did in 2013—the only available means by which Iraqis can win meaningful reforms. In order to avoid future conflict, several things will need to happen. There will need to be significant reform within the Iraqi government in order to weed out corruption and sectarianism and to create a government that serves all Iraqis instead of foreign, sectarian, or tribal interests. Equally important, the United States will need to abandon its imperial ambitions in Iraq. Far from being a liberator and a partner in Iraqi nation-building, the United States has been the source of much of the violence and instability in the country for over twenty-seven years. Lastly, there will need to be accountability for the crimes committed against the Iraqi people.

According to British commentator Jonathan Holmes, the 2004 sieges of Fallujah contravened seventy individual articles of the Geneva Conventions and were in breach of nearly every major area of concern identified by them.[31] "So careless is the U.S. military of the Conventions that it is difficult to see how it could continue to function were it to adhere to them," he said.[32] Following the U.S. sieges, Iraqi NGOs and civil society organizations have tried to attract attention to human rights violations in Fallujah, including taking cases to the UN Human Rights Council. Some international groups, journalists, and researchers have also undertaken investigations and authored reports. But on the whole, the Western media, the UN, and the U.S. government have either dismissed or remained silent on the myriad ethical and moral human rights questions regarding Fallujah.

Like all struggles for justice, it could take years, even decades, for Fallujans to get the accountability they deserve. It is a testament to the power of the United States that it is able to hold itself immune to international law and protect its partners in Iraq from prosecution. That said, there are a number of Iraqis and Iraqi institutions doing tremendous work to build the future that they want for their nation.[33] The main obstacles they face are the Iraqi elites and foreign interference.

For Westerners, especially citizens of those countries that invaded and occupied Iraq, the question arises as to what the travails of the Iraqi people mean to us? What is our moral debt to Iraq? What should we do? These are challenging questions, but particularly challenging for American audiences. The notion of American exceptionalism has traditionally carried with it not just ideas about the unique right of the United States to intervene in the affairs of other nations, but also an abiding belief in its duty to be a force for good in the world. Such lofty rhetoric has made it easy for warmongers to manipulate the goodwill of Americans, convincing them that military intervention is the only way to "help" the pitiful hordes they see on television. As we have shown throughout this book, the corporate media has been successful at promoting a culture of "humanitarian interventionism" that serves as a mask for U.S. imperialism. And conflict journalism too often presents Western audiences with tragic scenes that leave us feeling powerless and looking for a way to "help," either by sending in the troops or supporting charities and NGOs.[34]

However, our impulse to help can sometimes do more harm than good, given our position of power relative to our war victims. The sad irony is that the U.S. government has persuaded its citizens to support unjust wars by manipulating their feelings of goodwill as much as their fears and chauvinisms. Many Americans have failed to ask themselves, What should we do? This is because their government has encouraged them to go about their business as usual, assuring them that all necessary actions are being taken and that they do not need to think, act, or ask questions. For those of us who wish to disassociate ourselves from the actions of our governments, we must be careful not to act on our feelings of goodwill naively. How then can we stand in solidarity with Iraqis and resist the role that has been imposed on us as citizens of empire?

The events in Fallujah over the years have often served as topical fodder for Western commentators. Whether it be Jack Wheeler's invocation "Fallujah delenda est" or an activist's call to end the siege, Fallujah has been a topos of Western debate over what should be done in the Middle East or, more accurately, how the region can be made to fit Western agendas. Rarely have Fallujans, and Iraqis more generally, or any other colonized people for that matter, been allowed to intrude on this debate.

The Sacking of Fallujah: A People's History is an attempt to give voice to our victims, while also acknowledging our responsibility as citizens of empire to the subjects of this work. This project is both revisionist and action oriented. We have sought to break a pattern of irresponsible and self-serving justifications by putting the thoughts and experiences of Fallujans themselves at the heart of this history, while also issuing a call to action for Western audiences. It is also a direct challenge to those international bodies charged with investigating breaches of human rights and war crimes. We call not only for rigorous investigations and acknowledgment of what occurred in Fallujah and elsewhere in Iraq but also for a more comprehensive understanding of its consequences: the destruction of a way of life (sociocide) and the physical decimation of a city (urbicide). These are not simply words but rather signifiers of the nature and extent of the harm inflicted on a sovereign people.

Our hope is that this work acts as an impetus to interrogate what it means to do scholarship in an information war. But scholarship alone is not enough. We need to also rethink our role as citizens of empire, replace charity with reparations, supplement our feelings of goodwill with a sense of "politically specific responsibilities," and begin a process of material and social repair with our war victims.[35]

In many respects, this work is preliminary. Many relevant government documents remain classified, many important topics still need to be investigated, and more attention needs to be given to Arabic language sources. However, this work is a first step toward several goals: contributing to a rich historiography of this conflict, creating a balanced foreign policy debate that includes the perspectives of the people we are attacking, building an engaged citizenry and an active solidarity network with Iraqis, and, ultimately, mobilizing reparations for Iraq.

The final chapters of this history have yet to be written. As the people of Fallujah struggle to rebuild their lives, the citizens of those nations who embarked upon a reckless campaign of invasion and occupation are invited to reflect on the actions of their political and military leaders. Central to the Coalition's attempt to subdue the Iraqi people was a campaign to present a certain version of history that excluded ordinary people from the dominant narrative. This is a time-honored strategy used by Western powers, indeed of all those who seek to assert dominance over other nations. *The Sacking of Fallujah* is a contribution toward recentering the experiences of victims in the story of empire. It is a form of reckoning that gives expression to Milan Kundera's well-worn observation: "The struggle of man against power is the struggle of memory against forgetting."

AFTERWORD

FALLUJAH
My Lost Country
Feurat Alani

We lived in France in a little town outside of Paris. Even though it was the first day of winter vacation, I was feeling melancholy. My friends had all left to visit their families in the provinces, but we didn't have anyone to go and visit. I decided to ask my father (who is relatively sullen) a question about his past. Did we have a family?

Sensing my dismay, my father took out a piece of paper and a pen. He began to write down names. Nearly one hundred of them. My father gave me this piece of paper and told me, "You have a very big family." In the days that followed I kept that list in my pocket. I read it and reread it. On it there were masculine names like Auday, Mazen, Riad. And feminine names like Nahla, Souad, Hasna. One name stood out: Fallujah. My father had circled it and had written, "your hometown." It was then that I came to see the paradox of the situation: I was born in Paris when I should've been born in Fallujah. It left me with a feeling of guilt that has never left me.

According to my father, all these people knew my name and had even seen a photo of my sister and me. But the country was at war with Iran. Telephone calls were rare.

One summer day in 1988, we finally received the long-awaited phone call: "The war is over!" Several months later, in October of 1989, my mother, my sister, and I found ourselves on an Iraqi Airways plane bound for Baghdad, and from there we would go by car to Fallujah.

173

Fallujah. That city—whose name now has an infamous reputation—is the birthplace of my parents, bordered by the Euphrates River from which I inherited my name. I remember a clean city, green, certainly less illustrious than Baghdad, but charming nonetheless. In Fallujah I met the people whose lives I'd only been able to imagine up until then. Lots of aunts and uncles. Even more cousins. I had always felt alone in France, but here, I was overwhelmed by new faces.

Among my uncles, there was one mysterious Sufi, Khaled, the eldest. He had gray hair and blue eyes. His voice was as mysterious as his gaze was deep. He wasn't of this world. He lived away from others in his little house with his sons. I was very impressed by this well-respected figure. He emanated a peaceful aura, a sense of goodness. I also met my aunt Souad. Very white skin—she also had blue eyes. And my cousin Ahmed, stocky with no neck to speak of. A ball of muscle. He looked a lot like Mike Tyson. I'll never forget those beautiful summer encounters. The year 1989 was a year of peace. Fallujah was our Normandy.

Today, what do we know of Fallujah outside of its destruction in 2004 and its recent conquest by the Islamic State? Nothing. That nothing is everything to me. That nothing contains my origins, my history, my family tree. That nothing is my first trip to Fallujah in 1989. And in the years that followed that first encounter, its light began to fade. I returned in 1992 when an unstoppable embargo had begun to set in. Then again in 1995, nicknamed the black year of the blockade. The country had changed. The spectacular devaluation of the Iraqi dinar had multiplied prices by thirty or forty. A heavy silence fell over the country. Baghdad suffered. Fallujah, even more so. The city began to fold in upon itself. Everyone was hungry. Everyone was angry. I was fifteen when I saw my cousins go to work at the market instead of attending school. Fifteen years old when I learned that Iraq didn't have the right to import pencils. The country that had invented writing, deprived of pencils—how ironic. I saw hospitals without beds. Sick people without medicine. The Iraq I knew in 1989 slipped further and further away from me.

So I burned bridges. I lived in France and preferred to keep my eyes shut. Continued my studies. Went out with friends. Watching my country fall into darkness was too much for me. I was scared. I didn't have the strength to bear witness to the fall of a nation, especially knowing that I could just live in France given that I was lucky enough to have been born there.

I grew up. My family and I wrote letters to one another. My cousins grew up. Despite the embargo, the country managed to do as well as it could. The UN was in cahoots with Saddam and his "oil for food" plan. The people watched as the ones in power got richer. Dignitaries from all over the world stuffed their pockets. The Iraqi people—abandoned—had to make do. And they managed. But the anger and misery that defined the blockade years never went away. It was an anger that needed only the slightest nudge to explode.

After September 11, 2001, Iraq was once again on the world stage. We knew then that the biggest injustice of all was on its way. A lie, the likes of which no one had ever seen. I was sad, and I wanted to rediscover my country. I enrolled in a journalism school, which I finished around the same time that George W. Bush gave his ultimatum.

It wasn't until 2003, however, that I finally returned to Iraq, this time as a reporter. I covered news in Baghdad, then in Fallujah just after the horrible battle that took place in November 2004. Then I stayed through the full decade that preceded the arrival of the Islamic State. I reconnected with my uncles. And I witnessed the evolution of Fallujah's insurgency, composed of many different militias of various persuasions. Salafist, Sufi, nationalist, independent. A surprising amount of variety for a city that was relatively conservative. Family and friends reminded me consistently that the resistance army was legitimate and even officially recognized by the UN due to the occupied status of the country. They told me this while lowering the curtains with rage each time an American convoy passed by on the street.

In 2007, I met Abou Younis, a fixer and guide who became my friend.[1] That year, Abou Younis told me about deformed babies. Babies born with defects following the battles of 2004. Many of these babies die just after their birth. The ones that survive are hidden away in houses. They are taboo children. They can't have normal lives. In the beginning, Abou Younis's descriptions were so inconceivable that I struggled to believe them. What he told me stayed on my mind for several years, but I needed proof. And that's when the first photos reached me. I decided to pursue the case.

In 2010, for Canal-Plus, a French cable television channel, I conducted an investigation of babies born with deformities following the battles of 2004. This investigation of the weapons used by the American military brought me first to Fallujah then to the United States and the United Kingdom. My report appeared on over twenty television stations around the world from Japan to Russia and was broadcast throughout Europe and the Arab world. But not in the United States. I met U.S. Marines, Iraqi ex-combatants, families present during the battle, doctors from the Fallujah Hospital, researchers, scientists, activists, ordinary people. I filmed a baby born with deformities on the day she entered the world. The odds of witnessing such a heartbreaking scene were tragically high. To this day, one child out of five in Fallujah is born with a deformity. It was during this investigation that I met Ross Caputi, an ex-Marine who fought in Fallujah. An improbable meeting. This encounter with an eyewitness to the use of dirty weapons in Fallujah would soon become an unbreakable friendship. Ross, through his own humanity, moves this debate beyond questions of nationalism and even racism. This is a question of justice, of the oppressor and the oppressed, of the strong and the weak. Every honest and upstanding human being should be engaged in this fight. Whether in the case of Iraq, Palestine, or any other country where human rights are scorned and injustice reigns.

I chose the career of reporter in order to spread this idea. I am partisan to no cause, militant for no side, associated with no ideology if it is not that of justice. What I denounced in Fallujah I will also denounce in all other places where I may one day have the opportunity to work.

These histories within History should not be forgotten. What happened in Fallujah should be engraved in History. As for me, there is an underlying quest here—to find my lost country. In my younger years, I was that awestruck child of 1989, telling stories about my country to my friends. I became a journalist in order to keep telling these stories, stories about our world, even though over time my view of Fallujah has shifted. During my assignments and while writing articles on my parents' city, I never forget to talk about the peaceful moments. I also open up small windows into the past: 1920—the British occupation of Fallujah and the birth of a rebellion; 1958—the year of revolution in Iraq that gave way to the establishment of the republic, events in which the city of Fallujah played a central role; 1972—the year my father left Iraq to find refuge in France. These windows offer subjective perspectives as well as historical and narrative elements that help us to understand the situation in Fallujah.

Fallujah, my Normandy. My lost country. The war, the embargo, babies born with deformities, isolation—these are important elements for understanding the anger of Fallujah's inhabitants and the events that led to the Islamic State's "taking" of the city. Today, I feel as though Fallujah is slowly but steadily slipping away from me. I am now engaged in the nostalgic pursuit of a lost Iraq. To be a child of Fallujah and a journalist, telling stories about a city during its times of peace and everyday life as well as during its times of war, is to be one witness in this world among many.

NOTES

INTRODUCTION

1. Nicholas J. S. Davies, *Blood on Our Hands: The American Invasion and Destruction of Iraq* (Ann Arbor, Mich.: Nimble Books, 2010), 215–16.
2. Rashid Khalidi, "Fallujah 101: A History Lesson about the Town We Are Currently Destroying," *In These Times,* November 12, 2004.
3. "Coalition" refers to the allied armed forces—dubbed "the coalition of the willing" by President George W. Bush—that participated in the invasion and occupation of Iraq.
4. Ralph Peters, "Our Soldiers, Their Cities," *Parameters* 26 (Spring 1996).
5. Peters, "Our Soldiers, Their Cities."
6. David H. Petraeus, "Field Manual (FM) 3–24," in *Counterinsurgency* (Washington, D.C.: Department of the Army, 2006).
7. Gian P. Gentile, "A Strategy of Tactics: Population-centric COIN and the Army," *Parameters* 39 (Autumn 2009): 5.
8. Kanishka Goonewardena and Stefan Kipfer, "Postcolonial Urbicide: New Imperialism, Global Cities and the Damned of the Earth," *New Formations* 59 (2006): 23–33.
9. Michael Otterman, Richard Hil, and Paul Wilson, *Erasing Iraq: The Human Costs of Carnage* (New York: Pluto Press, 2010), 204.
10. Leigh Armistead, ed., *Information Operations: Warfare and the Hard Reality of Soft Power* (Dulles, Va.: Brassey's, 2004), 14.
11. Dan Kuehl, foreword to *Information Operations*, xviii. Emphasis added.
12. Joanna Bourke, "New Military History," in *Palgrave Advances in Modern Military History,* ed. Matthew Hughes and William J. Philpott (New York: Palgrave Macmillan, 2006), 259.

CHAPTER 1: THE ROAD TO FALLUJAH

1. Project for the New American Century, "Statement of Principles," Internet Archive, accessed March 14, 2018. Emphasis added, https://web.archive.org

/web/20130621044610/http://www.newamericancentury.org:80/statementofprin ciples.htm/.

2. Thomas Donnelly, "Rebuilding America's Defenses: Strategy, Forces and Resources for a New Century," Project for the New American Century, September 2000.

3. Donnelly, "Rebuilding America's Defenses," iv.

4. Henry R. Luce, "The American Century," *Life,* February 17, 1941.

5. Gideon Polya, "The US Has Invaded 70 Nations Since 1776—Make 4 July Independence from America Day," *Countercurrents,* July 5, 2013.

6. Irene Gendzier, *Dying to Forget: Oil, Power, Palestine, and the Foundations of U.S. Policy in the Middle East* (New York: Columbia University Press, 2015), xxxii.

7. Gendzier, *Dying to Forget,* 1–22.

8. Malcom Byrne, "CIA Confirms Role in 1953 Iran Coup," National Security Archive, August 19, 2013.

9. Lindsey A. O'Rourke, "The U.S. Tried to Change Other Countries' Governments 72 Times during the Cold War," *Washington Post,* December 23, 2016.

10. Rashid Khalidi, *Resurrecting Empire: Western Footprints and America's Perilous Path in the Middle East* (Boston: Beacon Press, 2004), 41.

11. Richard Sale, "Saddam Key in Early CIA Plot," in *Crimes of War: Iraq,* ed. Richard Falk, Irene Gendzier, and Robert Jay Lifton (New York: Nation Books, 2006), 192–95.

12. Andrew J. Bacevich, *America's War for the Greater Middle East: A Military History* (New York: Random House, 2017), 28.

13. Bacevich, *War for the Greater Middle East,* 98–108.

14. Tim Jacoby, "Islam, Violence and the New Barbarism," in *Evil, Barbarism and Empire: Britain and Abroad, C. 1830–2000,* ed. Bertrand Taithe, Tom Cook, and Rebecca Gill (New York: Palgrave Macmillan, 2011), 273–74.

15. Eric Herring, "Between Iraq and a Hard Place: A Critique of the Case for UN Economic Sanctions," in *Crimes of War: Iraq.*

16. Glenn Greenwald, "How Many Muslim Countries Has the U.S. Bombed or Occupied Since 1980?" *Intercept,* November 6, 2014.

17. Dag Tuastad, "Neo-Orientalism and the New Barbarism Thesis: Aspects of Symbolic Violence in the Middle East Conflict(s)," *Third World Quarterly* 24 (2003): 592.

18. Jacoby, "Islam, Violence and the New Barbarism."

19. Tuastad, "The New Barbarism Thesis," 596.

20. Matt Carr, "The Barbarians of Fallujah," *Race and Class* 50, no. 1 (2008): 21.

21. Stephen Graham, "Postmortem City: Towards an Urban Geopolitics," *City* 8, no. 2 (2004): 185.

22. Graham, "Postmortem City," 185.

23. Eduardo Mendieta, "The Literature of Urbicide: Friedrich, Nossack, Sebald, and Vonnegut," *Theory and Event* 10, no. 2 (2007): n.p.

24. Irene Gendzier, "Democracy, Deception, and the Arms Trade: The U.S., Iraq, and Weapons of Mass Destruction," in *Crimes of War: Iraq,* 202–12.

25. Joyce Battle, "The Iraq War—Part I: The U.S. Prepares for Conflict," National Security Archives, September 22, 2010; John Prados and Christopher Ames, "The Iraq War—Part II: Was There Even a Decision?" National Security Archives,

October 1, 2010; John Prados and Christopher Ames, "The Iraq War—Part III: Shaping the Debate," National Security Archives, October 4, 2010.

26. "Text of the Original Downing Street 'Memo,'" The Downing Street Memo(s): Seeking the Truth Since May 13, 2005, http://www.downingstreetmemo.com/.

27. Richard Falk, introduction to "Section One: A Legal Framework," in *Crimes of War: Iraq*, 4.

28. Bacevich, "War for the Greater Middle East," 240–45.

29. Raymond W. Baker, Shereen T. Ismael, and Tareq Y. Ismael, "Ending the Iraqi State," in *Cultural Cleansing in Iraq*, ed. Raymond W. Baker, Shereen T. Ismael, and Tareq Y. Ismael (New York: Pluto Press, 2010), 6.

30. Naomi Klein, *The Shock Doctrine: The Rise of Disaster Capitalism* (New York: Picador, 2007), 411–16.

31. For an overview of Bremer's role in shaping the new Iraq, see Klein, *Shock Doctrine*, 411–84.

32. Klein, *Shock Doctrine*, 436.

33. Klein, *Shock Doctrine*, 446.

34. Paul L. Bremer III, "Coalition Provisional Suthority [sic] Order Number 2: Dissoulution [sic] of Entities," National Security Archive, May 23, 2003.

35. Baker, Ismael, and Ismael, "Ending the Iraqi State," 35.

36. Klein, *Shock Doctrine*, 457–63.

37. Ahmed Mansour, *Inside Fallujah: The Unembedded Story* (Northampton, Mass.: Olive Branch Press, 2009), 183.

38. Leigh Armistead, *Information Operations: Warfare and the Hard Reality of Soft Power* (Dulles, Va.: Brassey's, 2004), 159.

39. See Amy Zalman's paper, "Narrative as an Influence Factor in Information Operations," *IO Journal Archives* 2 (2010), for an example of the U.S. military's strategic thinking about how to employ narrative.

40. See Lawrence Freedman's discussion of this so-called revolution in military affairs (RMA), *Strategy: A History* (Oxford: Oxford University Press, 2013), 214–16. He defines an RMA as operational and organization change spurred by technological change. For an overview of what believers in the RMA promised and what actually came to fruition, see his analysis, read to page 220.

41. Stephen Badsey, "Bridging the Firewall? Information Operations and US Military Doctrine in the Battles of Fallujah," in *Propaganda, Power and Persuasion: From World War I to Wikileaks*, ed. David Welch (London: I.B. Taurus & Co., 2014), 196.

42. Jeffery B. Jones. "Strategic Communication: A Mandate for the United States," *Joint Force Quarterly* 39, no. 4 (2005): 108–9. Emphasis in original.

44. See the definitions of "Information Operations" and "Offensive Information Operations" in US Joint Chiefs of Staff, *Joint Publication 3–13: Joint Doctrine for Information Operations* (1998 GL-7, GL-9).

44. Psychological operations have recently been relabeled as military information support operations (MISO). We use "PSYOP" in this section because this term was in use during the sieges of Fallujah in 2004.

45. Armistead, *Information Operations*, 153.

46. Steve Tatham, *Losing Arab Hearts and Minds* (London: Hurst and Co., 2006), 35.

47. Media Matters, "33 Internal FOX Editorial Memos Reviewed by MMFA Reveal FOX News Channel's Inner Workings," *Media Matters for America*, July 14, 2004.

48. See Emma Louise Briant, *Propaganda and Counter-terrorism: Strategies for Global Change* (Manchester: Manchester University Press, 2015), 2–16, for a review of the debate on the ethics of propaganda.
49. Briant, *Propaganda and Counter-terrorism,* 176.
50. Briant, *Propaganda and Counter-terrorism,* 180.
51. Badsey, "Bridging the Firewall?" 195.
52. Briant, *Propaganda and Counter-terrorism,* 48.
53. Badsey, "Bridging the Firewall?" 195–96.
54. Quoted in Adrian R. Lewis. *The American Culture of War,* 2nd ed. (New York: Routledge, 2012), 376.
55. Lewis, *American Culture of War,* 433.
56. Briant, *Propaganda and Counter-terrorism,* 57.
57. Thomas F. Metz et al., "Massing Effects in the Information Domain: A Case Study in Aggressive Information Operations," *Military Review* (May–June 2006): 113.
58. Badsey, "Bridging the Firewall?" 200.
59. United States Army National Ground Intelligence Center, "Complex Environments: Battle of Fallujah 1, April 2004," *WikiLeaks,* December 24, 2007 (2006): 14.
60. Metz et al., "Aggressive Information Operations," 113.
61. Tuastad, "The New Barbarism Thesis," 593.
62. Robert D. Kaplan, "The Coming Anarchy: How Scarcity, Crime, Overpopulation, Tribalism, and Disease Are Rapidly Destroying the Social Fabric of Our Planet," *Atlantic,* February 1994.
63. Robert D. Kaplan, *Imperial Grunts: On the Ground with the American Military, from Mongolia to the Philippines to Iraq and Beyond* (New York: Vintage Books, 2006), 4.
64. Kaplan, *Imperial Grunts,* 4.
65. Kaplan, *Imperial Grunts,* 319.
66. Kaplan, *Imperial Grunts,* 356.
67. Robert D. Kaplan, "The Real Story of Fallujah," *Wall Street Journal,* May 27, 2004.

CHAPTER 2: CONFLICTING NARRATIVES

1. Quoted in Jeremy Scahill, *Blackwater: The Rise of the World's Most Powerful Mercenary Army* (London: Serpents Tail, 2007), 106
2. Matt Carr, "The Barbarians of Fallujah," *Race and Class* 50, no. 1 (2008): 22–24.
3. Quoted in Scahill, *Blackwater,* 106–7.
4. Scahill, *Blackwater,* 107.
5. Quoted in Carr, "Barbarians of Fallujah," 23.
6. Scahill, *Blackwater,* 107.
7. Thomas E. Ricks, *Fiasco: The American Military Adventure in Iraq* (New York: Penguin, 2006), 331
8. Paul L. Bremer, III, *My Year in Iraq: The Struggle to Build a Future of Hope* (New York: Simon & Schuster, 2006), 317.
9. United States Embassy, "Bremer Congratulates Iraq's Newest Police Academy Graduates," April 2, 2004.
10. Bing West, *No True Glory: A Frontline Account of the Battle for Fallujah* (New York: Bantam Dell, 2005), 4–7.

11. Quoted in United States Embassy, "Arrest Warrant Issued for Iraqi Shi'ite Cleric al-Sadr," April 5, 2004.

12. David White, "Britain Admits Bomb Missed Target and Hit Town," *Financial Times,* February 18, 1991.

13. Rick Rowley, "Iraq, Part I—Counterinsurgency in Iraq," in *Hearts and Minds: A People's History of Counterinsurgency*, ed. Hannah Gurman (New York: The New Press, 2013), 141.

14. Charles Hanley, "US Troops, Conservative Religion a Fiery Combination in Heartland Town," *Standard Times,* May 2, 2003.

15. Hanley, "US Troops."

16. Peter Bouckaert and Fred Abrahams, "Violent Response," *Human Rights Watch,* 15, no. 7 (2003).

17. Bouckaert and Abrahams, "Violent Response," 23-24.

18. Bouckaert and Abrahams, "Violent Response," 27.

19. Andrew J. Bacevich, *America's War for the Greater Middle East: A Military History* (New York: Random House, 2017), 254.

20. Vincent L. Foulk, *The Battle for Fallujah: Occupation, Resistance and Stalemate in the War in Iraq* (Jefferson, N.C.: McFarland & Co., 2007), 13.

21. Rowley, "Counterinsurgency in Iraq," 141.

22. Rowley, "Counterinsurgency in Iraq," 141.

23. Muhamad Al-Darraji, "Civil Society Resistance in Fallujah," interview by Ross Caputi, May 30, 2013.

24. Quoted in Rowley, "Counterinsurgency in Iraq," 142.

25. Rowley, "Counterinsurgency in Iraq," 142.

26. Rowley, "Counterinsurgency in Iraq," 143.

27. West, *No True Glory,* 16

28. Foulk, *Battle for Fallujah,* 35.

29. Foulk, *Battle for Fallujah,* 12.

30. West, *No True Glory,* 16.

31. Rashid Khalidi, "Fallujah 101: A History Lesson about the Town We Are Currently Destroying," *In These Times,* November 12, 2004.

32. Muhamad Al-Darraji, *Fallujah' Secrets and Nuremberg' Barrier (sic)* (Dearborn, Mich.: Alpha Academic Press, 2016), 28.

33. John R. Ballard, *Fighting for Fallujah: A New Dawn for Iraq* (Westport, Conn.: Praeger Security International, 2006), 6–7.

34. West, *No True Glory,* 162.

35. Nir Rosen, *In the Belly of the Green Bird: The Triumph of the Martyrs in Iraq* (New York: Free Press, 2006), 139–73.

36. Dahr Jamail, *Beyond the Green Zone: Dispatches from an Unembedded Journalist in Occupied Iraq* (Chicago: Haymarket Books, 2007), 81.

37. Zaki Chehab, *Inside the Resistance: Reporting from Iraq's Danger Zone* (New York: Nation Books, 2005), 18.

38. Rowley, "Counterinsurgency in Iraq," 144–45.

39. Robert D. Kaplan, "Five Days in Fallujah," *Atlantic Monthly,* July/August 2004.

40. Quoted in Kaplan, "Five Days in Fallujah."

41. Patrecia Slayden Hollis, "Second Battle of Fallujah—Urban Operations in a New Kind of War," *Field Artillery,* March-April 2006, 6.

42. Foulk, *Battle for Fallujah,* 11.
43. Ballard, *Fighting for Fallujah,* 6.
44. Quoted in West, *No True Glory,* 43.
45. Thomas F. Metz, foreword to *New Dawn: The Battles for Fallujah,* by Richard S. Lowrey (New York: Savas Beatie LLC, 2010), xiv.
46. Way, "Operation al-Fajr," 92–93.
47. Hannah Gurman, introduction to *Hearts and Minds: A People's History of Counterinsurgency,* 9.
48. Ricks, *Fiasco,* 142.
49. Quoted in Scahill, *Blackwater,* 93.
50. Robert Orr, Bing West, and Tony Cordesman, interview by Margaret Warner, "Deadly Day in Iraq," *NewsHour,* PBS, March 31, 2004.
51. Quoted in Ricks, *Fiasco,* 330.

CHAPTER 3: THE FIRST SIEGE OF FALLUJAH

1. Bing West, *No True Glory: A Frontline Account of the Battle for Fallujah* (New York: Bantam Dell, 2005), 62.
2. Dick Camp, *Operation Phantom Fury: The Assault and Capture of Fallujah, Iraq* (Minneapolis: Zenith Press, 2009), 75.
3. Nir Rosen, *In the Belly of the Green Bird: The Triumph of the Martyrs in Iraq* (New York: Free Press, 2006), 139–72.
4. Rosen, *Belly of the Green Bird,* 172.
5. David Enders, "Iraq, Part II—February 2006–December 2012: New Allies, Old Tactics," in *Hearts and Minds: A People's History of Counterinsurgency,* ed. Hannah Gurman (New York: The New Press, 2013), 158–67.
7. Donna Mulhearn, "The Road to Fallujah," *Griffith Review,* 2007.
7. John R. Ballard, *Fighting for Fallujah: A New Dawn for Iraq* (Westport, Conn.: Praeger Security International, 2006), 13–14.
8. Ballard, *Fighting for Fallujah,* 14.
9. Jo Wilding, *Don't Shoot the Clowns: Taking a Circus to the Children of Iraq* (Oxford: New International, 2006), 228.
10. Wilding, *Don't Shoot the Clowns,* 227.
11. Vincent L. Foulk, *The Battle for Fallujah: Occupation, Resistance and Stalemate in the War in Iraq* (Jefferson, N.C.: McFarland & Company, 2007), 17.
12. Foulk, *Battle for Fallujah,* 28.
13. Foulk, *Battle for Fallujah,* 23.
14. Jamail, *Beyond the Green Zone: Dispatches from an Unembedded Journalist in Occupied Iraq* (Chicago: Haymarket Books, 2007), 123.
15. Timothy S. McWilliams, *U.S. Marines in Battle: Fallujah November–December 2004* (Quantico: Historical Division, United States Marine Corps, 2014), 2.
16. West, *No True Glory,* 93.
17. United States Army National Ground Intelligence Center, "Complex Environments: Battle of Fallujah 1, April 2004," *WikiLeaks,* December 24, 2007 (2006): 14.
18. Ahmed Mansour, *Inside Fallujah: The Unembedded Story* (Northampton, Mass.: Olive Branch Press, 2009), 79–85.

19. Mansour, *Inside Fallujah,* 103, 113–14, 123, 90.

20. Mansour, *Inside Fallujah,* 161–64.

21. Toshikuni Doi, *Fallujah: April.2004* [independent film], 2005, 47:40–53:43.

22. Mansour, *Inside Fallujah,* 134.

23. Jamail, *Green Zone,* 123, 135.

24. Associated Press. "U.S. Suspends Offensive Operations in Falluja," *New York Times,* April 9, 2004.

25. Jamail, *Green Zone,* 137.

26. Jamail, *Green Zone,* 138.

27. Mulhearn, "Road to Fallujah."

28. Mulhearn, "Road to Fallujah."

29. Rahul Mahajan, *Empire Notes* (blog), April 11, 2004, 2:00 p.m..

30. Mahajan, *Empire Notes,* April 11, 2004.

31. Robert D. Kaplan, "Five Days in Fallujah," *Atlantic Monthly*, July/August 2004.

32. See the definition of "human shields" provided by the International Committee of the Red Cross.

33. United States Army National Ground Intelligence Center, "Complex Environments," 12.

34. Foulk, *Battle for Fallujah,* 17.

35. Steve Connors and Molly Bingham. *Meeting Resistance* (Nine Lives Documentary Productions, 2006). (See 39:55–44:23 for a discussion of what these groups did to avoid civilian casualties.)

36. Ballard, *Fighting for Fallujah,* 5.

37. Robert D. Kaplan, "The Real Story of Fallujah," *Wall Street Journal,* May 27, 2004.

38. Rosen, *Belly of the Green Bird,* 165.

39. Ben Connable, "The Massacre That Wasn't," in *Ideas as Weapons,* ed. G. J. David Jr. and T. R. McKeldin III (Dulles, Va.: Potomac Books, 2009), 342.

40. Connable, "The Massacre That Wasn't," 342.

41. West, *No True Glory,* 113.

42. Mansour, *Inside Fallujah,* 143.

43. Rowley, "Counterinsurgency in Iraq," 140.

44. Rowley, "Counterinsurgency in Iraq," 145.

45. Mansour, *Inside Fallujah,* 158.

46. West, *No True Glory,* 72.

47. Associated Press, "U.S. Suspends Offensive Operations in Falluja," *New York Times,* April 9, 2004.

48. Rebecca Leung, "Abuse at Abu Ghraib," *CBS News,* May 5, 2004.

49. John D. Banusiewicz, "1st Marine Expeditionary Force Creating 'Fallujah Brigade,'" *American Forces Press Service,* April 30, 2004.

50. West, *No True Glory,* 208–20.

51. Dahr Jamail, "Fallujah Rebels, Residents, Police Celebrate Victory over U.S. Marines," *New Standard,* May 10, 2004.

52. McWilliams, *U.S. Marines in Battle,* 2.

53. Iraq Body Count, "No Longer Unknowable: Fallujah's April 2004 Civilian Toll Is 600," October 26, 2004; BRussells Tribunal, "List of Iraqi Civilian Martyrs Killed in Fallujah by Chemical Weapons Used by the Americans in Their Assault on the

City in April 2004," in *Remembering Fallujah: A Dossier of the BRussells Tribunal,* ed. the BRussells Tribunal, 38–53.

54. Rosen, *Belly of the Green Bird,* 173.
55. Quoted in Mansour, *Inside Fallujah,* 278.

CHAPTER 4: THE INTERSIEGE INFORMATION CAMPAIGN

1. John D. Banusiewicz, "1st Marine Expeditionary Force Creating 'Fallujah Brigade,'" *American Forces Press Service,* April 30, 2004.
2. John R. Ballard, *Fighting for Fallujah: A New Dawn for Iraq* (Westport, Conn.: Praeger Security International, 2006), 20.
3. Patrecia Slayden Hollis, "Second Battle of Fallujah—Urban Operations in a New Kind of War," *Field Artillery,* March–April 2006, 4.
4. Dick Camp, *Operation Phantom Fury: The Assault and Capture of Fallujah, Iraq* (Minneapolis: Zenith Press, 2009), 142.
5. Emma Louise Briant, *Propaganda and Counter-terrorism: Strategies for Global Change* (Manchester: Manchester University Press, 2015), 25.
6. Quoted in Briant, *Propaganda and Counter-terrorism,* 25.
7. Stephen Badsey, "Bridging the Firewall? Information Operations and US Military Doctrine in the Battles of Fallujah," in *Propaganda, Power and Persuasion: From World War I to Wikileaks,* ed. David Welch, 188–206 (London: I.B. Taurus & Co., 2014), 200.
8. John R. Way, "Fallujah—The Epicenter of the Insurgency: Interview with Lieutenant General John F. Sattler," in *Al Anbar Awakening, Volume 1, American Perspectives,* ed. Timothy S. McWilliams and Kurtis P. Wheeler (Quantico: Marine Corps University Press, 2009), 78.
9. Ahmed Mansour, *Inside Fallujah: The Unembedded Story* (Northampton, Mass.: Olive Branch Press, 2009), 287–88.
10. Way, "The Epicenter of the Insurgency," 79.
11. Hollis, "Second Battle of Fallujah," 6.
12. Ballard, *Fighting for Fallujah,* 44.
13. Ballard, *Fighting for Fallujah,* 42.
14. Way, "The Epicenter of the Insurgency," 80.
15. Martha Raddatz, "Inside the U.S.-Led Fallujah Airstrikes," *ABC News,* October 12, 2004.
16. Thomas F. Metz, foreword to *New Dawn: The Battles for Fallujah,* by Richard S. Lowrey (New York: Savas Beatie LLC, 2010), xvi.
17. Ballard, *Fighting for Fallujah,* 44.
18. Lowry, *New Dawn,* 77.
19. Dahr Jamail, "Media Repression in 'Liberated' Land," *Inter Press Service,* November 18, 2004.
20. Jamail, "Media Repression."
21. United States Army National Ground Intelligence Center, "Complex Environments: Battle of Fallujah 1, April 2004," *WikiLeaks,* December 4, 2007 (2006): 14.
22. Leigh Armistead, *Information Operations: Warfare and the Hard Reality of Soft Power* (Dulles, Va.: Brassey's, 2004), 153.
23. Badsey, "Bridging the Firewall," 200.

24. Metz, "Foreword," xv.

25. Way, "The Epicenter of the Insurgency," 79.

26. Bing West, *No True Glory: A Frontline Account of the Battle for Fallujah* (New York: Bantam Dell, 2005), 260.

27. Metz, "Foreword," xiii.

29. Badsey, "Bridging the Firewall," 201.

29. Metz et al., "Aggressive Information Operations," 109–10.

30. Nir Rosen, *Aftermath: Following the Bloodshed of America's Wars in the Muslim World* (New York: Nation Books, 2010), 176.

31. White House Archives, "Secretary of State Addresses the U.N. Security Council," February 5, 2003.

32. Thomas E. Ricks, "Military Plays Up Role of Zarqawi," *Washington Post,* April 10, 2006.

33. Rahul Mahajan, *Empire Notes,* April 4, 2004.

34. West, *No True Glory,* 225–26.

35. Dahr Jamail, "The Zarqawi Phenomenon," *Tom Dispatch,* July 5, 2005.

36. Jeremy Scahill, *Blackwater: The Rise of the World's Most Powerful Mercenary Army* (London: Serpents Tail, 2007), 164.

37. Ricks, "Military Plays Up Role of Zarqawi."

38. Way, "The Epicenter of the Insurgency," 78.

39. Quoted in Vincent L. Foulk, *The Battle for Fallujah: Occupation, Resistance and Stalemate in the War in Iraq* (Jefferson, N.C.: McFarland & Company, 2007), 155.

40. Rosen, *Belly of the Green Bird,* 171.

41. Rosen, *Belly of the Green Bird,* 172.

42. PBS, "Inside the Insurgency: Interview with Michael Ware," *Frontline,* February 21, 2006.

43. Michael Ware, "A Chilling Iraqi Terror Tape," *Time,* July 4, 2004.

44. Jon Lee Anderson, "A Man of the Shadows," *New Yorker,* January 24, 2005.

45. Mansour, *Inside Fallujah,* 238.

46. Camp, *Operation Phantom Fury,* 119.

47. West, *No True Glory,* 248–49.

48. Dexter Filkins, "Iraqi Government's Peace Talks with Fallujah Break Off; U.S. Drive against Rebels Expected," *New York Times,* October 19, 2004.

49. Jackie Spinner and Karl Vick, "Fallujah Talks, and Battle Planning, Continue," *Washington Post,* October 28, 2004.

50. Karl Vick. "Battle Near, Iraqi Sunnis Make Offer," *Washington Post,* November 6, 2004.

51. Scott Peterson, "Behind Fallujah Strategy," *Christian Science Monitor,* October 29, 2004.

52. Kassim Abdullsattar al-Jumaily, "Letter from the People in Fallujah Calling for Help to End the Bombardment and Prevent the Threatened Assault," International Action Center, 2004.

53. BBC, "Kofi Annan's Letter: Falluja Warning," November 6, 2004.

54. Ross Caputi, *Fear Not the Path of Truth: A Veteran's Journey after Fallujah* [amateur film], 2013. (See the discussion by Dr. Muhamad Al-Darraji at 36:57–39:26.)

55. Way, "The Epicenter of the Insurgency," 81.

56. John R. Way, "Operation al-Fajr and the Return to Security and Stabilization Operations: Interview with Major General Richard F. Natonski," in *Al Anbar Awakening*, 92–93.

57. Way, "The Epicenter of the Insurgency," 81.

58. Dahr Jamail, *Beyond the Green Zone: Dispatches from an Unembedded Journalist in Occupied Iraq* (Chicago: Haymarket Books, 2007), 229–30.

CHAPTER 5: THE SECOND SIEGE OF FALLUJAH

1. David Bellavia, *House to House: An Epic Memoir of War* (New York: Pocket Star Books, 2007), 182.

2. Bellavia, *House to House*, 75.

3. Quoted in Dahr Jamail, "An Eyewitness Account of Fallujah," *Ester Republic*, December 4, 2004.

4. United States Department of Defense, "News Transcript," November 8, 2004.

5. John R. Way, "Operation al-Fajr and the Return to Security and Stabilization Operations: Interview with Major General Richard F. Natonski," in *Al Anbar Awakening, Volume 1, American Perspectives*, ed. Timothy S. McWilliams and Kurtis P. Wheeler (Quantico, Va.: Marine Corps University Press, 2009), 93.

6. Vincent L. Foulk, *The Battle for Fallujah: Occupation, Resistance and Stalemate in the War in Iraq* (Jefferson, N.C.: McFarland & Company, 2007), 210.

7. Bing West, *No True Glory: A Frontline Account of the Battle for Fallujah* (New York: Bantam Dell, 2005), 260; Nicholas J. S. Davies, *Blood on Our Hands: The American Invasion and Destruction of Iraq* (Ann Arbor, Mich.: Nimble Books, 2010), 200.

8. John R. Way, "Fallujah—The Epicenter of the Insurgency: Interview with Lieutenant General John F. Sattler," in *Al Anbar Awakening*, 83.

9. UN Assistance Mission for Iraq, "Iraq: Emergency Working Group Falluja Crisis—Bulletin Update 11 Nov 2004," *ReliefWeb*, November 11, 2004. https://reliefweb.int/report/iraq/iraq-emergency-working-group-falluja-crisis-bulletin-update-11-nov-2004.

10. Timothy S. McWilliams, *U.S. Marines in Battle: Fallujah November–December 2004* (Quantico, Va.: Historical Division, United States Marine Corps, 2014), 19.

11. BBC, "US Strikes Raze Falluja Hospital," November 6, 2004. http://news.bbc.co.uk/2/hi/middle_east/3988433.stm.

12. Quoted in Jamail, "Eyewitness Account."

13. Quoted in Dahr Jamail, "Inside Fallujah: One Family's Diary of Terror," *Sunday Herald*, November 22, 2004.

14. Dahr Jamail, "Fallujah Refugees Tell of Life and Death in the Kill Zone," *New Standard*, December 3, 2004.

15. Quoted in Jamail, "Kill Zone."

16. Quoted in Jamail, "Kill Zone."

17. UN Assistance Mission for Iraq, "Emergency Working Group Falluja Crisis–Bulletin Update 11 Nov 2004."

18. McWilliams, *Marines in Battle*, 11.

19. UN News Centre, "UN Refugee Agency Voices Extreme Concern for Iraqis Fleeing Fallujah Assault," November 9, 2004.

20. Dahr Jamail, *Beyond the Green Zone: Dispatches from an Unembedded Journalist in Occupied Iraq* (Chicago: Haymarket Books, 2007), 232–33.
21. McWilliams, *Marines in Battle,* 57.
22. McWilliams, *Marines in Battle,* 60–61.
23. McWilliams, *Marines in Battle,* 8
24. Dick Camp, *Operation Phantom Fury: The Assault and Capture of Fallujah, Iraq* (Minneapolis: Zenith Press, 2009), 150.
25. Ross Caputi, "Seeing the Truth," *The Justice for Fallujah Project,* August 19, 2011. http://www.reparations.org/projects/fallujah/.
26. Quoted in Aaron Glantz, "The Fallujah Fall Guy," *Foreign Policy in Focus,* August 20, 2008.
27. Kevin Sites, "Marines Let Loose on Streets of Fallujah," *NBC News,* November 10, 2004.
28. McWilliams, *Marines in Battle,* 16
29. West, *No True Glory,* 270.
30. West, *No True Glory,* 270.
31. The SMAW-NE is a thermobaric rocket, which some have speculated could contain uranium.
32. Caputi, "Seeing the Truth."
33. John R. Ballard, *Fighting for Fallujah: A New Dawn for Iraq* (Westport, Conn.: Praeger Security International, 2006), 57–58.
34. Richard A. Oppel Jr., "Early Target of Offensive Is a Hospital," *New York Times,* November 8, 2004.
35. Camp, *Operation Phantom Fury,* 159.
36. Ballard, *Fighting for Fallujah,* 57–58.
37. Camp, *Operation Phantom Fury,* 160.
38. Quoted in Jamail, *Beyond the Green Zone,* 235
39. Camp, *Operation Phantom Fury,* 160.
40. Camp, *Operation Phantom Fury,* 161.
41. Foulk, *The Battle for Fallujah,* 213–14.
42. McWilliams, *Marines in Battle,* 61.
43. McWilliams, *Marines in Battle,* 48.
44. Richard S. Lowry, *New Dawn: The Battles for Fallujah* (New York: Savas Beatie, 2010), 246.
45. Way, "Operation al-Fajr," 95; Ballard, *Fighting for Fallujah,* 90.
46. West, *No True Glory,* 315–16.
47. Florian Zollmann, "Bad News from Fallujah," *Media, War & Conflict* 1, no. 23 (2015): 18.
48. Zollmann, "Bad News," 16.
49. Zollmann, "Bad News," 19.
50. Study Centre for Human Rights and Democracy in Fallujah, "A Brief Report on American Crimes in Al-Fallujah for the Period of November 7 to December 25, 2004," January 1, 2005.
51. Dahr Jamail, "Life Goes on in Fallujah Rubble," *Inter Press Service,* November 24, 2005.
52. Monitoring Net of Human Rights in Iraq, "First Periodical Report of Monitoring Net of Human Rights in Iraq," August 23, 2005.

53. See all the periodical reports at the Monitoring Net of Human Rights in Iraq website: https://mhriblog.wordpress.com.
54. Muhamad Al-Darraji, "Civil Society Resistance in Fallujah," interviewed by Ross Caputi, May 30, 2013.
55. Quoted in Robert H. Reid, "A Look at AP Photographer Bilal Hussein," *Associated Press,* November 21, 2007.
56. Jamail, "Fallujah Refugees."
57. Reporters without Borders, "Detention and Murder: The Nightmare Continues for Journalists," September 19, 2006.
58. Committee to Protect Journalists, "Bilal Hussein, Photographer, Associated Press."
59. The Pulitzer Prizes, "The 2005 Pulitzer Prize Winner in Breaking News Photography," 2005. https://www.pulitzer.org/winners/staff-60.
60. Similar arguments were raised about Israel's use of white phosphorous offensively in Gaza during the hostilities that lasted between December 27, 2008 and January 18, 2009. For a review of these legal arguments, see Human Rights Watch, *Rain of Fire: Israel's Unlawful Use of White Phosphorous in Gaza,* March 2009.
61. Jackie Spinner, Karl Vick, and Omar Fekeiki, "U.S. Forces Battle into Heart of Fallujah," *Washington Post,* November 10, 2004.
62. Spinner et al., "Heart of Fallujah."
63. Peter Popham, "US Forces 'Used Chemical Weapons' during Assault on City of Fallujah," *Independent,* November 8, 2005.
64. Sigfrido Ranucci and Maurizio Torrealta, *Falluja, The Hidden Massacre* (RAI, 2005).
65. "US Forces Used 'Chemical Weapon' in Iraq," *Independent,* November 16, 2005.
66. James T. Cobb, Christopher A. LaCour, and William H. Hight, "TF 2-2 in FSE AAR: Indirect Fires in the Battle of Fallujah," *Field Artillery,* March–April 2005, 22–28.
67. BBC, "US Used White Phosphorous in Iraq," November 16, 2005.
68. Ranucci and Torrealta, *Hidden Massacre,*19:35–19:58.
69. Popham, "Chemical Weapons."
70. Muhamad Al-Darraji, "Civil Society Resistance in Fallujah."
71. Jamail, *Beyond the Green Zone,* 237.
72. McWilliams, *Marines in Battle,* 28–29.
73. Noam Chomksy, *Failed States: The Abuse of Power and the Assault on Democracy* (New York: Owl Books, 2006), 65.
74. Ross Caputi, *Fear Not the Path of Truth: A Veteran's Journey after Fallujah* [amateur film] (2013), 40:20–43:25.
75. Francis A. Boyle, "Obliterating Fallujah," *Counterpunch,* November 15, 2004.
76. Ballard, *Fighting for Fallujah,* 66–67.
77. Nicholas Casey, "Civilian Court Tries Case from the Fog of War," *Wall Street Journal,* August 19, 2008.
78. Glantz, "Fallujah Fall Guy."
79. McWilliams, *Marines in Battle,* 64.
80. Way, "Operation al-Fajr," 95.
81. Oxford Research Group and Peace Direct, "Learning from Fallujah, Lessons

Identified 2003–2005," 20. https://web.archive.org/web/20160909230507/ http://www.oxfordresearchgroup.org.uk:80/sites/default/files/fallujah.pdf.

82. McWilliams, *Marines in Battle*, 64.

83. Scilla Elworthy, "Background: The Situation in Fallujah," in *Fallujah: Eyewitness Testimony from Iraq's Besieged City*, ed. Jonathan Holmes (London: Constable & Robinson, 2007), 23.

84. Democracy Now! "Iraq Through the Eyes of Unemebedded, Independent Journalist Dahr Jamail," April 28, 2005.

85. Dahr Jamail, "The Failed Siege of Fallujah," *Asia Times*, June 3, 2005.

86. Jamail, "Failed Siege of Fallujah."

87. Muhamad Al-Darraji, "Second Periodical Report of Monitoring Net of Human Rights in Iraq," *Monitoring Net of Human Rights in Iraq*, November 20, 2005.

88. Oxford Research Group and Peace Direct, "Learning from Fallujah," 20–21.

89. Juan Cole, "Fallujah Tent City Awaits Compensation," *Informed Comment*, March 13, 2005.

90. Elworthy, "Situation in Fallujah," 24.

91. Bellavia, *House to House*, 294.

92. Bellavia, *House to House*, 292.

93. Ali al-Fadhily, "Fallujah Now under a Different Kind of Siege," *Inter Press Service*, November 20, 2007.

94. Patrick Cockburn, "Return to Fallujah," *Independent*, January 28, 2008.

95. Keith Doubt and Jeff Boucher, "War in Iraq: Is It Sociocide?" *Academia.com*, 2009.

96. Study Centre for Human Rights and Democracy in Fallujah, "A Brief Report on American Crimes in Al-Fallujah for the period of November 7 to December 25, 2004," January 1, 2005.

97. Quoted in Elworthy, "Situation in Fallujah," 24.

CHAPTER 6: AFTERMATH

1. Nir Rosen, *Aftermath: Following the Bloodshed of America's Wars in the Muslim World* (New York: Nation Books, 2010), 17.

2. Quoted in Michael Hirsh and John Barry, "The Salvador Option," *Newsweek*, January 9, 2005.

3. The Guardian and BBC Arabic, *James Steele: America's Mystery Man in Iraq*, March 6, 2013.

4. Nicholas J. S. Davies, *Blood on Our Hands: The American Invasion and Destruction of Iraq* (Ann Arbor, Mich.: Nimble Books, 2010), 244–65.

5. Davies, *Blood on Our Hands*, 245.

6. Davies, *Blood on Our Hands*, 244.

7. Davies, *Blood on Our Hands*, 244–65.

8. Rosen, *Aftermath*, 69.

9. John Tirman, *The Deaths of Others: The Fate of Civilians in America's Wars* (New York: Oxford University Press, 2011), 239. Emphasis added.

10. Seymour M. Hersh, "Moving Targets," *New Yorker*, December 15, 2003.

11. Jeremy Scahill, *Dirty Wars: The World Is a Battlefield* (New York: Nation Books, 2013), 165.

12. Rosen, *Aftermath*, 25.

13. Rosen, *Aftermath*, 18.

14. SCIRI now goes by the Islamic Supreme Council of Iraq (ISCI).

15. Fanar Haddad, "Shia-Centric State-Building and Sunni Rejection in Post 2003 Iraq," Carnegie Endowment for International Peace, January 2016, p. 3.

16. Dahr Jamail, "Rivals Say Maliki Leading Iraq to 'Civil War,'" *Al Jazeera*, December 28, 2011.

17. Marisa Sullivan, "Maliki's Authoritarian Regime," Institute for the Study of War, Middle East Report, April 10, 2013, p. 6. https://web.archive.org/web/2016032 4133324/; http://www.understandingwar.org/sites/default/files/Malikis-Authoritar ian-Regime-Web.pdf.

18. Sullivan, "Maliki's Authoritarian Regime," p. 17–18.

19. Monitoring Net of Human Rights in Iraq, "Second Periodical Report of Monitoring Net of Human Rights in Iraq," November 20, 2005, p. 18.

20. Jacqueline Soohen and Brandon Jourdan, *Fallujah* (Deep Dish TV, 2006).

21. Monitoring Net of Human Rights in Iraq and Conservation Center of Environmental and Reserves in Fallujah, "Prohibited Weapons Crisis: The Effects of Pollution on the Public Health in Fallujah," March 4, 2008.

22. Chris Busby, Malak Hamdan, Entesar Ariabi, "Cancer, Infant Mortality and Birth Sex-Ratio in Fallujah, Iraq 2005–2009," *International Journal of Environmental Research and Public Health* 7, no. 7 (2010): 2828–37.

23. The International Coalition to Ban Uranium Weapons is one of the best sources of information on DU weapons. See their reviews of DU's environmental and toxicological effects: http://www.bandepleteduranium.org/en/general-papers.

24. IKV Pax Christi, "In a State of Uncertainty: Impact and Implications of the Use of Depleted Uranium in Iraq," January 2013, 18.

25. Feurat Alani, *Fallujah: A Lost Generation?* (Baozi Prod, 2011, 20:30–24:10; see interview with Dr. Chris Busby).

26. Patrick Cockburn, "Worse Than Hiroshima," *Independent*, July 23, 2010.

27. PAX and the International Coalition to Ban Uranium Weapons, "Targets of Opportunity: Analysis of the Use of Depleted Uranium by A-10s in the 2003 Iraq War," October 5, 2016.

28. George Monbiot, "Christopher Busby's Wild Claims Hurt Green Movement and Green Party," *Guardian*, November 22, 2011.

29. Hannah Gurman, "The Under-Examined Story of Fallujah," *Foreign Policy in Focus*, November 23, 2011.

30. Samira Alaani, Muhammed Tafash, Christopher Busby, et al., "Uranium and Other Contaminants in Hair from the Parents of Children with Congenital Anomalies in Fallujah, Iraq," *Conflict and Health* 5, no. 15 (2011).

31. Dai Williams, "Under the Radar: Identifying Third-Generation Uranium Weapons," *Disarmament Forum* 3 (2008): 35.

32. Williams, "Third-Generation Uranium Weapons," 36.

33. Williams, "Third-Generation Uranium Weapons," 36–38.

34. Williams, "Third-Generation Uranium Weapons," 38.

35. Alaani et al., "Uranium and Other Contaminants," 13.

36. *Mobilizing Faith for Women: Engaging the Power of Religion and Belief to Advance Human Rights and Dignity*, Report on the June 2013 Human Rights Defenders Forum (Atlanta: Carter Center, June 2013), 63–64.

37. *Mobilizing Faith for Women,* 63–64.
38. M. Al-Sabbak, S. Sadik Ali, O. Savabi, et al., "Metal Contamination and the Epidemic of Congenital Birth Defects in Iraqi Cities," *Bulletin of Environmental Contamination and Toxicology* 89, no. 5 (2012): 937–44.
39. M. Al-Sabbak et al., "Metal Contamination," 940.
40. M. Al-Sabbak et al., "Metal Contamination," 940.
41. See these reviews on the WHO's website for further information: http://www .who.int/mediacentre/factsheets/fs379/en/; http://www.who.int/mediacentre/fact sheets/fs361/en/
42. United States Environmental Protection Agency, "Health Effects of Exposures to Mercury." https://www.epa.gov/mercury/health-effects-exposures-mercury.
43. M. Savabieasfahani, S. Alaani, M. Tafash, et al., "Elevated Titanium Levels in Iraqi Children with Neurodevelopmental Disorders Echo Findings in Occupa-tion Soldiers," *Environmental Monitoring and Assessment* 187, no. 4127 (2015): 5.
44. For a more comprehensive review of the scientific research investigating Iraq's public health crisis, see Human Rights Now, "10 Years After the Iraq War: Inno-cent New Lives are Still Dying and Suffering"; and Mohamed Ghalaieny, "Toxic Harm: Humanitarian and Environmental Concerns for Military-Origin Con-tamination," Toxic Remnants of War, 2013.
45. Reliefweb, "Summary of the Prevalence of Reported Congenital Birth Defects in 18 Selected Districts in Iraq," 2013.
46. Nafeez Ahmed, "How the World Health Organisation Covered Up Iraq's Nuclear Nightmare," *Guardian,* October 13, 2013.
47. Neel Mani, "Politics and Science in Post-Conflict Health Research," *Huffington Post,* January 23, 2014.
48. Ahmed, "Iran's Nuclear Nightmare."
49. Ahmed, "Iran's Nuclear Nightmare."
50. Human Rights Now, "10 Years after the Iraq War, Innocent New Lives Are Still Dying and Suffering," Report of a Fact Finding Mission on Congenital Birth Defects in Fallujah, Iraq in 2013, April 2017.

CHAPTER 7: THE THIRD SIEGE OF FALLUJAH

1. Barack Obama, "Transcript: President Obama Iraq speech," *BBC,* December 15, 2011.
2. David Enders, "Iraq, Part II—February 2006—December 2012: New Allies, Old Tactics," in *Hearts and Minds: A People's History of Counterinsurgency,* ed. Hannah Gurman (New York: The New Press, 2013), 160–67.
3. Ross Caputi, "Iraqi Protests Defy the Maliki Regime and Inspire Hope," *Guard-ian,* January 17, 2013.
4. Caputi, "Iraqi Protests Defy the Maliki Regime."
5. Quoted in Dahr Jamail, "Maliki's Iraq: Rape, Executions and Torture," *Al Jazeera,* March 19, 2013.
6. Ross Caputi, "I Helped Destroy Falluja in 2004. I Won't Be Complicit Again," *Guardian*, January 10, 2014.
7. Victoria C. Fontan, "Sheikh al-Hamoudi and the Right to Peace," December 1, 2013. https://web.archive.org/web/20170203224637/http://www.victoriacfontan .com/blog/sheikh-al-hamoudi-and-the-right-to-peace.

8. At the start of the violence, ISIS was still an affiliate of Al Qaeda, but it later disassociated itself from its parent organization.

9. Mushreq Abbas, "Iraq: Four Armed Groups Fighting in Fallujah," *Al-Monitor,* January 8, 2014

10. Caputi, "I Helped Destroy Falluja in 2004."

11. Human Rights Watch, "Investigate Violence at Protest Camp," January 3, 2014.

12. Agence France Presse, "Iraq: Al Qaeda 'Controls Half of Fallujah,'" *Business Insider,* January 2, 2014.

13. Dion Nissenbaum, "Role of U.S. Contractors Grows as Iraq Fights Insurgents," *Wall Street Journal,* February 3, 2014.

14. Dan Murphey, "What's Really Going on in Iraq's Anbar Province?" *Christian Science Monitor,* January 9, 2014.

15. Peter Brooks, "Fallujah Fall Just the Beginning—Al Qaeda Virus Is Virulent and Spreading," *Fox News,* January 7, 2014; Mark Pomerleau, "Significance of the Fall of Fallujah," *Hill,* January 8, 2014; Charles Gray, "Fallujah's Fall Prompts Painful Reflection on US Failure in Iraqi Conflict," *Global Times,* January 14, 2014.

16. Charles R. Lister, *The Syrian Jihad: Al-Qaeda, The Islamic State and the Evolution of an Insurgency* (New York: Oxford University Press, 2015), 143.

17. Lister, *Syrian Jihad,* 41–43.

18. Lister, *Syrian Jihad,* 56–116.

19. Victoria Fontan, "Out beyond Occupy Fallujah and the Islamic State in Iraq and Sham, There Is a Field . . . ," in *Researching Terrorism, Peace and Conflict Studies,* ed. Ioannis Tellidis and Harmonie Toros (New York: Routledge, 2015), 168–73.

20. Lister, *Syrian Jihad,* 122–44.

21. International Crisis Group, "Falluja's Faustian Bargain," April 28, 2014.

22. International Crisis Group, "Falluja's Faustian Bargain."

23. Feurat Alani, phone conversation with author, January 10, 2014.

24. Jane Arraf, "Iraq's Sunni Tribal Leaders Say Fighting for Fallujah Is Part of a Revolution," *Washington Post,* March 12, 2014.

25. Victoria C. Fontan, "Resilience of Insurgencies in Iraq: Transcript of Abdullah Janabi's Sermon in Fallujah Friday January 17th 2014," January 18, 2014; "Resilience of Insurgencies in Iraq: Part 2 of Abdullah https:// web.archive.org/web/20160331184825; http://www.victoriacfontan.com/blog /resilience-of-insurgencies-in-iraq-tran script-of-abdullah-janabis-sermon-in-fallujah-friday-january-17th-2014; https: //web.archive.org/web/20160809213600; http://www.victoriacfontan.com/ blog/resilience-of-insurgencies-in-iraq-part-2-of-abdullah-janabis-sermon-in-fallujah -friday-january-17th-2014.

26. Fontan, "Occupy Fallujah and the Islamic State," 181.

27. Suadad Al-Salhy, "Iraqi Army Prepares to Storm Militant-held Falluja," *Reuters,* February 1, 2014.

28. This figure was received on June 1, 2016, in a personal correspondence with Dr. Ahmed Shami Jassem, head resident doctor of Fallujah General Teaching Hospital and Dr. Muhammad Al-Darraji, Director of the Conservation Center of Environment and Reserves in Fallujah.

29. Struan Stevenson, "Genocide in Fallujah," *UPI,* February 25, 2014.

30. Geneva International Centre for Justice, "Al-Anbar under Siege: Crimes against Humanity under the Pretext of 'Fight against Terrorism'!" January 2014.

31. Ross Caputi, "The Battle for Your Hearts and Minds in Fallujah," *Insurge Intelligence,* August 24, 2015.

32. Muhamad Al-Darraji, "Government War Crimes in Anbar Province: Fallujah as Example," *Conservation Center of Environment and Reserves in Fallujah,* February 6, 2014.

33. Human Rights Now, "Call for an Immediate Stop to Indiscriminate Attacks in Anbar Province That Have Resulted in Civilian Casualties and Thousands of IDPs," January 22, 2014.

34. Human Rights Watch, "Government Blocking Residents Fleeing Fighting," May 3, 2014.

35. Middle East Online, "Iraq Election Commission Withdraws Collective Resignation," March 30, 2014.

36. Mustafa Habib, "Iraq Votes 2014: New Electronic Voter Cards Result in Fraud, Privacy Fears and Unhappy Queues," *Niqash,* May 1, 2014.

37. Dirk Adriaensens and Iraq Surveys 2014, "Fraudulent Elections in Iraq" (parts 1 and 2), *BRussells Tribunal,* May 3, 2014.

38. Victoria C. Fontan, "Barrel Bombs in Fallujah—a Crime against Humanity?" *Strife,* May 13, 2014.

39. United Nations Assistance Mission in Iraq, *Situation Report: Anbar Humanitarian Crisis, Report #9,* February 13, 2014. https://reliefweb.int/sites/reliefweb.int/files/resources/Anbar%20Situation%20Report%20%23%209.pdf

40. Martin Chulov, "Isis Insurgents Seize Control of Iraqi City of Mosul," *Guardian,* June 10, 2014.

41. Ross Caputi, "Unthinkable Thoughts in the Debate about ISIS in Iraq," *Common Dreams,* June 15, 2014.

42. Feurat Alani, "À Mossoul, une alliance contre nature entre le Baas et les djihadistes," *Orient XXI,* June 12, 2014.

43. Tim Arango, "Iraqis Who Fled Mosul Say They Prefer Militants to Government," *New York Times,* June 12, 2014.

44. M. Cooke, "Tribes Matter in Iraq," *BRussells Tribunal,* June 30, 2014.

45. Michael David Clark and Renad Mansour, "Is Muqtada Al-Sadr Good for Iraq?" *War on the Rocks,* May 2, 2016.

46. Pedro Rojo, "Iraqi Revolution and the Specter of Jihadist Extremism," Anti-Imperialist Camp, June 20, 2014.

47. Middle East Monitor, "Prominent Shia Cleric Supports Sunni Uprising," July 10, 2014.

48. BBC, "Isis Chief Abu Bakr al-Baghdadi Appears in First Video," July 5, 2014.

49. Mushreq Abbas, "Fallujah Key to Defeating Islamic State," *Al-Monitor,* July 9, 2014.

50. Mustafa Habib, "Crowded Cemeteries, Flattened Buildings and Potential Revolution," *Niqash,* August 28, 2014.

51. Vice News and Reuters, "The US Is Sending Hundreds More Troops to Iraq to Retake Mosul," July 11, 2016.

52. Michael R. Gordon and Eric Schmitt, "Iran Secretly Sending Drones and Supplies into Iraq, U.S. Officials Say," *New York Times,* June 25, 2014.

53. Farzin Nadimi, "Iran Is Expanding Its Military Role in Iraq in a Bunch of Ways," *Business Insider,* September 10, 2014.

54. Dexter Filkins, "The Shadow Commander," *New Yorker,* September 30, 2013.

55. Jassem Al Salami, "Iran Sends Tanks to Iraq to Fight ISIS," *War Is Boring*, August 25, 2014.
56. Ranj Alaaldin, "Iran's Weak Grip," *Foreign Affairs*, February 11, 2016.
57. Sinan Salaheddin and Sameer N. Yacoub, "Islamic State Advances towards Kurdish Territory; 'All Christian Villages Are Now Empty,'" *Associated Press*, August 7, 2014.
58. Alissa J. Rubin, "For Refugees on Mountain, 'No Water, Nothing,'" *New York Times*, August 9, 2014.
59. Barack Obama, "Statement by the President, August 7, 2014," *The White House, Office of the Press Secretary*, August 7, 2014.
60. Combined Joint Task Force, "Fact Sheet: History," *Operation Inherent Resolve*.
61. Combined Joint Task Force, "Fact Sheet: History."
62. Denise Natali, "Event Report, Countering ISIS: One Year Later," Institute for National Strategic Studies, February 10, 2016, p. 2.
63. Natali, "Countering ISIS," 2.
64. Natali, "Countering ISIS," 11.
65. Brian Bennett, David S. Cloud, and W. J. Hennigan, "Pentagon Weighs Cyber-campaign against Islamic State," *Los Angeles Times*, December 20, 2015.
66. James Glassman, "Time to Whip ISIS on the Internet, Part 2: Crafting the US Strategy," *Tech Policy Daily*, August 21, 2015.
67. Benjamin Lee, "John Kerry Discusses Isis Strategy with Hollywood Studio Chiefs," *Guardian*, February 17, 2016.
68. Alireza Doostdar, "How Not to Understand ISIS," Martin Marty Center for the Advanced Study of Religion, October 2, 2014. https://divinity.uchicago.edu /sightings/how-not-understand-isis-alireza-doostdar.
69. Tim Jacoby, "Culturalism and the Rise of the Islamic State: Faith, Sectarianism and Violence," *Third World Quarterly* (2017): 4–5.
70. Jacoby, "Culturalism and the Islamic State," 5.
71. Victoria C. Fontan, "ISIS, the Slow Insurgency," June 13, 2014. https://web.archive .org/web/20161202024724/; http://www.victoriacfontan.com/blog/isis-the-slow -in surgency.
72. Martin Chulov, Luke Harding, and Dan Roberts, "Nouri al-Maliki Forced from Post as Iraq's Political Turmoil Deepens," *Guardian*, August 11, 2014.
73. Mushreq Abbas, "Abadi's New Government Will Face Challenges," *Al-Monitor*, September 10, 2014.
74. Tim Arango and Michael R. Gordon, "Next Leader May Echo Maliki, but Iraqis Hope for New Results," *New York Times*, August 19, 2014.
75. Omar al-Jaffal, "Sunnis Do Not Believe Abadi Is Solution to Iraq's Crises," *Al-Monitor*, August 21, 2014.
76. Omar al-Jaffal, "Number of Iraqi Orphans, Widows Rising with Conflict," *Al-Monitor*, September 17, 2014.
77. Casualty figures obtained through personal correspondence with Dr. Ahmed Shami Jassem, head resident doctor of Fallujah General Teaching Hospital.
78. Jacoby, "Culturalism and the Islamic State," 3.
79. Human Rights Watch, "After Liberation Came Destruction," March 18, 2015, p. 2.
80. Human Rights Watch, "Ruinous Aftermath," September 20, 2015, p. 9.
81. Amnesty International, "Absolute Impunity: Militia Rule in Iraq," October 14, 2014.

82. Bill Roggio and Amir Toumaj, "Iraq's Prime Minister Establishes Popular Mobilization Front as a Permanent 'Independent Military Formation,'" *FDD's Long War Journal*, July 28, 2016.

83. Ibrahim Al-Marashi, "How Iraq Recaptured Ramadi and Why It Matters," *Al Jazeera*, January 3, 2016.

84. Ahmed Ali, "Iraq Update 2014 #6 Sunni Tribal Dynamics in Fallujah and Ramadi," Institute for the Study of War, January 9, 2014 (blog post).

85. Nancy A. Youssef and Shane Harris, "How ISIS Actually Lost Ramadi," *Daily Beast*, December 30, 2015.

86. "UN: Destruction of Ramadi Worse Than Anywhere in Iraq," *Al Jazeera*, March 4, 2016.

87. Marina Koren, "The Civilian Toll in Fallujah," *Atlantic*, May 26, 2016.

88. Patrick Cockburn, "ISIS, A Year of the Caliphate: Day-to-Day Life in the 'Islamic State'—Where Any Breach of Restrictive, Divinely Inspired Rules Is Savagely Punished," *Independent*, June 26, 2015.

89. The New Arab, "Iraqis in Besieged Fallujah Face Starvation, Warn Local Activists," January 22, 2016.

90. Human Rights Watch, "Fallujah Siege Starving Population," April 7, 2016.

91. Human Rights Watch, "Fallujah Siege Starving Population."

92. Tim Arango, "In Bid to Counter Iran, Ayatollah in Iraq May End up Emulating It," *New York Times*, November 1, 2015; Nazli Tarzi, "A World Inured to Starvation in Fallujah," *Diagonal*, April 2016.

93. Clark and Mansour, "Al-Sadr Good for Iraq?"

94. Dan De Luce and Henry Johnson, "Who Will Rule Mosul?" *Foreign Policy*, April 29, 2016.

95. Patrick Martin, "The Campaign for Fallujah: May 26: 2016," *Institute for the Study of War*, May 27, 2016.

96. Saif Hameed, "Sunni Politicians in Iraq Condemn Visit by Iranian General Soleimani to Fallujah," *Haaretz*, May 28, 2016.

97. The New Arab, "Militias 'Disappeared' Hundreds from Fallujah Town, says MP," June 12, 2016.

98. Munaf al Obeidi, "Al-Hashd Al-Shaabi Burns Down Homes in Fallujah," *Asharq Al-Awsat*, June 29, 2016.

99. Geneva International Center for Justice, "Escaping Fallujah: From One Hell to the Other," June 2016.

100. Geneva International Center for Justice, "Fallujah: Inside the Genocide," June 14, 2016.

101. Human Rights Watch, "Fallujah Abuses Test Control of Militias," June 9, 2016.

102. Middle East Eye and Agencies, "UN Blames Iraq Shia Militia for Abductions and Beheadings in Fallujah," July 8, 2016.

103. Human Rights Watch, "Fallujah Abuses Inquiry Mired in Secrecy," July 7, 2016.

104. Suadad al-Salhy, "Iraq Says 17 Civilians Murdered by Shia Fighter in Fallujah," *Middle East Eye*, June 17, 2016.

105. Karl Schembri, Asmaa Nuri, and Hanne Eide Andersen, "Nuriya's Grandchildren Drowned Trying to Flee Besieged Fallujah," Norwegian Refugee Council, June 24, 2016.

106. Annie Slemrod, "The Failure in Fallujah," *IRIN News*, June 28, 2016.

107. Karl Schembri, "Welcome to Hell," Norwegian Refugee Council, June 24, 2016.

108. Caroline Gluck, "Families Struggle in Heat and Dust of Iraqi Desert Camp," *UNHCR*, August 2, 2016.

109. UN News Center, "UN Health Agency Expresses Concern over Disease Outbreaks in Besieged City of Fallujah," June 16, 2016.

110. The New Arab, "Iraq's Fallujah 'Laid to Waste' during Recapture from IS," June 29, 2016.

111. Quoted in Jennifer Newton, "'My Son Asked Me to Kill Him Because He Was So Hungry He Couldn't Take It Anymore': Iraqis Reveal the Horrors of Fallujah under ISIS and Say They Won't Return Even Though the City Is Liberated," *Daily Mail*, June 28, 2016.

CONCLUSION

1. Todd Phillips, dir. *War Dogs*, BZ Entertainment, 2016. DVD, 43:10–48:20.

2. Amnesty International, *At Any Cost: The Civilian Catastrophe in West Mosul, Iraq*, July 11, 2017.

3. Susannah George, "Mosul Is a Graveyard: Final IS Battle Kills 9,000 Civilians," *Associated Press*, December 21, 2017.

4. The New Arab, "The Iraq Report: War Crimes Continue in Mosul," July 19, 2017.

5. Samuel Oakford, "Mosul's Capture Sees ISIS Vanquished—but at a Terrible Cost," *Airwars*, July 1, 2017.

6. Samuel Oakford, "Trumps Air War Has Already Killed More Than 2,000 Civilians," *Daily Beast*, July 17, 2017.

7. Azmat Khan and Anand Gopal, "The Uncounted," *New York Times*, November 16, 2017.

8. Amnesty International, "Civilians Killed by Airstrikes in Their Homes after They Were Told Not to Flee Mosul," March 28, 2017.

9. Mohamed Mostafa, "Fallujah Needs US$2 Billion for Reconstruction: Official," *Iraqi News*, August 10, 2017.

10. Nazli Tarzi, "Iraqi Government Skimps on Reconstruction Preparations," *Arab Weekly*, January 7, 2018.

11. Haifa Zangana, "The Secret Public Auction of the 'Reconstruction' of Mosul," *Middle East Monitor*, November 16, 2017.

12. Margaret Coker and Gardiner Harris, "Iraq Wants $88 Billion for Rebuilding. Allies Offer a Fraction of That," *New York Times*, February 13, 2018.

13. Suadad al-Salhy, "Deadly Daesh Legacy Blights Iraq Reconstruction Plans," *Arab News*, February 12, 2018.

14. Sofia Barbarani, "A Sense of Claustrophobia Pervades Iraq's Fallujah," *Al Jazeera*, October 22, 2017.

15. Ahmed Aboulenein, "Iraq 'Forces' Displaced Civilians to Go Home," *Reuters*, January 9, 2018.

16. Renad Mansour and Faleh A. Jabar, "The Popular Mobilization Forces and Iraq's Future," *Carnegie Middle East Center*, April 28, 2017.

17. Martin Chulov, "Falluja after ISIS: A City of Ghosts and Graffiti," *Guardian*, July 9, 2016.

18. Mustafa Saadoun, "Security Trench around Fallujah Leaves Residents Feeling Trapped," *Al-Monitor,* August 5, 2016.

19. Tom Westcott, "The Battle of Ideas in Iraq's Most Dangerous City," *Middle East Eye,* November 13, 2017.

20. Patrick Cockburn, "Mosul's Sunni Residents Face Mass Persecution as ISIS 'Collaborators,'" *Independent,* July 13, 2017.

21. McKernan, Bethan, "Shocking Photos Emerge of Suspected ISIS Fighters Held Like Battery Chickens in Overcrowded Prison," *Independent,* July 19, 2017.

22. Human Rights Watch, "Displacement, Detention of Suspected ISIS Families," March 5, 2017.

23. Austin Bodetti, "Fallujah: The Iraq Victory That Could Lose the War," *Daily Beast,* June 21, 2016.

24. Kirk H. Sowell, "Understanding Sadr's Victory," *Sada: Carnegie Endowment for International Peace,* May 17, 2018.

25. Nazli Tarzi, "Iraq's Southern Uprising Could Ignite the Largest Revolt the Country Has Witnessed in Recent Memory," *Middle East Monitor,* July 18, 2018.

26. The National, "Over 800 Killed, Wounded Since South Iraq Protests Began," July 23, 2018.

27. Amnesty International, "Security Forces Deliberately Attack Peaceful Protesters While Internet Is Disabled," July 19, 2018.

28. Fanar Haddad, "Why Are Iraqis Protesting?" *Al Jazeera,* July 19, 2018.

29. Tarzi, "Southern Uprising."

30. Mustafa Habib, "Haunted by History, Iraq's Sunni Muslims Won't Join Shiite-Led Protests," *Niqash,* July 24, 2018.

31. Jonathan Holmes, *Fallujah: Eyewitness Testimony from Iraq's Besieged City* (London: Constable Limited, 2007), 113.

32. Holmes, *Fallujah,* 112.

33. Ali Issa, *Against All Odds: Voices of Popular Struggle in Iraq* (Washington, D.C.: Tadween Publishing, 2015).

34. Jim Hicks, *Lessons from Sarajevo: A War Stories Primer* (Amherst: University of Massachusetts Press, 2013), 30.

35. We take inspiration from the framework of grassroots reparations created by Kali Rubaii. See her work with the Islah Reparations Project (www.reparations.org) for examples of how grassroots reparations can be put into action. Also, her talk "Grassroots Reparations" (a panel presentation at the symposium *Envisioning the Postwar: A Dialogue with Scholars, Organizers, and Veterans,* organized by New York University's Cultures of War and Postwar Research Collaborative on April 7, 2016) offers a useful explanation for her philosophy of grassroots reparations.

AFTERWORD: FALLUJAH

1. A "fixer" is usually an indigenous person (in this case, an Iraqi) hired by foreigners to help them get around in an unfamiliar country by organizing transportation, logistics, and translators, and making introductions.

INDEX

al-Abadi, Haider, 154, 155, 156, 157, 166
Abdul-Aziz al-Samarrai Mosque, 62
Abizaid, John P., 111
Abrams, Elliott, 15
Abu Ghraib, 64, 110
al-Adnani, Abu Muhammad, 153
al-Aksari mosque, bombing of, 122
Alaani, Samira, 10, 119, 126–32, 135, 149
Alani, Feurat, 109
Alawi, Iyad. *See* Allawi, Ayad
Allawi, Ayad, 76, 83–87, 122
American Sniper, hero-villain binary
    in, 7
Amnesty International, 155, 165
Anbar Province, Iraq: fight for control
    of, 2; genocidal campaign against
    Sunnis in, 152; investigation into
    al-Maliki's assault on, 154; ISI
    strongholds in, 146; refugees in, 149;
    revolt of, 7, 147
Annan, Kofi, 10, 86
anti-American attitudes, 18, 39, 40
Arabian American Oil Company
    (ARAMCO), 16
Arab world, views of: Arab Other, 19;
    civilization vs. barbarism, 21; crude
    binaries, 46; dichotomization/dual-
    ization, 19; hero-villain binary in, 19;
    Orientalism, 19–20; "us vs. them," 19
ARAMCO. *See* Arabian American Oil
    Company
Arbour, Louise, 105
Association of Islamic Scholars, 53
Atlantic Charter (1941), anticolonial
    rhetoric of, 18

atrocities/crimes committed: by IS, 155;
    by U.S. military, 76, 104, 135, 169, 170

Ba'ath Party: as agent of U.S. influence,
    16; army, 146; assumption of power
    by, 17; "de-Baathification," 24; Fallujah
    support for, 59, 75; militias, 149, 150;
    removal from power, 44; as Sunni
    regime, 120
Badr Brigade, 121, 157
Baghdad, fall of, 40. *See also* govern-
    ment, Iraqi
al-Baghdadi, Abu Bakr, 150–51
Ballard, John R.: dispensing of human-
    itarian aid by, 98; on Fallujah curfew,
    54; on IED attacks, 61; on inaccurate
    press releases, 77; on media relations,
    111; on PA and IO, 74; on targets of
    ground assault, 101–2
barrel bombs, 149
Basra: protests in, 168; public health
    crisis in, 131–32
Bellavia, David, 113
Berg, Nicholas E., 81
bin Laden, Osama, 80
birth defects: caused by war pollution,
    5; contributing factors to, 131–33, 135;
    crisis of, 11, 124–26; hidden, 130; rates
    of, 10, 123, 129, 133–34
Blackwater ambush: conflicting narra-
    tives of, 37–47; killing of contractors,
    13, 53, 74
Blackwater USA, 37–39, 53
Blair, Anthony C. L. (Tony), 86
Brandl, Gareth, 95

ROSS CAPUTI is a PhD student in history at the University of Massachusetts Amherst. As a U.S. Marine, Caputi was deployed to Iraq in 2004 and participated in the second siege of Fallujah. He has since been involved in antiwar and solidary organizing. Caputi is also the curator of the People's History of Fallujah digital archive and he is a cofounder of the Islah Reparations Project.

DR. RICHARD HIL is adjunct professor in the School of Human Services and Social Work at Griffith University, Gold Coast, and convener of the Ngara Institute, Australia. Hil is coauthor of numerous books, including *Erasing Iraq: The Human Cost of Carnage* (with Michael Otterman).

DONNA MULHEARN is an Australian writer and activist. She was an eyewitness to the April 2004 attack on Fallujah and has returned several times in a bid to raise awareness of the legacy of the attacks. Her professional background includes more than thirty years as a journalist, human rights work in various war and conflict zones around the world, and being a sought-after speaker and media commentator on issues relating to the Iraq war and peace activism. She is the author of the memoir *Ordinary Courage: My Journey to Baghdad as a Human Shield,* published in 2010. Donna completed her master's degree at the University of Sydney's Centre for Peace and Conflict Studies. Her articles have appeared in various books, journals, and websites.